Performing Psychology

Performing Psychology

A Postmodern Culture of the Mind

Lois Holzman,
Editor

Routledge
New York • London

Published in 1999 by
Routledge
29 West 35th Street
New York, NY 10001

Published in Great Britain by
Routledge
11 New Fetter Lane
London EC4P 4EE

Performing psychology : a postmodern culture of the mind / Lois Holzman, editor.
    p.   cm.
Includes bibliographical references and index.
ISBN 0-415-92204-6 (alk. paper).—ISBN 0-415-92205-4 (pbk. : alk. paper)
    1. Psychology—Philosophy. 2. Postmodernism. 3. Newman, Fred—Views on psychology. I. Holzman, Lois, 1946– .
BF38.P38 1999
150'. 1–dc21

Contents

Foreword

It is sometimes said that the truly creative work in any discipline takes place at the borders—by those who understand the conventions governing the interior but who also understand something else. It is at the borders that we also find individuals who are sufficiently free from the tyranny of the normal—the pattern of expectations, obligations and swift sanctions within the core of most disciplines—that they can risk innovation. Fred Newman is just such a border dweller. Newman is deeply conversant with traditional paradigms of psychological inquiry, but with other things as well. For him, such inquiry must first be seen within the context of the philosophical tradition from which it was spawned, and must simultaneously be sensitized to the challenging transformations within philosophy since the period of psychological inception. Further, for Newman it makes little sense to pursue psychology without situating it within the political and social order. Again, the political and social context giving psychology its start in life has radically changed, and these changes should be reflected by transformations within the field. Newman's immersion in philosophical, political and social deliberations is finally complemented by a deep dwelling in the realm of aesthetics, and particularly the dramatic arts. For Newman, a psychology that fails to be informed by the expressive, the passionate, the ludic, and the communicative dimensions of aesthetic life is something much less than a full psychology.

In certain respects one may see Newman's professional life in terms of his travels across these various borders, and his concerted attempt to explore new potentials—new ways of understanding knowledge, methodology, and conceptual work on the one hand, and the place of the psychologist within historical, political, cultural, and aesthetic context on the other. These explorations have also been accompanied by a singular willingness to take risks—to move from talk about ideals and alternatives to precedent-breaking action. In building a community-based institution, generating an alternative form of therapy, forming a political party, writing and producing plays, organizing forums for public debate, and countless other innovative projects, Newman and his colleagues have surprised, unsettled and antagonized. At the same time they have placed into orbit a galaxy of new stars—images, institutions, and practices against which we can fruitfully compare our traditions and ask for more.

One might say that in his crisscrossing borders Newman has indeed created a new land for visitation and illumination. In the present volume he is joined by his colleagues, Lois Holzman and Dan Friedman, to give us a glimpse of recent installations. We are confronted with probing questions concerning the nature of psychology's subject matter, the status of traditional science in a postmodern world, the process of therapy and diagnosis, the relationship of theater to human development, and finally to three short plays that delightfully and powerfully transform theory into practice, practice into drama, and drama again into the realm of the theoretical. For me one of the chief contributions of this work lies in its shift away from the traditional view of the person as living within a private psychological world, attempting desperately and often in vain to understand and communicate with other subjectivities. Rather, we are invited to see the individual not as separated from the social surrounds, but as integrally interrelated. Drawing sustenance particularly from Wittgenstein and Vygotsky, Newman sees us as intimately tissued with each other; psychology and social practice are one. And if psychological functioning is essentially the living out of social practice, then psychological action is essentially performance. With this turn, we gain new and significant purchase on the metaphor of life as theatre. Yet, for Newman entertainment is scarcely the only goal for life theatrics. We are speaking here on the one hand of the full flowering of human potential and on the other of challenging the social and economic conditions that suppress these potentials.

I have joined Newman in writing one of these chapters. The experience was both stimulating and enjoyable. Yet, in the end what was perhaps most important to me about this and other encounters with Newman is his response to our points of disagreement. For me the litmus test of any body of ideas resides in the way these ideas are embedded in practice. Joy is easily derived from a community of shared ideas and practices; the more difficult challenges emerge when differences are encountered. It is in these dances of difference that I came most fully to appreciate the performative movement as crafted by Newman and his colleagues. My voice of difference has neither been ignored nor annihilated. Rather, it has been treated as an integral part of the play. Without difference there is scarcely drama, and without drama what is life as theatre?

Kenneth Gergen
July 1998

Introduction

LOIS HOLZMAN

This book addresses the shifting nature of the discipline of psychology through a series of "performance pieces" by and about Fred Newman, the controversial American philosopher, psychotherapist, playwright and political activist. As Kenneth Gergen comments in his eloquently phrased foreword to this volume, "Newman and his colleagues have surprised, unsettled and antagonized [and] at the same time placed into orbit . . . images, institutions and practices against which we can fruitfully compare our traditions . . . " (Gergen, this volume). It is primarily because of this that showcasing Newman's method of developmental performance (in the practice of social therapy and developmental theatre) can shed light on the crossroads at which psychology stands.

My task in this introduction is to set the stage. The essays and plays contained in this volume are, in a certain sense, parts of extended dialogues on psychology, philosophy, culture and politics that have been conducted on the margins of mainstream psychology for several years. No doubt, some readers will frequently feel as though they have stepped into the middle of a conversation. But there is nothing unusual or prima facie problematic about that. On a typical day, all of us regularly walk into conversations that have already begun, and whether we feel included or excluded has to do with many factors. One thing that usually facilitates inclusion is knowing the speakers. The conversationalists in *Performing Psychology* are mainstream psychology on the one side, and on the other Fred Newman and other critics of mainstream psychology (some of them colleagues of Newman's). In the following pages, I will introduce them to you.

PSYCHOLOGY ON THE DEFENSIVE

Performing Psychology: A Postmodern Culture of the Mind is a response to current challenges to the century-long domination of experimentally based, laboratory-located, behavior-oriented scientific psychology by two opposing forces—cognitive science and neuro-science on the one hand and sociocultural psychology and postmodern psychology on the other. From the outer edges of mainstream psychology, each calls into question many of the basic categories of psychologists' object of study and method of analysis.

If they are no longer "the mind experts," do psychologists still have a bona fide subject matter? While the popular (mass) perception of psychology has never come close to being an accurate picture of the discipline, the public image has shifted over the past two decades: Where once the picture that came to the layperson was an analyst's couch, today it is a human brain. Can the traditional experimental paradigm of psychology survive in the face of the dazzling sophistication of neuropsychology and neurophysiology? How serious a threat is the transition to managed care and the popularity of psychotropic drugs to the livelihood of psychologists involved in mental health treatment and clinical research? The recent popular media coverage of "theories of mind" and consciousness research is a (usually subtextual) reminder of the failure of psychological research to deliver scientific answers to the most compelling puzzles and problems of human life. More and more people from all walks of life—practitioners, theoreticians, policy makers and consumers—are disillusioned with scientific psychology and question whether it can help us understand or deal successfully with pressing contemporary problems and their related human-social phenomena, for example, emotional pain, anger and violence, identity, sexuality, prejudice and bigotry, depression, learning failure, memories false and true, to name just a few.

Mainstream scientific psychology suffers a challenge of another sort from scholars within its ranks who believe that psychology has serious ideological and methodological biases. From different vantage points (sociocultural-historical, critical, and postmodern) they offer up critiques of the philosophical and political underpinnings of psychology's investigative practices. To these critics, a major source of psychology's current crisis is its misguided effort to emulate the natural sciences. Human-social phenomena simply cannot be understood with the tools and conceptions that are used to study nature, they say. When psychology is subjected to 'postmodern deconstruction'—that is, an exploration of the hidden assumptions of its categories and methods of analysis—what is found are philosophical biases, some going as far back as ancient Greek philosophy and others stemming from the last 400 or so years since the advent of modern science. What is being questioned is psychology's belief in and commitment to reality, truth, objectivity and universals—ideas and terms that exemplify the historical era known as modernism and that have become completely insinuated into our ordinary and everyday perceptions, language, experiences and understandings. Psychology's core conceptions—such as development, behavior, the individual, the self, stages and patterns, rationality and irrationality, normality and abnormality—are themselves said to be rooted in philosophical-scientific assumptions about what it means to understand and to know. A new psychology (or many new psychologies) are called for, ones that are socially, culturally and historically (rather than reality) based.

The response of mainstream psychology to these challenges has been pragmatic and self-serving. This is especially striking, but not surprising, in the United States. A brief look at the 150,000+ member American Psychological Association (APA)—the official voice of American psychology—suggests where international psychology might be heading. Over the past few decades, the APA has become dominated by practitioners. The so-called "scientist-practitioner split" within psychology continues to be a major subject within the organization and, with an unfortunate lack of self-examination, its publications lament the rift and present recommendations for healing it, at the same

time as they continue to perpetuate it, both institutionally and methodologically (see Rice, 1997, for a recent example). Over the last few
years, the APA successfully organized its membership to rally for pre-
scription privileges for psychologists so that, in this age of managed
care and psychotropic drug treatment, they can compete with psychia-
trists. In addition, through member publications and its annual convention, the APA is addressing the need for psychologists to find some new
avenues of research and practice in the rapidly changing marketplace.

In 1995 the APA launched a multimillion dollar campaign to
improve the faltering public image of psychology. Through a variety of
public education and public relations activities, it has been attempting to
market psychology as exceedingly relevant and, at the same time, stead-
fastly scientific. Programs have been designed "to better inform the
public, policymakers, and the media about the value of psychological
science" (Fowler, 1997, p. 765). According to former APA president
Dorothy Cantor, the organization has come out of its "isolationist" period when all efforts were focused on the association itself (Cantor, 1997,
p. 780) to join forces with nonpsychological organizations in order to
deal with the varied problems of contemporary life and, hopefully, have
greater impact on policy. For example, the association has created an
Urban Initiatives Model with the goal of "improving life in America's
cities" (Cantor, 1997, p. 780), developed a Bill of Rights for consumers
of mental health services, and is working with unions and organizations
involved in training and employment efforts. The APA has also become
the largest publisher of psychology books in the world (Fowler, 1997, p.
766). Its hundreds of books, journals, pamphlets and its electronic
archives and information sources promote the status quo in psychology,
as they bring the "psychological perspective" to an ever-widening
group of contemporary issues. Critical, radical, alternative and postmodern views are conspicuously absent from its offerings.

Along with steps to upgrade the public image of psychology as scientifically relevant and socially practical, the association began in 1998
to make moves to focus psychologists in a new direction—then-presi-
dent Martin Seligman urged members to seriously consider a reorienta-
tion of research and practice "from deficits and wounds to strengths

and virtues" (Seligman, 1998, p. xxv). According to Seligman, "the future of the discipline" might well depend on abandoning its fifty-year focus on mental illness because the mood of the country has shifted: "We are enjoying, as a nation, economic prosperity. It has been at the few times like this throughout history that different cultures have turned their attention from concerns about defense and damage to the promotion of the highest qualities of life" (p. xxv). In order to remain in sync with the consumers of psychology, Seligman proposes "that we . . . reorient ourselves from being a victimology to becoming a positive social science for the twenty-first century. We've done an excellent job of learning how to validly assess such negative states as depression, fear, anomie, aggression, and hopelessness. *Now we can call upon these same methods to measure and understand how to build personal human strengths and civic virtues*" (p. xxv, emphasis added).

Whether scientific psychology can resurrect itself through efforts of this kind remains to be seen. Certainly, Seligman's pollyanna-ish assessment of the US 'mass psychology' doesn't inspire confidence. But it is his complete lack of reflection on method that so irks mainstream psychology's critics; he never considers the possibility that building "strengths" might involve an entirely different methodological 'orientation' from treating "weaknesses," so entrenched in the scientific paradigm of measurement and validity is he.

Keeping a watchful eye on scientific psychology's attempts to create a future for itself, *Performing Psychology: A Postmodern Culture of the Mind* is primarily concerned with advancing alternatives to that psychology. The scientific paradigm that underlies psychological research and practice is the book's focus because, along with many other psychologists, I believe that it is this paradigm that renders psychology conservative and ineffectual in contributing to humane social change. *Performing Psychology* intersects current intellectual trends, among them the increased popularity of narrative, discourse, social constructionist and constructivist psychologies and therapies; the international interest in sociocultural-historical approaches (e.g., activity theory and Vygotskian psychology); the growing interest among psychologists in synthesizing theatre (performance, drama) and psychology proper; and the beginning concern with what lies beyond postmodernism.

As the term is used throughout this book, *postmodernism* is both a way to describe the historical moment in which we are living and the name given to a broad and interdisciplinary intellectual movement that studies and analyzes this historical moment from a particular vantage point. Whether or not you personally experience "living in a postmodern world," it's more than likely you have on occasion gone about your day 'accompanied by' at least one of these postmodern characteristics—a "saturated" self or multiple selves; the loss of meaning; the disappearance or relativity of truth, the blurring of boundaries between the real and unreal, subject and object, self and other, politics and entertainment, popular and high culture, etc.[1] Postmodern scholars look at how we are living (or how they think we are living), they look at the kinds of studying, teaching and policy-making being done in our name, and they find a huge gap. They point out that we live in a postmodern world but we don't have postmodern tools. It is conceptual tools more than technological tools that we lack; we're still using modern conceptual tools to help us understand and navigate in a world which is no longer modern.

In my opinion, the best of postmodernism raises questions about what we (human beings) can do in this predicament. Can we move ahead without the conceptual tools (assumptions, presuppositions, categories and biases) of modernism? Is it possible that much about the ways of understanding the world that were necessary for the extraordinary advances made in science and technology are now limiting our further advancement? Do we need what got us here, historically speaking, or is it now holding us back? Are we, as a species, stuck?

The modern era came into being over an extended period of time during which human life was transforming in every way—politically, socially, economically, and intellectually. The religious world view faced its greatest challenge from an extraordinarily liberating and powerful new way of seeing—science. Science eventually won and, while religion continues on to this day, the scientific worldview is what dominates. To appreciate the profound transformation that occurred in human history, compare the premodern (religious) era, when only God knew how the world works, with the discoveries of modernism. Not just God but human beings could know how nature works, how human beings work and how the two work (and don't work) together. Today, science's reign faces as great a challenge as religion did centuries ago, as postmodernists question whether we can know anything and whether there is any objective reality to know.

Broadly speaking, from the postmodern perspective three core modernist conceptions—truth, reality and objectivity—are especially troubling. They are so deeply entrenched in our thinking and speaking, so embedded in our knowledge-seeking activities and so intertwined with modern science, that they have come to define what it is to know and understand. They are the modern gods and often function with a similar level of authority. To many postmodern philosophers and critics, it is important to expose the gods of modernism (its "grandnarratives," its foundational presuppositions) for what they are—stories and myths.

Bringing the postmodern perspective to psychology has meant bringing philosophy, from which it had separated around the turn of the century, to bear on psychology once again. The early pioneers in psychology were not only trained in philosophy, they saw their enterprise—investigating the nature of human experience—as compatible with philosophy. However, as Danziger (1994) reports, psychology rather quickly rejected philosophy when it transformed its goal from studying individuals as "subjects of experience" to studying them as "objects of intervention." Putting on a scientific veneer, psychology fashioned itself into the premier academic discipline able to provide "knowledge that could be quickly utilized by agents of social control so as to make their work more efficient and more rationally defensible" (Danziger, 1994, p. 66). Thus, the postmodern challenge to psychology does not so much return to the philosophical concerns of the early philosophically trained psychologists as much as it attempts to incorporate advances in the philosophy of science and of language that have been made since the mid–twentieth century. Contemporary philosophically inclined psychologists direct their attention to psychology's core conceptions. They deconstruct these conceptions—in the discourse of the psychological literature, and in the way ordinary people talk, think and act—in order to expose their philosophical and ideological biases. Many postmodernists work to develop new research methodologies and educational and therapeutic approaches that are not grounded in these conceptions and the overall scientific paradigm in which they are put to use. *Performing Psychology* is a discussion of how to get beyond the limitations of both scientific psychology and its postmodern critique and, in this sense, it is part of the recent tradition of philosophical psychology.

NEWMAN'S PRACTICE OF METHOD

As a sampling of performance pieces by and about Fred Newman, this book breaks new ground in philosophical psychology. By training, Newman is a philosopher of science and language, and he looks at psychology with a philosopher's eye rather than a social scientist's. By avocation, he is a psychotherapist, playwright and political organizer who has been developing—in practice—a challenge to mainstream psychology for over thirty years. His challenge shares much with those of the postmodernists although, more than most, Newman's work examines assumptions about knowing and knowledge that permeate the discipline of psychology and people's everyday experiences. It is, perhaps, his radical stance against any epistemological (knowing) methodology whatsoever for the study and/or help of human beings that sets him apart. It is the methodology of psychology that, to Newman, makes it pseudoscientific, a methodology based in the primacy of knowing (as in the widespread conviction that knowing about things is a prerequisite for doing anything). As a long-time psychotherapist, he developed an approach that rejects this bias toward knowing (as manifest, for example, in the prevailing assumptions that change comes through understanding and that understanding consists of some kind of knowing, e.g., interpretation, explanation or description). Newman has characterized his therapy—social therapy—as "philosophizing without philosophy" (Newman, 1996). As a political playwright, he rejects the rationalistic and pedagogical traditions of "left" theatre as they have been overdetermined by German playwright and theorist, Bertolt Brecht (see Dan Friedman's essay in this volume).

Newman's methodological challenge to psychology also confronts the conservative ideology embodied in its (and modernism's) conception of change. Along with Marx and some non-Marxist philosophers, Newman is convinced that discrete particulars (psychology's objects of change) are fictions. What there is—and therefore what is changeable—are totalities. His work has been dedicated to changing the conception of change that currently dominates mass culture and the social sciences as a necessary part of the activity of changing the world.

Newman occupies a precarious and, perhaps, unique position within academic psychology circles. He is a long-time outsider: by discipline—he is not a psychologist; by choice—he left academia in the 1960s and never returned; and by how he and his work have been related to. For most of his career, Newman has been either ignored or maligned. It is only during the 1990s that his work has begun to receive serious response by scholars and significant numbers of practitioners. While he is best known as the founder in the 1970s of the radically humanistic and highly controversial clinical practice known as social therapy, today Newman is recognized for the highly effective development projects he has initiated, his provocative theoretical writing and his work as a playwright and director.

The location for the varied work Newman has spearheaded is a non-university setting—a network of organizations and projects in psychology, education, culture and politics located in several US cities. That is not completely accurate—the work is equally the creating of this non-university setting—it doesn't come ready-made but has to be brought into existence. In Newman's work, environments and settings are not physical locations but ongoing activity. The organizations and projects are independently funded; by design, they receive no government funding but instead reach out to ordinary Americans for financial support and participation. Some of the projects are decades old, while others were begun within the last two years. They include: the East Side Institute for Short Term Psychotherapy; the East Side Center for Social Therapy and its sister therapy centers in Atlanta, Boston, Brooklyn, NY,

Hempstead, NY, Philadelphia, San Francisco, Saratoga, NY, and Washington, DC; the Castillo Theatre; the Community Literacy Research Project, Inc., a nonprofit organization that supports the 30,000 member All Stars Talent Show Network and the Development School for Youth; Performance of a Lifetime, a performance school for nonprofessionals; and numerous efforts to build an independent political party in the US.

The number of people involved in or impacted on in some way by Newman's approach through this network of community-building organizations is estimated to be in the several hundreds of thousands.[2] While projects vary in focus, they share a common methodology central to Newman's work: developmental performance—the ongoing collective activity of creating new kinds of environments where people can be active performers of their lives.

As Newman's close colleague and friend for more than twenty years, I have collaborated in nearly every aspect of this ongoing community-building effort, what we call "the developing development community" (Holzman, 1997; Newman and Holzman, 1995, 1997) and what Gergen calls "the borders" (Gergen, this volume, p. 1). My own training and degree are in psychology (developmental psychology and psycholinguistics). In the mid-1970's I decided to take the "independent route" with Newman but, unlike him, I stayed tied to academia through university appointments (a research position at the Laboratory of Comparative Human Cognition at Rockefeller University from 1976–1979 and a faculty position at the State University of New York's nontraditional Empire State College from 1979–1996) and by nurturing relationships with academic colleagues. Located both inside and outside academia and institutional psychology for so many years, I have been in a fascinating and challenging position—less an outsider than Newman but not wholly an insider either.

This location/experience/activity has given me a unique view of mainstream psychology and challenges to it (including Newman's and my work)—a differently based and differently biased view from my progressive colleagues who are located at universities. How I see psychology, including the "new psychologies" that challenge it, led me to think it timely to bring together some of Newman's most recent provocations to institutionalized psychology. Thus, this volume of "performed conversations" which were designed to support postmodern and other progressive challengers to move forward. All but four of them were first presented in mainstream psychology contexts. (The exceptions are two essays written especially for this volume: my "Life as Performance" and Friedman's "Twenty-two Weeks of Pointless Conversation;" Newman's talk "A Therapeutic Deconstruction of the Illusion of Self," delivered at an East Side Institute event; and his play "What Is To Be Dead? (Philosophical Dialogues") which was performed at the Castillo Theatre.)

One reason for examining Newman's work is that it goes to the heart of the current crisis in psychology, what Newman calls its *methodological conservatism*. The modern scientific paradigm adopted by psychology holds rigidly to a particular (and particularly narrow) conception of methodology which has as one of its major features that it is necessarily dualistic. First, theory and practice are presumed to be necessarily and always separate; theories are developed and then they are tested in practice. Second, method is understood instrumentally, that is, as a means to an end, an approach to be applied, a tool that is used to yield a result. (The most common examples in psychological research are the experimental and clinical methods.) These dualisms—theory separated from practice, tool separated from result—are what, presumably, maintain scientific objectivity.

There have been earlier voices in psychology's history who challenged this dualistic conception of methodology. What Newman adds is not merely a new conception (as in theoretical statement) of methodology that does not embody this dualistic bias, but a new *conception of conception of methodology* that rejects the theory-practice dualism "in (dialectical) practice." Newman did not mentalistically *conceive* of the methodology of developmental performance. He engages with others in the activity of creating noninstrumental methodology—without knowing how to do it—and, in so doing, they collectively create method as simultaneously the tool *and* the result. In the practice of this method, the mode of study is inseparable from what a human being is.

This unorthodox way of working (and what it has generated) is one source of what is currently a controversy within the field of psychology over how to relate to Newman.

There is a second source of interest in and controversy over Newman's work. As a community-building project encompassing psychology and theatre, for over twenty years it has not merely been sustained, but has grown substantially without any government or corporate funding or university affiliation. Newman's methodology is at once theoretically sophisticated and enormously practical. That it has been conducted *outside* of academic institutions yet is highly relevant to academics raises some important questions. For example, what are the implications for institutionalized psychology if it is the case that an effective approach to human development has been created outside its boundaries—not only its physical boundaries but its methodological ones as well? How will clinical psychology and psychotherapy in particular deal with evidence that people who have emotional problems grow emotionally through engaging in the collective activity of breaking down psychology's methodological dualisms? Could such a wide-reaching practice be sustained within academia? If not, what issues does this raise both for academics and for Newman and his colleagues? This book was written in the hopes of stimulating dialogue on these and similar questions.

Not surprisingly, at this early stage of academic openness to Newman's work conflicts and tensions arise. To illustrate, I share a conversation I recently had with a close colleague and friend. She and I had just returned from an international conference on cultural-historical approaches to societal practice where we attended many of the same sessions, including a symposium at which both of us presented. My colleague told me that many times during the conference she could see the 'inside academia/outside academia' tension that Newman's and my work generates. As an example, she mentioned how some members of the audience at our symposium seemed to be put off when, during my talk, I gave some facts and figures about the size and scope of the community building projects I'm involved in—she thought they took it as self-promoting. In her opinion, this set up an unnecessary barrier (a statement of difference between me and them) that made it difficult for them to hear what, according to her, were sophisticated and important theoretical points that these scholars would be greatly interested in. She wondered if next time I should just omit those details and speak to the theoretical issues.

I feel sympathetic to my colleague's position, the more so because it stems from her own experiences being outside the officially sanctioned institutions. At the same time, however, omitting this information would not only violate the very methodology I was trying to communicate, but I think it would be problematic even on their (academic) terms. I wanted those in the audience to take notice of the fact that my data base is, on the one hand, analogous to their "30 subjects" or "two suburban high schools" or "three mother-infant dyads" and, on the other hand, it's fundamentally different. The thousands of people who have been touched by our activity-based methodology of community building are not the subjects of a research study designed to test a theoretical position; their behavior is not to be construed as the result of our intervention nor as some natural phenomenon subject to objective (or even relativistic) analysis. These people are, rather, both the tool and the result of our method. As Newman and I have said many times, it is the activity of the builders and users of these independent projects that give us (as authors) something to say.

Additionally, there is an ethical issue. Rather than risk being seen as self-promoting, wouldn't I wind up being self-serving in the name of protecting the institution? For regardless of whether our activity ultimately has value, it really is the case that Newman and I believe that psychological research is fundamentally ill-suited to discovering things about human life. We also believe that challenges to psychology that remain academically located will, at best, lead to reforms of the discipline. They cannot—by virtue of their institutional location—bring about a radical transformation in ways psychologists try to understand and improve human life. We further believe that we have data (albeit, of an unusual kind) that not only support these beliefs but take a practical and positive step toward such a transformation of the discipline. Given these beliefs, to present only half the argument (the theoretical part) and leave out the environment in and by which the theory was produced (that is, our data/practice) on the grounds that presenting it might seem self-promoting, seems to me to be a very conservative position. It is relatively easy to defend a particular interpretation or application of Vygotskian and/or activity theory in a debate with psychologists who have a cultural-historical orientation. It is quite another thing to insert into the dialogue a statement that raises questions about the total enterprise and, thereby, challenges the very rules of the debate, which currently count only certain kinds of data, produced under certain conditions, as legitimate.

The question of legitimacy is the very soul of Newman's practice. More importantly, it is the soul of the postmodern challenge. For, at its best postmodernism in psychology and elsewhere questions the *epistemological authoritarianism* of science, that is, its claim to have discovered the one true path to knowledge and understanding. Encapsulated in what has come to be called "the Science Wars," the controversy about the nature of knowledge and understanding (including, most importantly, the understanding of what it means to understand) is all about legitimacy (see Newman's "Science Can Do Better Than Sokal: A Commentary on the So-called Science Wars," this volume). It's a debate that has frequently grown vitriolic: To the postmodern charge that science is not Truth but a story (or worse, a hoax), the modernists—prominent professors of chemistry, physics, biology and the like—retaliate by calling their postmodern academic critics irrational and delusionary hypocrites and frauds (see Gross, Leavitt and Lewis, 1996 and Newman and Holzman, 1997, pp. 1–7). Apparently, to these representatives of the scientific establishment, it is illegitimate to suggest that the scientific paradigm is not the only legitimate way to understand phenomena! Moreover, if you do question the authority of science, then you've raised an unallowable question which makes you yourself illegitimate and drummed out of the club.

The self-protective and sometimes irrational response on the part of our culture's models of rationality (the hard core scientists) to their postmodern critics, coupled with the extensive popular media coverage the Science Wars has received, can tell us something about the intellectual and political issues facing science today. Whether always intentional or not, postmodernism raises the question of whether or not science has reached its limits. Along with discussions taking place among some natural and physical scientists (see for example, the collection of interviews in Horgan, 1996), the so-called Science Wars is but one indication that we are living through an historical crisis where what is at stake is "whether the 400-year reign of modern science as the exemplar of human knowledge is coming to an end" (Newman and Holzman, 1997, p. 1). For this reason, it deserves a close watch.

The conflicting response to Fred Newman's work raises a similar issue about psychology. Has it, too, reached its limits? Some of the developments within the APA discussed above suggest that this might be the case. Exactly how open to critical questioning and constructive recommendations for change is the psychological establishment before, like the threatened science establishment, it claims its authority to decide what is allowable to question and change and what is sacred? Exploring the ongoing and changing relationship between scientific psychology, its postmodern and sociocultural critics, and Newman's work provides an opportunity to learn more about the intellectual and political issues facing psychology today. In particular, it can help us understand better the roots of the new psychologies and their limitations. I explore these issues below and, when appropriate, in the introductions to each chapter.

It is, however, important to state here that Newman is by no means a critic of science. On the contrary, he is quite a fan of the physical and natural sciences and has no quarrel with how they employ the scientific paradigm—which developed alongside and for these disciplines. What he is critical of and what he directs his provocations toward is the misguided application of the natural and physical science model to areas of human social life and—inseparable from this—the misguided conception of what it is to be human.

CONTEMPORARY PSYCHOLOGY AND *CONTEMPORARY PSYCHOLOGY*

Looking at how Newman's published writings have been received

by the psychological establishment can give a sense of academia's relationship to his ongoing work. There is a fascinating history of vastly
different responses here, of which readers who are unfamiliar with the
controversiality of the work should be made aware. I analyze a part of
this history in some detail to both meet that need and in order to provide specific examples of the general points made above about mainstream psychology, postmodern and critical philosophical psychology,
and methodology. We now turn to reviews of three of Newman's books
that have appeared over the past six years.

From 1966 (when his dissertation, *Explanation by Description*, was
published by Mouton) until 1993 (when our co-authored *Lev Vygotsky:
Revolutionary Scientist* was published by Routledge), Fred Newman
had, by academic standards, not written very much. Moreover, what he
had written was essentially self-published through the institutions we
had built (e.g., Practice Press and Castillo International). A case in
point is the 1991 *The Myth of Psychology*, a collection of talks
Newman had delivered over the preceding nine years. In its totality, the
book argues that psychology is a myth that impacts profoundly (and
mostly negatively) on all of us. *Myth's* specific target is psychotherapy,
with individual chapters "deconstructing" some cherished (and lucra-
tive) psychotherapeutic conceptions, categories, treatment tools and
claims, including transference, addiction, depression and anxiety. The
book also presents a beginning description of Newman's practice,
social therapy—which he thinks of not as another alternative psychology, but as an anti-psychology: "The only way to engage a myth is to
develop an anti-mythical historical (pro-human) *practice*. . . which does
not simply offer a *cognitive* critique (myths eat cognitive critiques for
breakfast) but which organizes people (the rabble) to destroy the myth
and then to use the rubble to build something of use for us—for our
species, for our class-for-itself" (Newman, 1991, p. xix).

In 1993 *Myth* was reviewed in the most mainstream of mainstream
psychology journals, the APA's monthly journal of reviews of books in
psychology, *Contemporary Psychology*. Here is an excerpt from the
brief review by Benjamin Harris:

> For those who follow political sects, Fred Newman is best
> known as a former collaborator with Lyndon H. LaRouche
> who went on to found the New Alliance Party (NAP) . . . part
> of an interlocking network of small businesses and political
> fronts that are based in New York and staffed by devotees of
> Fred Newman . . . Preaching to the choir, Newman rejects all
> other alternative psychologies. (Harris, 1992, p. 216)

Needless to say, Newman, I, other social therapists and our clients
found it upsetting and odd that such a statement would appear in an
academic journal review. And so did many of our colleagues—well
over a hundred of them from across the country signed an open letter to
the APA voicing their concerns that the journal might be violating its
own ethical and scientific standards by publishing what amounted to a
personal attack on Newman. They submitted their statement for publication in either *Contemporary Psychology* or *American Psychologist*,
another APA journal. (APA refused to print the open letter, even as a
paid advertisement, citing existing columns in these journals that it felt
were appropriate for such an interchange.)

It is interesting to speculate as to why *Contemporary Psychology*
paid any attention to *Myth* in the first place since, according to reviewer Harris (an associate editor of *Contemporary Psychology* at the time),
it "reads like an internal document for a political movement" (Harris,
1993, pp. 1134–5). Perhaps a clue to the reviewer's (and maybe the
journal's) motive is to be found in Harris' opening sentence which
directly precedes the above quote citing Newman's political "creden-
tials." Says Harris: "This is a very imaginative book. Its author imag-
ines to have discovered a treatment, 'social therapy,' that helps 'tens of
thousands directly, and perhaps millions indirectly,' with emotional
problems" (Harris, 1992, p. 216). I still sometimes wonder whether
Harris meant that Newman imagined social therapy altogether or that
he only imagined its effectiveness. Either way, Harris is calling
Newman a liar (or delusional) and issuing a warning to readers. Why
did he bother?

At the time, Newman's name and our work were known in left political and radical psychology circles, but no more than a handful of the

100,000+ APA members had ever heard of social therapy. The number of people in the general population who had first-hand experience with social therapy and/or Newman was far greater, but still only many thousands. Social therapists had been working with adults and children in therapy centers in New York and other large US cities for well over ten years, and the approach was becoming known to increasing numbers of direct service providers in the mental health and education fields across the country and worldwide. Many of them found it effective, refreshingly new and provocatively non-psychological.

Harris had to have known this—or else why the red flag? There would be no reason to alert readers about Newman's social therapy if he wasn't worried that it was gaining influence. Rather than checking out Newman's claim or at least acknowledging (no doubt, in this case, suspiciously) that such a claim merits investigation—as befits a scientist and editor—Harris utilized a ploy that is common practice in political circles but usually considered a bit too crass for the ivory tower of academia. He justified his refusal to relate to the substance of Newman's claims by dismissing Newman as a suspicious character with dangerous political affiliations and by dismissing social therapy as a figment of Newman's imagination. In so doing, Harris abandoned the standards of his profession; arguments ad hominem should play no part in scientific investigation or historically oriented social science. Perhaps worse, he seems to have lied to his readers.

It's important to note that while *Contemporary Psychology* was the first academic journal to attack Newman politically, it was not the first publication to do so. Ten years earlier, the New York-based *Village Voice* (a weekly with a long history as a progressive/left paper) ran a front-page story entitled "Psychopolitics: What Kind of Party Is This, Anyway?" in which writer Joe Conason accused Newman of being a cult leader and social therapy of brainwashing people into joining a left political party (the New Alliance Party) (Conason, 1982). Newman, who was interviewed by Conason, willingly gave him names of social therapy clients to contact. Conason did, in fact, interview several of them but not one client is quoted in the article, nor did Conason even mention that he interviewed people who had had experience in social therapy.

This became the political strategy employed for many years with regard to social therapy: ignore the empirics. In the case of the *Contemporary Psychology* review, Harris could have contacted Newman and/or former and current clients to find out whether social therapy existed and/or was effective. For its part, the journal itself all but ignored readers who had firsthand experience with social therapy. In addition to the open letter which *Contemporary Psychology* decided not to print, the journal received several personal letters from clients in social therapy, practitioners in social work and the mental health field, and academic psychologists. However, instead of printing as many of them as possible in the column designated for reader response to reviews, it gave Harris space to cite still more political journalistic pieces devoid of empirics. As we will see, this absence of the most elementary level of investigation is characteristic of those on one side of the debate about Newman's and my work both in and out of academia.

The publication of Harris' personal-political attack by *Contemporary Psychology* is helpful in exposing the mechanisms of institutionalized psychology's conservatism and self-protective isolationism. What Harris was allowed to say by the psychological establishment is, for me, evidence of what it *won't* allow someone to say. Apparently, you can say that mental illness is a myth as Thomas Szasz did in 1961 (from an academic location at Syracuse University), but saying that psychology is a myth (while mental illness, tragically, is all too real)—and that you can back up the claim with real world practical evidence that an anti-psychological therapeutic approach is effective—is over the top. The message is that a challenge *to the totality of the institution* made by someone *outside* the institution is one that psychology will not tolerate.

Three years later, Newman was reviewed again in *Contemporary Psychology*. The occasion was our *Lev Vygotsky: Revolutionary Scientist* (1993), which received a full page review (rather than the few hundred words in *Contemporary Psychology's* "Briefly Noted" column that *Myth* merited). Notably, this review is devoid of reference to Newman's political activities (real or alleged). No doubt the serious tone of the review had something to do with the fact that the book was published by a prestigious academic press (Routledge) instead of being self-published, and that it was contracted by three highly respected academic scholars as a volume for their Critical Psychology series. Both the publication of *Lev Vygotsky: Revolutionary Scientist* and its review are indications that Newman was being invited into the "academic club."

However, here too, the picture is not without controversy. According to Ian Parker, one of the first academic psychologists to take a serious look at social therapy and the community-building effort of which it is a part, the debate surrounding Newman and social therapy apparently raged across the Atlantic. In an article in which he gives his own critical assessment of social therapy while dismissing several of the attacks made against it by others, Parker noted the following: "There have also been (denied) rumors that the Routledge 'Critical Psychology' series editorial team (John Broughton, David Ingleby and Valerie Walkerdine) were put under pressure by some American radical psychologists for the publishers to cancel the contract for the Newman and Holzman (1993) volume on Vygotsky" (Parker, 1995, p. 2).

In the *Contemporary Psychology* review, entitled "Vygotsky as Therapist," Michael Tomasello addressed the substance of our work as he placed the book in the context of other discussions of Vygotskian theory:

> The current volume has as its avowed aim "Introducing Lev Vygotsky to college and university students" (p. 1). But it does this not from the traditional point of view of Vygotsky's cognitive psychology, as do the other recent volumes, but rather from the point of view of Vygotsky as an intellectual revolutionary who has much to say to modern citizens of the Western world about life in general . . . The book thus begins with a chapter on the role of Marxist philosophy in Vygotskian theory and ends with a chapter on Vygotsky and psychotherapy. Its central theme is that psychological change (revolutionary activity) is a fundamental aspect of normal psychological development . . . The authors do a very good job of expressing and arguing for their own views of modern life and the possibility of psychological change, but the use of Vygotsky in the argument is highly selective. This is fine, of course, given such a goal, but it makes the title somewhat misleading. (Tomasello, 1995, p. 768).

In spite of its scholarly tone and favorable comments about the book, Tomasello winds up conveying a similar message as Harris did, namely that there's something self-promoting at best, and devious at worst, about the book. In addition to references to the book's "avowed aim," our "highly selective" use of Vygotsky to make our arguments, and the "somewhat misleading" title, Tomasello explicitly denies that the book has any relevance to psychology: "The book is not about Vygotsky's revolutionary theories and their impact on the practice of psychology as a science" (p. 768). In his view, that the book reflects our views makes it a book *about* our views and not about psychology or even about Vygotsky: "Readers interested primarily in the views of Newman and Holzman, therefore, will be very well served by this passionately argued and engaging volume. Readers interested primarily in Vygotsky would best look elsewhere" (p. 768).

Without the political smokescreen Harris employed, this review reveals more clearly the boundaries of psychology as a discipline and its methods for refuting methodological challenges to its institutional authority. Tomasello apparently respects the nontraditional approach we take, but cannot treat it as psychology. Newman and I come at Vygotsky with our own frame of reference. While not a philosopher, Vygotsky was, in our view, deeply concerned with questions of methodology. In our reading of his life and work, he was attempting to find a way to break down the instrumental dualism of the psychological paradigm. Other contemporary readers of Vygotsky disagree (that is, they present Vygotsky from within their own frame of reference). Given that our frame of reference is a revolutionary one and our location a nonacademic one, the charge is made that our work is not about advancing psychology, but instead it is about advancing our own work. In this way, this review is a kinder, gentler variation of the attack on *The Myth of Psychology*—both de-legitimize our data/practice/methodology.

Tomasello does, however, raise an important issue: Is our work psychology? If by psychology we mean the institutionalized discipline, then he is correct—social therapy and developmental performance are not psychology. If, however, by psychology we mean the study of the vast and complex activity of creating human subjectivity (the culture of the mind), then we would argue that psychology is not psychology!

Newman's next academic book was our coauthored *Unscientific Psychology: A Cultural-Performatory Approach to Understanding Human Life* (1995) which was reviewed in *Contemporary Psychology* in 1998. Under the title "The Case for 'Unscientific Psychology': Perplexingly Paradoxical," reviewer Daniel Fishman places the book within the critical psychology tradition, which he describes as "psychology based on postmodern, critical theory" (Fishman, 1998, p. 277). He has praise for the book's theory and method of argumentation, calling it "a philosophically and historically sophisticated, impressively scholarly, neo-Marxist, deconstructive critique of all of psychology" (p. 277).

The paradox, as he sees it, is that while the book's "purported theme is the importance of the authors' own brand of 'social therapy' . . . this book is as far from concrete, innovative, practical action as I can imagine. There are no specific examples of what social therapy looks like . . . in contrast to its subtitle, this is not a book that effectively sets forth a cultural-performatory approach to understanding human life which can be translated into a specific method of social therapy for alleviating distress and alienation" (p. 277).

From Newman's and my perspective, the seeming paradox that perplexes Fishman stems from his modern scientific framework. He locates *Unscientific Psychology* and its authors squarely in the postmodern camp, but then proceeds to ignore the (post-) postmodern methodology of the book. He presumes the theory-practice dichotomy, in which theory comes first and then is "translated into a specific method." He thus reads the bulk of the book as theory and then, when he looks for its therapeutic application, he cannot find any. Not because we, the authors, failed to give one, but because in the dialectical methodology of Newman's therapy and our collective writing, there is none; method is practiced, not applied. No doubt it would never occur to Fishman to consider the possibility that the conversations created by people in social therapy are no different in kind from those in the book, that is, that they are creative philosophical dialogues (whether they are 'good' philosophy or 'bad' philosophy is not relevant to this point).

This is unfortunate, since there are likely some psychologists who would be interested in pursuing our therapeutic claim that creating philosophical conversations is emotionally growthful.

There is something interestingly paradoxical about the direction Fishman goes with his "perplexity." Given his criticism that the book is all theory, and his frustration that it contains no examples of social therapy, it is rather surprising that he feels confident and knowledgeable enough to conclude his review with an evaluative statement about social therapeutic practice: "Certainly the passionate anger, philosophical complexity, conceptual abstractness, and grand scale of their rhetoric, though making dramatic reading, does not engender in the reader visions of an open, accepting, accessible, and compassionate mode of social therapy" (p. 278).

A leap of this magnitude—conjuring up an image of social therapeutic practice from his reading of a book he takes to be entirely theoretical—seems difficult to justify on the dualistically based scientific grounds Fishman adheres to up until this point. It seems, well, entirely too "theoretical." After all, Fishman did not have to speculate; he could have found out for himself if clients find social therapy too theoretical, compassionate or not, open and accessible or not, etc. Scientifically speaking, what is perplexing is that Fishman, like others before him, eschews empirical investigation when it comes to questions of the substance, effectiveness and client experience of social therapy. Newman and I continue to be perplexed by the lack of interest in our practice— even if interest originates in a desire to refute it—especially as interest in our theoretical formulations increases.

Within the span of six years, judgments about social therapy have gone from denying its existence altogether (Harris, 1992); to denying that it has anything to do with Vygotsky or psychology (Tomasello, 1995); to accepting its existence—but finding it problematic (Fishman, 1998). The three reviews illustrate the conflicted relationship academic psychology has to Newman's (and my) work and the dilemma we face as "border dwellers." We find a certain irony in the fact that after an extended period during which our "theory" had no credibility (it was denied that our practice might have some theoretical implications of interest to psychologists), now mainstream psychologists find the "theory" interesting—and use that to imply that the "practice" is somehow troublesome. In this way, the reviews reveal how locked into its methodological paradigm mainstream psychology is.

The radical change from politically attacking Newman in 1992 to engaging the substance of our writings in 1995 and 1998 also suggests that the debate within psychology over how to respond to our work is becoming more interesting. Over the years, what Newman and I had to say gradually became subsumable within certain theoretical trends emerging in the field. For example, what we were saying about the philosopher Ludwig Wittgenstein and the Russian psychologist Lev Vygotsky—that they were brilliant methodologists with a practical therapeutic bent—came to be relevant to some postmodern, language-oriented, and sociocultural psychologists. As the body of work has become respected by some of the leading spokespersons for alternative approaches in psychology (particularly social constructionism, critical psychology, and sociocultural-historical approaches in developmental psychology and education), it has been taken more seriously by the mainstream. Yet, there is a catch—what receives serious treatment is the work *as theory*. But treating the work as theory distorts it. It is the totality of the work—not just abstracted theory—that Newman and I believe has any chance of making some difference in the world. In our view, the important questions to ask about our work have to do with whether and how a new understanding of therapeutics as a developmental way of life, and a new therapeutic approach that is fundamentally anti-psychological and, thereby, anti-epistemological might contribute to a cultural transformation in which people learn how to live together.

Newman has often said that the most startling thing to him about social therapy is that people love it. In informal conversation, anecdotal storytelling and survey reports, they say they find it exciting, fun, useful and growthful.[3] Newman did not begin doing therapy with a particular vision other than to do something with people in emotional pain that *was not harmful*. It has taken many years of working with many hundreds of people who have come to social therapy for help with emotional problems to convince him that the joint activity of creating philosophical conversation on the mundane and practical matters of everyday life is emotionally growthful. (See Newman's "A Therapeutic Deconstruction of the Illusion of Self", this volume.) There are some academic psychologists who recognize this innovation and, regardless of whether they agree or not, appreciate the dilemma it poses to psychology and psychotherapy. Kenneth Gergen, whose preface opens this volume, is one of them. In our view, no small part of his well-earned reputation as the leading postmodern psychologist is the philosophical sensibility Gergen displays in his expansive body of theoretical work (Gergen, 1982; 1991; 1994; McNamee and Gergen, 1993). Moreover, it is this sensibility, we think, that makes him one of the few colleagues to appreciate the centrality of the activity of philosophizing to Newman's therapeutic approach.

Gergen's principled positioning and intellectual respect for Newman's work illustrate another interesting paradox our methodological approach creates for psychology. For some colleagues, getting to know our work and community firsthand contradicts the intellectualized opinion of it that they had formed at a distance. Indeed, it was just such personal experience—the contrast between his theoretical objections and his appreciation for the actual ongoing real-life activity—that led Parker, as discussed earlier, to examine our claims, ideology and therapy in light of polemical attacks (Parker, 1995) and that continues to stimulate philosophical conversations among the three of us.

Early on in my coming to know Fred Newman, he provided a metaphor that strongly affected me and that I quickly adopted. He likened qualitative transformation, changing the world (what Karl Marx called practical-critical, revolutionary activity) to taking an ocean voyage—but with a twist. Imagine leaving New York harbor on a ship, he said. As you and the other passengers and crew travel across the Atlantic, you painstakingly rebuild the ship so that by the time you arrive in Southampton, it is not the same ship with which you started. Fred attributed this image to Neurath. But the clincher—you never actually arrive anywhere; the voyage doesn't end—was his own.

It is impossible to fix our current location on this journey from behavior to activity and performance (performed activity), just as it is impossible to fix its end point, for activity has none. The essays and plays of this volume are points along the way in what has been, thus far, an arduous yet exhilarating voyage away from mainstream scientific psychology. The points are very near each other temporally—these creative works were all written in the last three years—and reflect the valuable contributions of postmodern theorizing, both to the continued development of critiques of mainstream psychology in general and to Newman's and my own work in particular.

NOTES

1. These and other characteristics of our times are discussed by many writers, both those who identify as postmodernists and those who don't. Among the most influential are Baudrillard (1986); Gergen (1991; 1994); Latour (1993); and Lyotard (1984).

2. The following figures range from exact numbers to the roughest of estimates:

East Side Institute and Center for Developmental Learning training and research: 7,000–10,000 adults

Nine Social Therapy Centers: 900 adults, children and families in 1997

All Stars Talent Show Network: 30,000 young people, mostly in the New York metropolitan area

Development School for Youth: 60 high school students in 1998

CLRP, Inc.: 100,000 individuals contributed $1.75 million in 1997

Castillo Theatre: since 1983 has produced 76 plays by 18 playwrights; since 1996, audiences have totaled 10,000 people (in a theatre with 71 seats)

Performance of a Lifetime: since 1996, approximately 600 students, 250 performances with average audience of 75; 40 agency and corporate trainings

Let's Develop! Weekly call-in radio show: reaches thousands of listeners in the New York metropolitan area

Independent politics: Local and national electoral campaigns have reached millions.

3. In the spring of 1998, we surveyed current and former social therapy clients. Our questionnaire was designed with psychotherapy effectiveness studies in mind (e.g., the *Consumer Reports* survey as discussed in Seligman, 1995). The responses of social therapy clients—who fit the general profile of clients in other psychotherapies that have been subject to effectiveness studies—suggest that social therapy is more effective on several measures than these other psychotherapies. A report of the study is available from the East Side Institute for Short Term Psychotherapy.

REFERENCES

Baudrillard, J. (1968). *Le systéme des objets*. Paris: Denoel-Gonthier Cantor.

Conason, J. (1982). Psychopolitics: What kind of party is this, anyway? *Village Voice, 27* (22).

Cantor, D. W. (1997). A paradigm shift. (President's Address). The APA 1996 Annual Report. *American Psychologist, 52 (8)*,780–786.

Danziger, K. (1994). *Constructing the subject: Historical origins of psychological research*. Cambridge: Cambridge University Press.

Fishman, D. B. (1998). The case for "Unscientific Psychology": Perplexingly paradoxical. *Contemporary Psychology, 43 (4)*, 277–278.

Fowler, R. D. (1997). The report of the Association, 1996. The APA

Annual Report. *American Psychologist, 52(8)*, 764–779.

Gergen, K. J. (1982). *Toward transformation in social knowledge*. London: Sage.

Gergen, K. J. (1991). *The saturated self: Dilemmas of identity in contemporary life*. New York: Basic Books.

Gergen, K. J. (1994). *Realities and relationships: Soundings in social construction*. Cambridge, MA: Harvard University Press.

Gross, P. R., Levitt, N. and Lewis, M. W. (Eds.) (1996). *The flight from science and reason*. New York: New York Academy of Sciences.

Harris, B. Review of Fred Newman, "The Myth of Psychology." *Contemporary Psychology, 38(2)*, 216.

Holzman, L. (1997). *Schools for growth: Radical alternatives to current educational models*. Mahwah, NJ: Lawrence Erlbaum.

Horgan, J. (1996). *The end of science: Facing the limits of knowledge in the twilight of the scientific age*. Reading, MA: Addison-Wesley.

Latour, B. (1993). *We have never been modern*. Cambridge, MA: Harvard University.

Lyotard, J-F. (1984). *The postmodern condition: A report on knowledge*. Minneapolis: University of Minnesota Press.

McNamee, S. and Gergen, K. J. (Eds.) (1992). *Therapy as social construction*. London: Sage.

Newman, F. (1991). *The myth of psychology*. New York: Castillo International.

Newman, F. (1996). *Performance of a lifetime: A practical-philosophical guide to the joyous life*. New York: Castillo International.

Newman, F. (in press). Does a story need a theory? (Understanding the methodology of narrative therapy). In D. Fee (Ed.), *Pathology and the postmodern: Mental illness as discourse and experience*. London: Sage.

Newman, F. and Holzman, L. (1993). *Lev Vygotsky: Revolutionary scientist*. London: Routledge.

Newman, F. and Holzman, L. (1996). *Unscientific psychology: A cultural-performatory approach to understanding human life*. Westport, CT: Praeger.

Newman, F. and Holzman, L. (1997). *The end of knowing: A new developmental way of learning*. London: Routledge.

Parker, I. (1995). "Right," said Fred, "I'm too sexy for bourgeois group therapy": the case of the Institute for Social Therapy. *Changes, An International Journal of Psychology and Psychotherapy, 13(1)*, 1–22.

Rice, C. E. (1997). The scientist-practitioner split and the future of psychology. *American Psychologist, 52(11)*, 1173–1181.

Seligman, M. E. P. (1995). The effectiveness of psychotherapy: The *Consumer Reports* study. *American Psychologist, 50(12)*, 965–974.

Seligman, M. E. P. (1998). Message from the President of APA. *APA Annual Convention Program*. Washington, DC: American Psychological Association, p. xxv.

Szasz, T. (1961). *The myth of mental illness*. New York: Harper & Row.

Tomasello, M. (1995). Vygotsky as therapist. *Contemporary Psychologist, 40(9)*, 768.

Life Upon the Wicked Stage

Since 1996, Newman has written short plays expressly for presentation at American Psychological Association Annual Conventions. The impetus for these "psychology plays" was Kenneth Gergen's invitation to Newman and me to participate in an innovative symposium he was putting together for the APA's 1996 convention. Entitled "Performative Psychology Redux," the symposium was a continuation of a successful experiment launched the year before to expand the narrow limits of the "representations of knowledge" psychologists make use of in talking to each other. Performative psychology, as Gergen uses the term, refers to representations (e.g., statements about the nature of psychological processes) that are simultaneously expressive acts. The symposium offered us a wonderful opportunity. For many years, I had been urging Newman (who had been writing and directing plays since 1986) to write a play with Vygotsky as a central character (he had already written "Outing Wittgenstein"). An APA symposium seemed the perfect venue. Newman wrote the 14-minute "Beyond the Pale" which was performed live as one of four "expressive acts" of Performative Psychology Redux, and I served as discussant. In the play Lev Vygotsky, the early Soviet developmental psychologist, and Ludwig Wittgenstein, the Austrian-born philosopher of language (both major influences on our work) are having a social therapy session. Their therapist is Bette Braun, a longtime social therapist and colleague of Newman's (played, in the original production, by herself). "Beyond the Pale" is a performance of their relational activity within social therapy. (It appears in

Chapter 5 of The End of Knowing: A New Developmental Way of Learning, *Newman and Holzman, 1997.) The enthusiastic response to "Beyond the Pale" suggested that there might be a wider audience for live theatre/performative psychology among convention participants. In 1997, the APA ad hoc Committee on Films and Other Media tested this out by sponsoring a session for which Newman wrote another (longer and more complex) play. "Life Upon the Wicked Stage" was performed in Chicago in front of an audience of nearly 450 attendees of the APA convention. As Friedman (1998) has pointed out, "Life Upon the Wicked Stage" contains a number of "inside" jokes which require, for full appreciation, some knowledge of history, psychology and philosophy. For example, the "seal car" of the Swiss National Circus in which Trotsky proposes to smuggle Lenin back into Russia, is a pun on the "sealed car" in which the Germans helped to smuggle Lenin into St. Petersburg in 1917. The argument between Vygotsky and Piaget over the name of the street upon which they are supposed to meet—is it "Stage Street" or "Zone Street"?— is based on one of the major differences between them. Piaget's view holds that human development consists of a fixed set of predetermined stages; Vygotsky held to a more fluid, transformational view, maintaining that human development is a social/performatory activity with no fixed stages and no necessary limit. The concept of "language games" that Kafka mentions in passing to Wittgenstein is a major component of Wittgenstein's later writings. Newman thinks of this play (and others like it) as "learning-leading-development" plays, in contrast to Brechtian "learning plays" which offer lessons and construct frameworks for solutions. "Life Upon the Wicked Stage," consisting of philosophical conversations between some of Newman's favorite thinkers, offers no lessons and certainly no solutions; it is simply a performance of performance.—L. H.*

CHARACTERS

LEV VYGOTSKY
JEAN PIAGET
V. I. LENIN
LEON TROTSKY
FRANZ KAFKA
LUDWIG WITTGENSTEIN
SIGMUND FREUD

Offstage (taped)

ANNOUNCER
SIR MALCOLM MUCKEREX

PROLOGUE

*JEAN PIAGET and LEV VYGOTSKY sit frozen at a small cafe table as
the song "Life Upon the Wicked Stage" from Showboat plays. They
slowly become animated, stand, and do a tap dance to the music.
Then they sit, and engage in silent, animated conversation, until the
music ends and the lights fade.*

SCENE 1

ANNOUNCER: History Theatre. Your host: Sir Malcolm Muckerex.

MUCKEREX: The world is a wicked stage upon which we all perform our
lives. The paradox of people trying to perform decent lives on a
wicked stage sometimes becomes overwhelming. So with modernism, which in the early years of this century generated achievements of almost unbelievable magnificence, even as the stage for
the remainder of the century was being built—a set for 50 years of
devastating warfare. But although the stage is wicked it does not
follow that life is wicked. Modernism's failure has been brought
about by the inability of genius to make a better world for all. World
War I, the War To End All Wars, turned out to be the beginnings of a
new level of human atrocities. Yet the pre-World War I period was
an exceedingly optimistic moment of great scientific, technological
and humanist accomplishment. It was a time of great and powerful
thinkers creating and dialoguing on great and powerful ideas. It was
a time of exiles debating these great ideas within the growing intellectual urban centers. Often the setting for such dialogue was not
the formal environment of the university, but the street cafe or the
dingy, cigarette-smoke-filled restaurant. These settings turned out
to be the unknown and unheard-of sites of new developments; the
wicked off-Main Street stages on which was exposed the paradox of
the greatness of modernism and its inability to change a wicked
world. A small sidewalk cafe in Geneva, Switzerland; the early
summer of 1916.

(Enter LENIN and TROTSKY. They sit at the cafe table.)

LENIN: I did not know you would come here, Leon. I was led to believe you would remain in America until the time was ripe.

TROTSKY: The time might well be ripe today, Comrade Lenin. Combined and uneven development governs history all the time. And in a historical moment such as this matters can leap forward in what we, overdetermined in our thinking by the temporal mode of society, call a week or a fortnight, Comrade Lenin.

LENIN: Yes, Comrade Trotsky, you are right—as always. I also think the conditions for revolution are more ripe than meets the eye. Though, as you know, I have never felt completely comfortable with your theory of combined and uneven development.

TROTSKY: And why not?

LENIN: I suppose I am not completely at ease with any *psychological* notion of development—not yours or Freud's or anyone else's for that matter. I am concerned that the historicalness, the sensuousness of Marx's notion of dialectics is in some ways corroded by these psychological notions of development that now consume so many bourgeois thinkers as well as yourself.

TROTSKY: Comrade Lenin, are you calling me a bourgeois thinker?

LENIN: Leon, Leon, don't be so sensitive. All of us are bourgeois thinkers. We live still in a bourgeois world. My concern is that our bourgeois thoughts not *totally* overdetermine our actions. I am constantly touched and motivated by the stories of Marx's reactions to the Paris Commune; his immediate and intense support for the communards in the face of his stern opposition before the commune began. So, in my view, must our actions be more determining than our words. Leon, I fear most of all the brilliance and purity of your thought. You might well be as much a danger for your being right about everything as other Bolshevik leaders are for being wrong about everything.

TROTSKY: Lenin, Lenin, Lenin, Marx was first and foremost a scientist.

LENIN: No. No, never. He was first and foremost a revolutionary.

TROTSKY: Well then, enough of this gibberish. What is to be done? The Western world is at war and so is Mother Russia. Our people are dying in droves. We cannot afford to sit here in a cafe in Geneva.

I'm sure we both agree on that. What is to be done? I've come here from the Bronx, New York—in America—to find out what is to be done? My theory of combined and uneven development does not tell me that. You, my leader, V. I. Lenin, must do so.

LENIN: I do not know what to do. I sit here in Geneva day after day rereading Hegel's *Logic* like a school boy preparing for an examination. But I do not know what to do.

TROTSKY: This must be a result of your extended stay in Western Europe. Everywhere there are brilliant theories of how to understand everything—but their world is not working. Not even the social democrats here know what to do. Kautsky creates theories, theories, theories, and betrayals in action every day. But we are Russians. We are making a revolution. You must know what to do.

LENIN: But I don't, Leon! I don't.

TROTSKY: Then you must return to Russia.

LENIN: Easier said than done, Leon. I am nowadays easily recognized even in disguise.

TROTSKY: *(Thinking hard)* Maybe I can help. I have a friend here in Geneva. He is a ringmaster in the Swiss National Circus and he told me yesterday, they are going to St. Petersburg next February.

LENIN: The Swiss Circus?

TROTSKY: Yes. I'm sure you've heard of them. They are famous the world over for their trained seals. He said he could get me or a couple of Bolshevikis back to St. Petersburg in one of the seal cars. It would be smelly but safe.

LENIN: *(Laughs)* And what will the headlines say: Lenin returns to St. Petersburg on seal train.

TROTSKY: You will make something positive of it, Comrade Lenin. You are our very best propagandist.

LENIN: I like it, Leon. I like it. You will put me in touch with your seal man.

TROTSKY: *(Nods)* Yes.

SCENE 2

MUCKEREX: We choose to fictionalize matters altogether. We have our characters come together as their total historical becomings, rather than presenting them in their space-time straitjackets. Lenin and Trotsky abandoned their table at around 5:30 in the afternoon. They are quickly replaced on the historical performatory stage by Jean Piaget and Lev Vygotsky. They never met, you say? Good. Here they can meet! They were only 19, you say—both having been born the same year, 1896, but never having seen each other in their entire lifetimes? Again, you are right. But this is only a story.

Truth was a passion for our civilization in the early years of this century. But we now know that passion, not truth, ruled the day. Our postmodern story continues with the meeting of Piaget and Vygotsky in Geneva, 1916 on June 19 at 5:45 p.m.

(Enter JEAN PIAGET in his late teens, dressed like a student, carrying books. He sits down at the table and starts to read. LEV VYGOTSKY enters, also looking like a student. He looks around trying to find a seat and finally comes over to PIAGET's table, seeing no other place to be seated.)

VYGOTSKY: Might I join you? There appear to be no other tables available.
PIGET: *(Stands and extends his hand)* Oh, of course. Please. My name is Jean Piaget.
VYGOTSKY: *(Shaking hands)* Thank you so much. I am Lev Vygotsky.

(They sit.)

PIAGET: I take it you are not from Switzerland.
VYGOTSKY: Oh, no. I am not from Switzerland. I am from Russia— Gomel. I am here on spring break from the university. And you?
PIAGET: Yes. Yes, I am from Switzerland, though also on spring break from the university. *(Pause.)* What is happening in Russia? Things seem so chaotic. I heard Lenin speak at a forum the other night. But I could tell nothing from what he said. He is such a fanatic. And

there is a rumor going about that Trotsky is in the city. Do you follow Lenin or Trotsky? Are you a leftist? Or should I not ask?

VYGOTSKY: No, No. Please. It's quite alright. Yes, indeed I am a leftist—a Marxist. And I would say I follow Lenin and Trotsky and the Bolsheviki line. But I have not been active. I have been studying in school mainly. Trotsky is very popular in Gomel where there are many Jews. He is a Jew, you know.

PIAGET: I did not know. I am not so political. Switzerland is a peculiar place. In many ways we have no politics. We are a kind of permanent neutral state in Western Europe—a home to exiles of every variety. It makes us all too neutral in every respect. But what can I do? We are put wherever we are put. And our place on the world stage determines the role.

VYGOTSKY: Perhaps. Perhaps you are right. Perhaps my place in Russia makes me a revolutionary. But I do not feel comfortable with the passivity of your observation.

PIAGET: Nor do I. Nor do I. But I am afraid it's so. We are, after all, animals not unlike the lower phyla. We transform as they do. In stages. In accordance with relatively rigid biological laws. And, I suspect, laws determining stages of consciousness which we merely have not yet discovered.

VYGOTSKY: And culture?

PIAGET: Not so much of a factor, I think. *(Pause.)* But, listen, speaking of culture, I have two tickets to a play this evening. Chekhov. Do you like Chekhov? You must. *(Smiling.)* He is a Russian.

VYGOTSKY: I do like him very much. But I do know many Russians who hate him. Yes I would love to join you. It's nice of you to invite me. Maybe this bit of Russian culture can have more of an impact than you think possible. Where is the theatre? And when does the play begin?

PIAGET: It is at the Leo Tolstoy Theatre. Downtown. At eight.

VYGOTSKY: Really? I was there just yesterday. To a photographic exhibition. It's on that small curvy street, right off of the main square in the center of town . . . right next to the post office. Yes, I remember it well. It's on something called Zone Street, isn't that right?

PIAGET: You have a good memory, Lev Vygotsky. But actually that street is called Stage Street.

VYGOTSKY: No, no I am certain. It's Zone.

PIAGET: Lev, I have lived here all my life. It's Stage Street. I am absolutely certain. Stage. Stage Street.

VYGOTSKY: Do the tickets say? I am certain it is Zone, Jean.

(PIAGET pulls out tickets.)

PIAGET: It does not say. As you know, it is not a very formal theatre.

VYGOTSKY: Well, I am absolutely certain it is Zone Street.

PIAGET: *(Slightly frustrated)* Well, Vygotsky. You go to your Zone Street Theatre and I'll go to my Stage Street Theatre and if we both wind up at the same place, we'll see the play together. But now I must be going. I have a prior meeting. I hope we see each other again.

(PIAGET exits.)

SCENE 3

MUCKEREX: The world of 1916 was a strange mixture of optimism and pessimism. In Europe, dying monarchism and unborn communism mixed to form a confusion that was not easily articulated. Real politics, which have no capacity to deal with the subtleties of history, resolves these contradictions by bureaucratic means and ultimately by the most extreme of bureaucratic moves—war. But those thinkers, famous and ordinary, for whom war was not a serious or moral solution—those who identified these confusions as more cultural or more psychological or more historical and less in terms of the game playing of nation states—they searched the fields of science and the humanities, of literature and music, of philosophy and theatre, more generally of culture, to better understand what was going on. Our table hosts still another conversation on that summer day in 1916.

(FRANZ KAFKA is seated at the table as WITTGENSTEIN wanders aimlessly— with a knapsack on his back.)

KAFKA: Ludwig. Ludwig Wittgenstein.

(WITTGENSTEIN looks around bemusedly until he sees who is calling him.)

KAFKA: Kafka. Franz Kafka. *(He stands, reaches his hand out to WITTGENSTEIN.)* We met at a conference on aeronautics . . . in Prague . . . last summer.

WITTGENSTEIN: I remember, I think. Franz . . . uh . . . .

KAFKA: Franz Kafka. Do you really remember?

WITTGENSTEIN: *(Stiffens)* I do not lie, Mr. Kafka. I do not lie.

KAFKA: No offense, Wittgenstein. I mistakenly thought you were being polite. I should have known better. Please have a seat.

WITTGENSTEIN: I was looking for Freud . . . Sigmund Freud. Do you know him? We had an appointment. He is a friend of my sister, Gretl . . . we are all from Vienna.

KAFKA: I do not know him, though I have heard of him. He is becoming quite famous. *(WITTGENSTEIN sits.)* Perhaps we could chat until he arrives. What are you up to these days, creating model airplanes, are you?

WITTGENSTEIN: No. I have given up aeronautics. I am just now completing a tractatus which shows positively the precise nature of language.

KAFKA: Impressive, Ludwig. I am impressed.

WITTGENSTEIN: There is a problem, Kafka.

KAFKA: And what is that?

WITTGENSTEIN: Language is not precise.

KAFKA: Then what have you shown?

WITTGENSTEIN: Either that I am wrong or that one can show something to be precise which isn't.

KAFKA: Well, I guess everything can be bureaucratized—even

language. Everything can be shown to be what it isn't. Using language is a kind of game, don't you think, Ludwig?

WITTGENSTEIN: A game? What kind of game? What is a game?

KAFKA: There are endless kinds of games. Some are very precise; follow very clear rules. Others are like randomly moving about in a complex maze with no rules at all.

WITTGENSTEIN: What are you doing now, Kafka?

KAFKA: Oh, I'm still working as an accountant. But I've begun to think more and more about writing stories.

WITTGENSTEIN: Then you think writing stories is like playing a game with language?

KAFKA: Perhaps.

WITTGENSTEIN: There will be no rules in your stories?

KAFKA: I hope not. The stories are all about the endless rules of our bureaucratized lives. And the alienation and madness created by living in such a world. But I hope my stories do not create still more rules.

WITTGENSTEIN: I'm returning home to enter the Austrian Army. I think I will carry my tractatus with me and see how it appears to me by war's end.

KAFKA: I hope it is not filled with bullets by the war's end. This is a stupid war. A wholly rule-governed game played by bureaucrats with the lives of young men.

WITTGENSTEIN: I agree. But I feel morally bound to participate on the side of my homeland.

KAFKA: Wittgenstein, you have only the duty of genius to consider. Your genius. Do not let them turn you into cannon fodder.

WITTGENSTEIN: I am not so sure as you are, Kafka, as to the nature of life. I cannot even discern the nature of mathematics and language and they're infinitely less complex than life. In any event, my family, in particular my father, who is a wealthy man in Vienna, needs for me to fulfill this obligation.

KAFKA: Do not die Wittgenstein. It would be a great waste.

WITTGENSTEIN: When the war is over I will think more about games. *(Looks offstage and points.)* Oh, there's Freud looking through the window.

(KAFKA turns, looks where WITTGENSTEIN is pointing.)

KAFKA: I'll go now. I'll tell Freud where you are as I leave. Have a good . . . what does he call it . . . ?
WITTGENSTEIN: I don't know.
KAFKA: . . . session. *(Stands and starts offstage. Turning back to WITTGENSTEIN.)* Take care, Ludwig Wittgenstein. Do not let them squish you out like a roach. Take care. *(He exits.)*

SCENE 4

MUCKEREX: Does the world determine the mind or does the mind determine the world? Modern psychology is born in this paradoxical quagmire. It is an old paradox, to be sure, but it is a new day. The mind-body dilemma appears quite different when the bodies are creating great technology and building more and more sophisticated elements of the wicked stage while the mind stays relatively the same. Geneva, June 19, 1916; 6:31 in the afternoon.

(Enter FREUD. WITTGENSTEIN stands.)

WITTGENSTEIN: Dr. Freud. Over here.

(FREUD recognizes him and heads toward the table extending his hand.)

FREUD: Ludwig. Ludwig Wittgenstein. I've not seen you for years. You've grown up. I have regards from your sister Gretl whom I saw just last week. *(Sits.)* What have you been studying?
WITTGENSTEIN: I've been studying the philosophy of mathematics and the philosophy of language. Do you know anything of that, Dr. Freud?
FREUD: Not a thing, Ludwig. Not a thing.
WITTGENSTEIN: What then is the relationship of the language of our

dreams, the language of our unconscious, as you have called it, and the language of everyday life?

FREUD: I would say it is the same language, only it is used differently. And the pictures it conjures up are not so constrained by the representations language has in real life.

WITTGENSTEIN: Well, would that not eventually make the language itself different?

FREUD: I would suppose so, Ludwig. I have not thought as much about it as I probably should. But it seems quite important. Since in my opinion the language and structure of the mind, both conscious and unconscious, determine our understanding of the world. It would be important to better understand the language of the mind as part of understanding the activity of the mind.

WITTGENSTEIN: But what if the mind has no language? What if the mind determines, amongst other things, the language that we use in life without itself having a language?

FREUD: That might well be what I am saying. The mind might not need language for it has no one to talk to, save itself. Representing it as an inner conversation might just be the language that we use in reality imposing itself on the mind.

WITTGENSTEIN: And, in turn, this understanding of the mind in conversation might in turn be imposing itself on reality.

FREUD: You are too clever for me, Ludwig.

WITTGENSTEIN: I do not mean to be clever.

FREUD: I know, but you are. Does it seem a curse to you?

WITTGENSTEIN: No, not a curse, but a burden. Would your method of analysis help?

FREUD: I fear not. Brilliance is not psychopathology.

WITTGENSTEIN: Yet brilliance perhaps creates more pain than stupidity. Brilliance abounds in Europe and more generally in Western civilization. And yet it appears to be of little value in making our world work.

FREUD: It's hard to live a good life on so wicked a stage.

WITTGENSTEIN: But how could it have gotten to be so wicked on your theory?

FREUD: We are wicked, Ludwig. Not only wicked, but wicked enough.

WITTGENSTEIN: So yours is a theory about the wickedness of men?

FREUD: No, Ludwig. Mine is a theory about the workings of the mind of man, which surely must include its capacity for wickedness.

SCENE 5

MUCKEREX: And so we live our lives on our wicked stage. Our performances are constrained by the theatre space. Or so it appears. Sometimes the performance almost seems to go beyond the stage. Sometimes in a story. Sometimes in a life performance. Many doubt that it can. It is the old paradox in its latest form.

(VYGOTSKY seated at the table. PIAGET enters. VYGOTSKY notices him and waves to him to come sit.)

VYGOTSKY: Piaget. Good to see you. I was hoping you would be here again today. Please sit. I must apologize for my pig-headedness yesterday. You, of course, were right. The Tolstoy Theatre is on Stage Street. I have been obsessed lately with zones. I do not understand it. My apologies.

PIAGET: What precisely is a zone?

VYGOTSKY: I don't know. Though so far as I can tell, it is the opposite of a stage. If you could tell me then exactly what a stage is, it might help me understand better what I am thinking.

PIAGET: A stage is a point in a temporal line. It is then, following Kant, a unit of time, of succession, necessary for perception. It is the *a priori something that comes next* in our experience of the world.

VYGOTSKY: And what of the experience of the transition itself? Is there not danger here of an infinite regress—a kind of Parmenidian paradox?

PIAGET: Such is our limitation, Vygotsky. As scientists. As students of our own selves and our world, we are limited by such categories of perception.

VYGOTSKY: Again, Jean Piaget, limitation. I think a zone is perhaps a rejection of limitation. It is a place from which becoming—transaction—can be studied and, simultaneously, lived.

PIAGET: This seems too Hegelian for me. A practical use. Give me a practical example.

VYGOTSKY: *(Long pause, thinking)* Tell me the strangest thing you do—you know—something you don't tell anyone about. I will not laugh! Please.

PIAGET: *(Thinks hard)* I tap-dance!

VYGOTSKY: You tap-dance, too?

PIAGET: You are also a tap dancer?

VYGOTSKY: Incredible. This must be what made us attractive to each other at first sight.

PIAGET: You dance in public?

VYGOTSKY: Never. I am in the tap-dance closet.

PIAGET: Me too. Me too . . . You think, perhaps, a zone is where embarrassed tap dancers hide out?

VYGOTSKY: *(Laughs)* Could be, Jean. Could be . . . . We continue. How do you tap-dance?

PIAGET: Am I to show you? Right here . . . in public? Are we coming out, Lev?

VYGOTSKY: Why not? Let us tap-dance together. Piaget and Vygotsky—the tapping thinkers.

(Music comes up on chorus of "Life Upon the Wicked Stage." They tap-dance for about 30 seconds.)

VYGOTSKY: *(Stops the dancing)* Now tell me, Piaget, what have we just done? Let us study the relationship between what we have done and our characterization of what we have just done.

PIAGET: I have actually thought about this often . . . My understanding is that tapping begins in the feet. The feet move first and the rest of the body follows.

VYGOTSKY: Aha! To me nothing moves first. Everything moves at once; the body—not just the feet—taps. Our obsession with stages—with what comes first—distorts history where there is no beginning and no end. A zone, it seems to me, is a methodological construct for examining the processes of life and history as process. We must not make things stand still in order that they might be studied.

PIAGET: But what of objectivity, Vygotsky? The theatre, I must remind you, was on Stage Street. By the way, did you get to the theatre?

VYGOTSKY: No. I didn't. You neither? *(PIAGET shakes his head "no.")* I wound up at an informal discussion with Leon Trotsky at the Workers' Salon. He laid out his theory of combined and uneven development.

PIAGET: Did he tell you what is happening in Russia?

VYGOTSKY: No. He did not.

PIAGET: I went to have dinner with my mother and she would not permit me to leave. Besides, I was angry at you and didn't want to see you.

VYGOTSKY: We'll be talking about zones and stages for the rest of our lives, Piaget . . . you think?

PIAGET: But we will, I fear, never explain our strange meetingyesterday.

VYGOTSKY: Maybe it needs no explanation. We lived it. And we can communicate it to others as a story rather than an explanation.

PIAGET: Piaget and Vygotsky—the tap-dancing thinkers.

(They laugh, and return to the table. "Life Upon the Wicked Stage" music plays again, and they converse animatedly with each other. Near the end of the song they again perform a tap dance, after which they embrace and bow.)

Life As Performance
(Can You Practice Psychology If There's Nothing That's "Really" Going On?)

LOIS HOLZMAN

This discussion is meant to introduce the "basics" of Newman's methodology. On the one hand, it is a conversation in which nearly all psychologists have taken or can easily take part. All the same, it is a piece of an ongoing debate among psychologists with a sociocultural orientation on both the substance and politics of Lev Vygotsky and his psychology. As such, the following remarks serve to fill in the blanks of what Tomasello, in reviewing Newman's and my Lev Vygotsky: Revolutionary Scientist, *referred to as our "point of view of Vygotsky as an intellectual revolutionary who has much to say to modern citizens of the Western world about life in general" (see the Introduction).—L.H.*

WHAT ARE REVOLUTIONARY PSYCHOLOGISTS TO DO?

Lev Vygotsky, the Russian/Soviet psychologist who has been an inspiration for current cultural-historical approaches in psychology, worked throughout his life to change the culture of the psychology of his day. He tried to escape the Stalinist dogma of many of his Soviet colleagues and refused to be an ideologue. He took seriously the ideas of European and American psychologists, even as he was troubled by the linear, dualistic and reductionistic idealism and scientism of many of them. He deeply appreciated the creativity of Piaget's work, for example, while at the same time he rejected Piaget's premise of the asocial and ahistorical child who possessed "pure thought" and did not communicate until the age of 7. Vygotsky was, in his own words, searching for method—to create a new psychology inseparable from creating a new environment for (the creating of) that new psychology.

This search was as much a cultural study as it was a scientific one. According to contemporary Vygotskian Alex Kozulin, psychology was not even Vygotsky's object of study; rather, he saw psychology as a tool with which to study culture (Kozulin, 1986, 1990). Indeed, Vygotsky's cultural-scientific enterprise was equally a political one. Among present-day Vygotskian scholars who share this assessment are Jerome Bruner, who views Vygotsky's work as a form of revolutionary political activism (Bruner, 1996, p. 4) and James Wertsch, who described the cultural environment in which Vygotsky worked as "one of upheaval, enthusiasm, and energy unimaginable by today's standards [in which] people such as Vygotsky and his followers devoted every hour of their lives to making certain that the new socialist state, the first grand experiment based on Marxist-Leninist principles, would succeed" (Wertsch, 1985, p. 10).

Fred Newman and I call Vygotsky a revolutionary scientist (Newman and Holzman, 1993). In our opinion, when Vygotsky raised the question, "What is the proper unit of analysis for a psychological science?" he was doing so as a *revolutionary scientist*. After all, these were revolutionary times. The first successful socialist revolution was only minutes old, and the transformation from a feudal Russia to a

Soviet Union characterized by a planned economy was a monumental task. There were dozens of 'learning and development' problems to deal with, such as nearly universal illiteracy, cultural differences among the hundreds of ethnic groups that formed the new nation, absence of services for those unable to participate fully in the formation of the new society, and millions of abandoned and homeless children who roamed the country.

There is another way in which Vygotsky's question was revolutionary—it treated science itself as open to scrutiny and radical transformation. The nature of the science activity—human social-cultural-historical activity—was what concerned him. By the 1920s the field of psychology was well on its way to becoming an empirical and experimental science, and questions of method and units of analysis were hotly debated. For example, would following the experimental path mean excluding from psychological investigation the very nature of human consciousness? Vygotsky was not willing to give up the study of consciousness (nor the "higher psychological processes" that are its manifestations). Nor was he willing to settle for two kinds of psychology (one for mental and one for nonmental events) or one psychology if it bypassed consciousness by reducing mental events to nonmental ones. He recognized the need to break with the dualism of existing psychological method.

Moreover, the issue was not merely theoretical. Vygotsky and his colleagues were a part of a great real-life experiment in creating culture (the hoped-for new society). To understand and accomplish the process of this actual construction required a new method of study. Even more, it required a new *understanding* of method. Here is how Vygotsky phrased the challenge:

> The search for method becomes one of the most important problems of the entire enterprise of understanding the uniquely human forms of psychological activity. In this case, the method is simultaneously prerequisite and product, the tool and the result of the study. (Vygotsky, 1978, p. 65)

Vygotsky is making a solid break with the accepted scientific paradigm, in which method is understood as a tool which, when applied, yields results. With this model, the relation between tool and result is linear, instrumental and dualistic. Vygotsky is proposing a nonlinear, noninstrumental, nondualistic method—a dialectical method—in which the "tool" and the "result" come into existence together. They are neither separate nor identical, but elements of a unity (totality, whole). Vygotsky's way of seeing is dialectical; he is relating to the totality, not to any particular. His great insight was that human development—on the individual, societal and species levels—is the transformation of totalities, not the changing of individual particulars. This is how he understood method: create/practice ("search for") method—this was both his question and his answer as a revolutionary scientist.

Vygotsky's revolutionary conception of method as "tool-and-result" cannot be separated from his (equally revolutionary) conception of what it means to be human. Among the many wonderful and terrible things we are and do, human beings have the capacity to "do dialectics." We transform totalities; we create "tools-and-results." Vygotsky understood the human developmental process dialectically, as an ongoing, continuously emergent social-cultural-historical collective activity. In contemporary language, we human beings create our development; it doesn't happen to us. The evidence? Our capacity for dialectics: From infancy through old age we are "who we are" and, at the very same time, "who we are not."

For Vygotsky, living at the historical juncture of the beginning of modern science's fourth century of cultural hegemony and the birth of what was seen by its creators as the most significant cultural transformation since capitalism, science and revolution were historically (practically-critically) intertwined:

> To the naïve mind, revolution and history seem incompatible; it believes that historical development continues as long as it follows a straight line. When a change comes, a break in the historical fabric, a leap—then this naïve mind sees only catastrophe, a fall, a rupture; for the naïve mind history ends until back again straight and narrow. The scientific mind, on the contrary, views revolution as the locomotive of history forging ahead at full speed; it regards the revolutionary epoch as a tangible, living embodiment of history. A revolution solves only those tasks which have been raised by history: this

proposition holds true equally for revolution in general and for aspects of social and cultural life. (Vygotsky, quoted in Levitin, 1982, front cover)

In our post-Cold War, post-revolutionary, post-Marxist (and to some, post-scientific) times, Vygotsky's words may seem quaint and romantic; his turn of phrase, certainly, is modern as opposed to post-modern. He was seeking to discover/create a Marxist science. A product of modernism (as, of course, was Marx), he could not help but be susceptible to some of the idealistic claims of science and the scientific world view, in particular, that human liberation would have a scientific face. For, modern science was nothing if not politically, culturally and philosophically revolutionary. It made an ontological and epistemological break with religion, the world view that had dominated for centuries. Modern science brought a new view of the world—as being naturally in motion rather than naturally at rest, a new view of "Man"—as uniquely *other than* Nature, and a new view of their relationship—the universe was governed by rules which Man alone can make and know and by which he can, thereby, establish control over it. Human beings thus came to be characterized as knowers (viewers, perceivers, technological interveners) of the world. In fact, our very existence and identity became contingent on our knowing, or epistemic, capabilities (see Newman and Holzman, 1996, pp. 31–32). This epistemological paradigm has been the basis for remarkable advances in the biological and physical sciences and technology.

Given the success and promise of modern science and the epistemological paradigm, it is all the more remarkable that Vygotsky was able to break as sharply as he did with some of modernism's most cherished conceptions about method and units of analysis. In the best tradition of Marx, he was an historical materialist and a dialectician, thus his sensitivity to the historical necessity of transforming the accepted instrumental conception of method— as a tool to be applied—into non-instrumental, dialectical *tool-and-result* methodology. And, as we will explore further, in the best tradition of science, Vygotsky was sensitive to the particularities of his subject matter—human beings.

We are living in an historical moment very different from

Vygotsky's. The interconnectedness of politics and science is far less obvious, to a large degree because it is obscured (sometimes deliberately) by both the scientific and political establishments. Is Vygotsky's question, "What is the proper unit of analysis for a psychological science?" still revolutionary? Is it still relevant? Are science and revolution (and history) still intertwined? Can we even ask "What are revolutionary psychologists to do?" in such politically nonrevolutionary/reactionary times as these?

Along with some other contemporary psychologists who are admirers and/or followers of Vygotsky, Newman and I find his question as relevant as ever. Political events of the past decade have erased the capital *R* from Revolution, and intellectual events equally threaten the god of Science. These circumstances create possible openings for dialogue on the methodological issues that consumed Vygotsky's short life. (He died at the age of 38, having lived his adulthood sick with tuberculosis). In this essay, I want to explore the current quite particular relevance of Vygotsky's questioning activity to the task of creating environments of and for human liberation and what, if anything, psychology and psychologists have to do with this.

Vygotsky's method did not win the day, either for the Soviet Union or for psychology as a human science. His work came under severe attack from academicians/ideologues during the last years of his life and was suppressed after his death. His publications were withdrawn from libraries and universities and only the efforts of a small group of his followers kept his writings intact and his work alive (Vygodskaya, 1996). While psychologists at Soviet (and now Russian) psychological institutes and universities continued his legacy, his ideas about child development, learning and language have never been put into practice through large scale educational initiatives.

As it developed over this century, the discipline of psychology took a very different path from the one Vygotsky suggested. It virtually ignored the methodological issues he raised and, instead, created itself in the image of the natural and physical sciences. It rejected dialectics in favor of linearity and causality. It adopted the narrow and dualistic conception of method as something to be applied (tool-for-result

methodology) and rejected Vygotsky's search (tool-and-result methodology). It adopted an understanding of human beings that combined a
natural science view—we are a behaving species—with a technological
metaphor—we are like machines. Having fashioned the image of
human beings as isolated individuals separated from each other and our
environment, psychologists created for themselves the task of figuring
out how any of us ever get "socialized." Having conceptualized an
"inner world" and "outer reality" they had to posit theories, devise
research strategies and conduct investigations in order to answer the
puzzling questions of how the "inner" gets externalized and the "outer"
becomes internalized.

Many critics and historians of mainstream scientific psychology
have discussed the unfortunate consequences arising from psychology
having gone in the direction of a natural as opposed to a human science
(e.g., Danziger, 1994, 1997; Gergen, 1982, 1994; Parker, 1989; Parker
and Shotter, 1990; Polkinghorne, 1983; Shotter, 1990). The present discussion will not review this interesting and valuable literature but
instead focus on efforts to refashion psychology as a sociocultural-historical field of inquiry. Vygotsky's question, "What is the proper unit of
analysis for a psychological science?" will remain in the forefront of
this discussion. First, I summarize how mainstream scientific psychology answered the question by creating behavior as psychology's unit of
analysis. Next, I discuss one strain of the sociocultural-historical (neo-
Vygotskian) movement—cultural psychology—which offers *mediated
activity* as the unit of analysis that can serve to remind psychologists to
"keep culture in mind" while remaining scientific (Cole, 1996).

Finally, I present the approach of Newman and myself as an unscientific, cultural-performatory practice of tool-and-result (dialectical)
methodology. As the primary example of our practice, Newman's performative social therapy emulates neither explanatory nor interpretive
science, as do other forms of psychotherapy. Dealing with emotional
problems and pain does not require insight, objectification or analysis.
Rather, as we see it, it requires creating new emotions (developing
emotionally). This is a creative activity people do with each other. In
dialectial, tool-and-result fashion, growing emotionally is inseparable

from creating environments that support emotional growth. The next three essays in this volume discuss specific aspects of the unscientific, cultural-performatory nature of social therapy. For example, in "Diagnosis: The Human Cost of the Rage to Order," Newman and Gergen state that the problem with diagnosis is "the diagnostic form of life, the identificational form of discourse, the analytical form of therapy and emotive language." Their distinctly unscientific suggestion is to eradicate the authoritarianism and pseudo-scientific "truth" of therapy by diagnosing in a radically democratic, performatory environment. In "Beyond Narrative to Performed Conversation," Newman and I urge narrative therapists to appreciate the therapeutic implications of the fact that while we human beings believe that we can distance ourselves from ourselves, we cannot. The value of stories is in their making. Finally, in "A Therapeutic Deconstruction of the Illusion of Self," Newman describes social therapy as, among other things, an ensemble performance of discourse that helps people gain a practical and activistic sense of their capacity to create (rather than helping them "express themselves," communicate, persuade, and so on).

Just as changing the culture of the psychology of Vygotsky's day required a transformation of the totality of the science activity, so too does changing the culture of the psychology of our day. The difference, given the changed days, is that the transformation now required is from a scientific to a cultural methodology.

HOW PSYCHOLOGY CREATED BEHAVIOR

Kurt Danziger has written extensively about how American psychology created itself in the image of the natural sciences in a little over 100 years. In his most recent book, *Naming the Mind: How Psychology Found Its Language*, he examines the most significant categories and concepts of psychological theory, research, and practice. His work is useful in showing the role of discourse in creating and maintaining scientific psychology. Danziger identifies some of psychology's problematic philosophical assumptions:

Although psychologists are conventionalists in the definition of their theoretical concepts, they act like naive naturalists with respect to the domains that their theories are meant to explain. They tend to proceed as though everyday psychological categories represented natural kinds, as though the distinctions expressed in their basic categories accurately reflected the natural divisions among psychological phenomena. Psychological discussions typically assume that there really is a distinct kind of entity out there that corresponds exactly to what we refer to as an attitude, say, and it is naturally different in kind from other sorts of entities out there for which we have different category names, like motives or emotions. (Danziger, 1997, p. 8)

In order to expose the hidden level of theory, Danziger contends, we need to analyze the discourse from which psychological categories derive their sense. But to do so requires that we recognize that discourse is an historical formation—and this would reveal that psychology had nothing "natural" to talk about—but only what it had invented:

> This runs counter to one of the most deeply embedded features of modern Psychology—its ahistoricism. Why? The most obvious reason is based on Psychology's wishful identification with the natural sciences. Psychological research is supposed to be concerned with natural, not historical, objects, and its methods are considered to be those of natural science, not those of history. Psychology is committed to investigating processes like cognition, perception, and motivation, as historically invariant phenomena of nature, not as historically determined social phenomena. (Danziger, 1997, p. 9)

Its "wishful identification with the natural sciences" led psychologists to believe that the proper unit of analysis was a "natural" object. This has had unfortunate consequences for, to the extent that we create a psychology *about* us in the ways that zoology is about animal life, physics is about matter and astronomy is about stars, we (the studiers) wind up distorting us (the studied) to such a degree that the object of our investigation is lost. Such is the curious nature of the "aboutness paradigm"—it cannot be applied to human life-as-lived (see Newman's and my "Beyond Narrative to Performed Conversation," this volume; Newman, in press; Newman and Holzman, 1997). With apparent ease, psychology thus dismissed that which is most fascinating and interesting about being human—our subjectivity (historicalness, socialness, consciousness and self-reflexivity)—in order to apply research methods constructed to investigate objects that do not have these qualities. Human subjectivity and its paradoxicality were subjects left to the philosophers to ponder.

In this age of behavioral science, however, it is worth being reminded that many of the late nineteenth- and early twentieth-century pioneers of psychology were as well versed in philosophy as they were in physics. They concerned themselves with subjectivity and its paradoxes—and considered psychology to be as much a philosophical, historical and cultural enterprise as a scientific one. In this age of the naive experimental subject, it is worth noting, as Danziger does, that a century ago the scientific community served as its own data source (1994, p. 52). In Wilhelm Wundt's Leipzig laboratory, the psychological investigation was a collaborative effort among scientists who would serve interchangeably as "subject" and "experimenter" as a matter of practical convenience. For Wundt, human subjectivity—far from being a problem to be overcome in the name of unattainable scientific objectivity—was an asset to be utilized in efforts to understand even simple psychological processes. Wundt thought he could devise a method to scientifically study perceptual experience—not the self-reporting of the experience but the actual perceptual experience itself. One of the things we see in his failure to achieve the desired results is the paradoxicality of human subjective experience—we cannot distance ourselves from ourselves without distorting that part of ourselves we seek to understand; we cannot help but be self-reflexive; we cannot study human subjective-social phenomena scientifically. Ironically, Wundt is remembered as the father of scientific psychology and the complexity of his thinking, even on the manner of experimentation, has been all but lost except to those who delve into the history of psychology.

Philosophical considerations of the nature of subjectivity, consciousness, agency and activity rather quickly faded from consideration as psychology, in the first quarter of this century, found the perfect candidate for its object of scientific study—behavior. According to Danziger, this new psychological category was key to establishing the legitimacy of the discipline. Behavior (and, to a lesser extent, learning) unified Psychology—providing the common "scientific" laws and the common discourse that made it possible for psychology to claim the existence of phenomena important to (and belonging to) all fields of psychology.

> Behaviour became the category that Psychology would use to define its subject matter: Whether one was trying to explain a child's answers on a problem-solving task, an adult's neurotic symptomotology, or a white rat's reaction to finding itself in a laboratory maze, one was ultimately trying to explain the same thing, namely, the behaviour of an organism. Classifying such diverse phenomena together as instances of "behaviour" was the first necessary step in establishing the claim that Psychology was one science with one set of explanatory principles. (Danziger, 1997, p. 86).

Here was a phenomenon that seemed to meet the criteria necessary for a proper unit of analysis for a new discipline fashioning itself after the natural and physical sciences. Behavior seemed to be the kind of phenomenon about which something could be said. Here was a phenomenon that could be measured and quantified. Here was a phenomenon that could be "found" over and over again to be the unifying factor in all the varied things human beings do. And so, psychology became the study of behavior, psychologists presuming (and convincing the rest of us) that they had identified a naturally occurring phenomenon, a naturally occurring psychological category.

As the great unifier, behavior came to be what psychologists see. Psychologists of our day seek to discover the psychological foundations of violence and aggression in order to gain insight into (and reverse the tide of) the increase in *violent and aggressive behavior*; the widespread use and often devastating effects of drugs has shaped a billion dollar addiction industry in the US which includes the psychological study of *addictive behavior*; the information highway challenges psychologists to rethink *learning behavior*; the pressure of identity politics made clear the need for intensified study of variations in the *communicative behavior* of various groups as compared along gender, race, ethnic and class lines, and so on.

The choice of behavior as "the proper unit of analysis for a psychological science" is deliberately contrary to who/what human beings are (and are not)—continuously emergent and dialectical, simultaneously agents and products (tools-and-results) of qualitative change. Behavior relates to human beings as unchanging in character, just as the units of study in the natural and physical sciences are. Chemists, biologists and the like are aware that their objects of study—e.g., chemical elements, atoms, genetic material and planets—do not transform their character and still remain chemical elements, atoms, genetic material, planets. But human beings are different in this respect; we do undergo fundamental, qualitative transformations in our character—yet, we remain human beings.

Identifying behavior as the subject matter of psychology, the basic unit of analysis no matter what, where, when, how or who, has had significant social, cultural and political consequences. It accounts, in large part, for the conservatism of psychology as an approach to understanding human life. Understanding human beings as essentially, fundamentally and naturally *a behaving species* is an acceptance of alienation as a universal human condition. Indeed, it is the perfect unit of analysis for a culture dominated by alienation, a culture in which the process of production, not only of material goods but of human experience of all kinds, is separated from its "products" which are then reified (as "natural") and commodified (as "behavior"). Scientific psychology, in this way, perpetuates a conservative view of human life and produces a limited research strategy for discovering anything profound or, more importantly, creating anything transformative about human life. Behavior, it seems to me, is a particular human-social phenomenon produced under definite social-historical-cultural conditions (specifically, conditions of extreme alienation), not "the constant," not the meta-category, but a variable. It is no more "natural" to human beings than surfing the Net, hitchhiking or undergoing open heart surgery.

Consciousness still remains a mystery to psychologists, but there is agreement that, whatever it is, it plays a key role in our capacity to transform our environment (which includes, in dialectical fashion, ourselves). The fate of self-consciousness—the remarkable twin human capacities of reflection and abstraction—has been even worse. The paradox of psychology as a discipline is that the very capacities that make science, and pseudo-science (and distinguishing between them) possible are, at the same time, the capacities that make the scientific (objectified and presumably reality-based) study of human consciousness impossible.

THE ACTIVITY ALTERNATIVE OF CULTURAL PSYCHOLOGY

Many critics of experimental psychology and laboratory studies object that psychology—fashioned as a "behavioral science"— ignores the critical role of culture or, at best, treats culture as a variable that impacts on behavior. Among those who want to place culture at the center of the discipline are psychologists who identify with one or more of the following approaches: sociocultural psychology, cultural-historical psychology, cultural psychology, and activity theory. What ties them together is a shared belief that culture *mediates* behavior and is therefore essential in any attempt to gain understanding of human thought and action. (The acronym CHAT—cultural-historical activity theory— is sometimes used as a shorthand for these approaches, although it does gloss over differences.)

Because CHAT approaches draw upon the work of Vygotsky in their attempt to create an alternative to the paradigm of mainstream scientific psychology, it is worth having a look at its methodology and unit of analysis. I draw heavily upon Michael Cole's recent *Cultural Psychology: A Once and Future Discipline* (1996). This choice is not meant to imply consensus among researchers (there are many hotly debated methodological, theoretical, and political issues among these groupings); rather, as the most well-known and mainstream of sociocultural-historical psychologists, Cole occupies a particular place and takes a particular stance that bears examination.

Cole sees cultural psychology as a return to psychology's beginnings, a chance to start out again "on the road not taken, the road along which culture is placed on a level with biology and society in shaping individual human natures" (Cole, 1996, p. 101), by which he means "to study culture's role in the mental life of human beings" (p. 1). The cultural psychologist's task is to discover "how to ground one's psychological analysis in the culturally organized activities of everyday life" (p. 5). What Cole hopes to achieve is "a broad reconciliation of cultural-historical ideas with the traditional paradigm of psychology" (p. 218).

Such a reconciliation strikes me as the same road—only now repaved—rather than the road not taken. It would appear to have little chance of changing the culture of the psychology of our day, for it is methodologically psychology as we know it. Cole's formulations—for example, "culture's role in mental life"—reiterate traditional (noncultural) psychology's biases and assumptions, such as the separation of person and environment, and the split between so-called inner life and so-called outer reality. If culture plays a role in mental life, then culture and mental life are necessarily separate. We have a dualistic picture—on the one hand, there is an outside world which is presumably where culture resides, and on the other hand, there are individuated selves which possess inner minds that generate mental life. If culture plays a role—that is, has an influence on mental life, then it is reasonable to conclude that mental life itself is not a cultural phenomenon. By implication, psychological processes of all kinds are not cultural phenomena.

The origins of CHAT and cultural psychology in particular are many and diverse. One strand of its history is the early work of Cole and associates at the Laboratory of Comparative Human Cognition at the Rockefeller University during the 1970s in which I participated. At that time, we coined the term *ecological validity* to describe our concerns about the direction studies of cognition, language and learning were taking. Most theory and findings about cognition were being generated in laboratory settings under strict conditions that constrained what people did so that there could be systematic measurable outcomes. We asked, how could we then generalize to everyday life—which does not have the same constraints? How could such data be valid? We set about trying to create a new methodology for investigating learning, literacy and schooling in everyday life contexts. Concerned with inequality, we saw schools as perpetuators of class, race, and gender bias and also as potential forces for transforming such bias. We believed that the dominant psychological paradigm—its view of what a person is, what learning and development and culture are—played a significant role in allowing certain children to succeed in school and others to fail. Our approach had roots in ethnography and ethnomethodology, Marxist thought and Soviet psychology—especially the writings of Vygotsky and his followers. Just as important, our approach was rooted in the political activism of the times.

We looked for individual cognitive acts—in real time and on hundreds of hours of video. But we could not find any, and became convinced that psychology was ecologically invalid because it excluded critical features of the human-social life space. The laboratory became for us much more than a physical site; we saw it as a methodology that systematically gives a distorted picture of human activity. People learn, think and solve problems through joint activity. The unit of analysis for psychology, then, cannot be the individual, but what we called the person-environment interface and mind-in-society[1] (see Cole, Hood and McDermott, 1978; Hood, McDermott and Cole, 1980; McDermott, 1993; and McDermott and Hood, 1982).

Understanding psychological processes as social and cultural, as historically constructed, as something human beings *do* was a big step. Observing the person-environment interface may allow you to see some new things, just as emphasizing the role of culture on mental life can open up new research areas. Yet, the model remains rooted in scientific objectivity. The new "seeing" that is made possible through studying everyday life activity is still a scientific, experimental kind of seeing–it is methodology no different from the typical psychological laboratory experiment. The environment remains a context and a tool *for* analysis, rather than self-reflexively, dialectically *being* the analysis. After all, from the vantage point of the people who are being "observed" in their everyday life situations, this is no experiment; it's a scene in their continuous life performance. But to the psychologist, it *is* an experiment. Ironically, we did not heed our own warning that the laboratory is more than a physical space.

The need to impose some objectification on people's activity is the source, Newman and I believe, of the radical difference between our reading of Vygotsky and that of most proponents of CHAT. To illustrate, I quote a section from Cole (1996) in which he responds to a statement made by Vygotsky. I then present Newman's and my response.

> The Russian cultural-historical approach begins with everyday activity only in an abstract manner. Rather than concern themselves with concrete parameters of everyday scenes, the Russians focused on what they considered to be the central core of all activity—its mediated nature. Work of Vygotsky's published well after we concluded our cross-cultural research makes it clear that he was not particularly sympathetic to the kind of ethnographic approach which has been so important to us. Regarding strategies of experimentation, he commented: 'It might seem that analysis, like the experiment, distorts reality—creates artificial conditions for observation. Hence the demand for closeness to life and naturalness of the experiment. If this idea is carried further than a technical demand— not to scare away that which we are looking for—it leads to the absurd. The strength of analysis is in the abstraction, like the strength of the experiment is in artificiality' (quoted in Van der Veer and Valsiner, 1991, p. 147).
>
> While I agree with Vygotsky's general point that analysis is central to the scientific enterprise, my experience has led me to believe that he underestimated the intellectual task condensed into the idea of a 'technical demand' not to 'scare away' the phenomena of interest. This characterization of the problem overlooks the analytic achievement involved in specifying a cognitive task in its context, and overestimates the experimenter's ability to re-create a task in a new context and still have it remain the same task. (Cole, 1996, pp. 338–339)

Newman and I find Cole's worry that Vygotsky would not be enamored of ethnography quite reasonable. We also find Cole's criticism of Vygotsky's position equally reasonable (although we happen to agree with Vygotsky). As we understand it, the desire to create a psychology grounded in everyday life activity grows in part out of the concern to not distort, through your analysis, what is "really going on." And ethnographic study is (at least in theory) far less imposing and constraining than laboratory research. Yet, the desire to get a true ("native," "emic," "from the ground up") picture of reality presumes that there is some objective truth and some objective reality. Cole faults the Russian cultural-historical approach for its lack of interest in the "concrete parameters of everyday scenes" and chastises Vygotsky for failing to appreciate both the importance and the difficulty in staying grounded in *concrete reality*. Granting that Cole is a realist, it seems to us that he fails to recognize objectivity (even ethnographic objectivity) as abstract, which is problematic on his own account.

We, in contrast, agree with Vygotsky that "closeness to life" can lead to the absurd. The strength of analysis *is* in the abstraction and the strength of the experiment *is* in the artificiality. So the strategy of holding to a reality-based, truth-referential scientific paradigm, while at the same time grounding your study in the concrete uniqueness of everyday activity in the hopes of seeing the real (instead of the artificial), and then claiming that your analysis is not an abstraction because your object of study was not artificially produced—seems to be the effort of trying to be all things to all people. Cole wants to satisfy the objectivity requirement of the experimentalists while at the same time assuring the more culturally and historically oriented activity-ists that he has something to offer them.

PSYCHOLOGICAL ACTIVITY AS PERFORMANCE

The tool-and-result methodology of Newman's developmental performance/social therapy is an attempt to create a method of study that is not only suitable to human subjectivity and its paradoxicality, but that relishes and even "exploits" it. Its roots are not in Vygotsky but in what Kenneth Gergen eloquently described as "Newman's immersion in philosophical, political and social deliberations . . . complemented by a deep dwelling in the realm of aesthetics, and particularly the dramatic arts" (Gergen, this volume). Nevertheless, Newman's and my practice has been greatly aided by Vygotsky's writings. It is not only his radically dialectic and "pre-postmodern" insights that we have learned from, but also the glimpses of his conflicted commitment to reality, truth, objectivity and dualism.

It seems to us that Vygotsky's attempt to create a dialectical conception of human developmental activity and a dialectical methodology for studying it answered one of the questions raised by twentieth-century advances in relativity theory, quantum physics, and foundations of mathematics: How could something be both what it is and what it is not?

Mainstream scientific psychology has yet to even entertain such a question, yet nearly 70 years ago, Vygotsky put forth an analysis of children's learning and development which, if not a complete explication of this phenomenon, gives us some methodological insight with which to tackle it. Newman and I have written extensively on this topic (Holzman, 1997; Newman and Holzman, 1993, 1995, 1997), and specific features of it are displayed throughout the essays and plays in this volume. Here I will give a brief summary of the way in which we read Vygotsky's analysis.

Vygotsky broke through the linear and causal (both dualistic) understandings of learning (or instruction) and development and how they are related. Rather than development being the foundation necessary for learning, or there being some kind of unspecified mutual interaction between them, he believed that, "Instruction is not limited to trailing after development or moving stride for stride along with it. It can move ahead of development, pushing it further and eliciting new formations" (Vygotsky, 1987, p. 198). Vygotsky did not see learning (instruction) and development as discrete particulars that interact; he saw, instead, a dialectical unity in which learning leads development. In so doing, he was not merely identifying another way in which learning and development are "related." He was introducing a new conception of relationship itself, one not premised on particulars but on totalities. He was identifying human beings as dialectical process. Further, he showed that young children are related to as dialectical process (as who they are and who they are not), and that this is how they develop. Through their joint activity, young children and their caretakers, siblings, etc., create environments for learning leading development (what he called zones of proximal development or zpds) and, in the practice of that dialectical activity, they create the unity, learning and developing.

How do they (we) do it? Vygotsky describes it as being a head taller than you are; we call it performing. Either way, it is the activity of being who you are/being who you are not. Development, in this understanding, is the activity of creating who you are by performing who you're not. It is, significantly, an ensemble—not a solo—performance. And the zpd is not a zone at all, nor a societal scaffold, but an activity—simultaneously the performance space and the performance. Newman's practice of developmental performance is, in Vygotsky's language, the ongoing creation of many, many overlapping zpds. The success thus far of this practice leads us to believe that performance—the human capacity to transform ourselves, sometimes in a matter of seconds, into who we are not—is a likely candidate for a "proper" postmodern, post-scientific unit of analysis.

We also think that it does away with the worry about distorting reality that troubles Cole and that underlies ethnographic approaches in psychology. "Performance pulls the rug out from under truth-referentiality," Newman is fond of saying. Neither performance nor the study of performance (itself a performance) requires explanation. Indeed, they invite explicative analysis instead. In our view, performed activity cannot be studied by psychology's (even cultural psychology's) quantitative or qualitative research methods which presume reality and try to devise an analysis that can get as close to capturing it as possible. However, performed activity is *study-able*. Its analysis is an abstraction (a transformation "into the realm of the theoretical" is the way Gergen described Newman's method, this volume) whose strength *as abstraction* lies not in its dualistically based "closeness to life" but in its inseparability, as tool and result, from life activity. With no "ontic underpinning," no presumption of a connection to the real, we human beings can gain understanding about ourselves as we transform what it means to understand ourselves.

Newman and I believe that there is nothing social, cultural or historical other than what we human beings create. Accepting this requires that we give up the belief that we can distance ourselves enough from our activity to study it as a scientific phenomenon. Accepting this requires that we stop imposing objectification onto what we do. It requires Vygotsky's revolutionary search for method, the ongoing process of changing totalities, what we refer to—after Marx and Vygotsky—as revolutionary (with a small r) activity. It requires, in the practice of therapy, speaking to people as if they can change the world.

It does *not* require, as far as we can tell, the kind of knowing and explanatory analysis that psychologists tend to do.

Nearly ten years ago (for a journal article), I interviewed several Vygotskian researchers on the relevance of Vygotsky's work to today's world. James Wertsch, one of the most respected American followers of Vygotsky, had this to say:

> What I see as potentially very important is the lesson that Vygotsky's work might be able to teach Americans . . . namely, that there are very legitimate well-grounded alternative world views or modes of thinking . . . in an era when the Berlin Wall comes down, the Soviet Union is falling apart, South Africa's changed, all the things in Eastern Europe that are going on, psychologists in the traditional American mode have practically nothing to say about any of this stuff! The reason we can't is not because we're neutral—although that's the claim—but because we presuppose our own world view as the ideal one . . . all the while hiding the fact that [psychology] is grounded in American individualistic ideology. Exposing this and "proving" it scientifically is what I see as the powerful lesson that is potential in Vygotsky. (Wertsch, quoted in Holzman, 1990, pp. 21–22)

I have two friendly—but critical—amendments to Wertsch's valuable words. The first concerns what he identifies as American individualistic ideology. I agree with Wertsch that it is important. But individualism cannot be the only target if the critique of traditional psychology is to have any serious impact on our culture. The methodological issues raised in this essay and in all of Newman's work are equally troublesome components of American political and scientific culture. Changing the subject from the so-called isolated individual to the social unit (the group, the community of learners) merely results in gathering data on groups as if they were individuals.

My second amendment to Wertsch addresses the culture of psychology. The point he makes about psychology's inability to say anything about social upheaval in other parts of the world is telling. What he has left out is the fact that psychologists have much to say about the social-political problems in this country. They study crime, violence, school failure, substance and alcohol abuse, mental illness, family breakdown, etc., make remarkably little headway in solving any of these problems, and yet claim they are scientists.

The revolutionary spirit with which Vygotsky was embraced by a handful of psychologists in the 1960s and 1970s has, it seems to me, been abandoned as American culture has become more and more conservative. Ecological validity was radical in "the 60s" because the 60s were radical. It was, I think, ecologically valid then. But in becoming cultural psychology, it has gone from locating "mind" in—yet inseparable from—society to making society and culture a mere "context" for mind. In my opinion, this return to the traditional scientific dichotomy stems at least in part from a failure to do the hard self-reflexive work of considering the ecological validity of ecological validity. If we were to engage in such an exploration, I think we would find that much of sociocultural/cultural-historical psychology is, today, ecologically invalid.

As suggested at the beginning of this essay, I believe that Vygotsky's question, "What is the proper unit of analysis for a psychological science?" was asked in the revolutionary spirit of transforming the culture of psychology as a necessary part of transforming the broader culture toward human growth and liberation. Still relevant and still revolutionary today, this modern question has a paradoxically postmodern answer: The proper unit of analysis for a psychological science cannot be scientific. It must be cultural and performatory.

NOTES

1. It is interesting to compare the original "ecological validity" research report (Cole, Hood and McDermott, 1978) with subsequent descriptions provided by Cole (Newman, Griffin and Cole, 1989 and Cole, 1996). As one of the researchers and authors of the original report, I find the representation of our work seriously revisionist. However intentionally reconciliative cultural psychology is today, its Rockefeller University laboratory origins were, perhaps naively and preliminary, an attempt to develop an alternative, nondualistic methodology and unit of analysis.

REFERENCES

Bruner, J. (1996). Celebrating divergence: Piaget and Vygotsky. Keynote Address, Growing Mind Conference, Geneva, September, 1996.

Cole, M. (1996). *Cultural psychology: A once and future discipline.* Cambridge, MA: Harvard.

Cole, M., Hood, L. and McDermott, R. P. (1978). *Ecological niche-picking: Ecological validity as an axiom of experimental cognitive psychology.* (Monograph). New York: Rockefeller University, Laboratory of Comparative Human Cognition. [Reprinted in *Practice, 4(1),* 117–129].

Danziger, K. (1994). *Constructing the subject: Historical origins of psychological research.* Cambridge: Cambridge University Press.

Danziger, K. (1997). *Naming the mind: How psychology found its language.* London: Sage.

Gergen, K. J. (1982). *Toward transformation in social knowledge.* London: Sage.

Gergen, K. J. (1994). *Realities and relationships: Soundings in social construction.* Cambridge, MA: Harvard University Press.

Holzman, L. (1990). Lev and let Lev: An interview on the life and works of Lev Vygotsky. *Practice, The Magazine of Psychology and Political Economy,* 7(3), 11–23.

Holzman, L. (1997). *Schools for growth: Radical alternatives to current educational models.* Mahwah, NJ: Lawrence Erlbaum.

Hood, L., McDermott, R. P., and Cole, M. (1980). "Let's try to make it a good day"—Some not so simple ways. *Discourse Processes, 3,* 155–168.

Kozulin, A. (1986). Vygotsky in context. In L. S. Vygotsky, *Thought and language.* Cambridge, MA: MIT Press.

Kozulin, A. (1990). *Vygotsky's psychology: A biography of ideas.* Cambridge, MA: Harvard University Press.

Levitin, K. (1982). *One is not born a personality: Profile of Soviet education psychologists.* Moscow: Progress Publishers.

McDermott, R. P. (1993). The acquisition of a child by a learning disability. In S. Chaiklin and J. Lave (Eds.), *Understanding practice: perspec-*

tives on activity and context. New York: Cambridge University Press.

McDermott, R. P. and Hood, L. (1982). Institutionalized psychology and the ethnography of schooling. In P. Gilmore and A.A. Glatthorn, (Eds.), *Children in and out of school: Ethnography and education* (pp. 232–249). Washington, DC: Center for Applied Linguistics.

Newman, D., Griffin, P. and Cole, M. (1989). *The construction zone: Working for cognitive change in school.* Cambridge: Cambridge University Press.

Newman, F. and Holzman, L. (1993). *Lev Vygotsky: Revolutionary scientist.* London: Routledge.

Newman, F. and Holzman, L. (1996). *Unscientific psychology: A cultural-performatory approach to understanding human life.* Westport, CT: Praeger.

Newman, F. and Holzman, L. (1997). *The end of knowing: A new developmental way of learning.* London: Routledge.

Parker, I. (1989). *The crisis in modern social psychology and how to end it.* London: Routledge.

Parker, I. and Shotter, J. (1990). *Deconstructing social psychology.* London: Routledge.

Polkinghorne, D. (1983). *Methodology for the human sciences: Systems of inquiry.* Albany: SUNY Press.

Shotter, J. (1990). *Knowing of the third kind: Selected writings on psychology, rhetoric, and the culture of everyday social life.* Utrecht: ISOR.

Vygodskaya, G. (1996). Remembering Lev Vygotsky. In L. Fulani (Ed.), *Women who won't sell out* (pp. 158–163). New York: Castillo International.

Vygotsky, L.S. (1978). *Mind in society.* Cambridge, MA: Harvard University Press.

Vygotsky, L. S. (1987). *The collected works of L. S. Vygotsky,* Vol. 1. New York: Plenum.

Wertsch, J. V. (1985). *Vygotsky and the social formation of mind.* Cambridge, MA: Harvard University Press.

Diagnosis:
The Human Cost of the Rage to Order

FRED NEWMAN AND KENNETH GERGEN

D*ebates on the issue of psychological diagnosis have been rag-ing for decades. In recent times, both sides in the debate have become more stubborn and self-righteous. The critics, especially, appear to be ineffectual and impotent. Poking fun at the more ludicrous of the hun-dreds of categories of mental disorder catalogued in the* DSM-IV *(the fourth edition of the* Diagnostic and Statistical Manual *that mental health professionals and their clients have to dance to) has become a favorite pastime not only at cocktail parties but professional confer-ences as well. But, still, diagnoses are made, infirm identities are solid-ified and treatment is prescribed.*

In Realities and Relationships, *Gergen describes the cultural dynamic of diagnosis as "the cycle of progressive infirmity":*

> *Mental health professionals exist in a symbiotic relation-ship with the culture, drawing sustenance from cultural beliefs, altering these beliefs in systematic ways, dissemi-nating these views back to the culture, and relying on their incorporation into the culture for continual sustenance. Yet the effects of this symbiosis seem increasingly substantial. In particular, a cyclical process seems to be operating that, once activated, expands the domain of deficit to an ever-increasing infirmity; hierarchies of discrimination, denatu-ralized patterns of interdependence, and an expanding arena of self-deprecation. The historical process may be viewed as one of "progressive infirmity." (Gergen, 1994, p. 155)*

Independent of each other, Gergen and Newman had been pursuing the philosophical assumptions that underlie diagnosis and that perpetuate this cycle, both of them in theoretical writings and Newman in the practice of social therapy. In this essay, originally delivered at the 103rd Convention of the American Psychological Association in New York in August, 1995, the two join forces and, with the aid of Wittgenstein, flex their philosophical and psychological muscles to present a methodologically sophisticated and radically humanistic call for an end to Truth and for the democratization of diagnosis.—L.H.

Let us distinguish and contrast "two views on the vocabulary of mind," the pictorial and the pragmatic (Gergen, 1994). The *pictorial* view which, we believe, remains dominant in practice in our culture (for mental language in particular and language in general) identifies mental vocabulary as fundamentally referential, i.e., its primary function is to accurately (truthfully) describe *states of mind* (in ordinary emotive, attitudinal and cognitive terms, in physiological terms, in phenomenological terms, in intra-psychic terms, in behavioral terms, if you happen to believe that the discrete and discernible events of mental life are the behaviors associated with it, and so on). These descriptions *correspond*, on the *pictorial* view, to objective states of inner and, sometimes, outer "reality," and the utterances of these descriptions (in therapy) are typically either first person efforts to *express* and/or communicate a mental state or second and third person efforts to *attribute* one to the first person, a.k.a. the patient, client, group member, etc.

In accordance with this view the clinical client is typically urged (by the therapist) to say "what's going on," i.e., is urged to *describe* in as much detail, honesty and depth as she or he can the "inner realities" to which she or he has a special, though presumably by no means omniscient, observational relationship. The therapist is, characteristically, skilled in supporting the client to do so and, moreover, is equipped to offer alternative descriptions of the client's state of mind which nurturingly or at least neutrally challenge the truth, the meaning, the coherency, the clarity, the value, etc. of the client's first-person descriptions. Diagnosing is, so it seems to us, but one element of this describing and redescribing (defining) process. While the diagnosis per se may or may not be literally conveyed to the client directly (in more liberal therapeutic settings it typically is, although in the most liberal-radical environments it may be "officially" renounced), it at least informs the therapist's nondiagnostic redescriptions. Indeed, as we and others (Guattari, Deleuze, etc.) have pointed out, such redescription in medical or pseudomedical pictorial-based language often receives a very positive response from the client since it may normalize her or his subjective state of mind. In effect,

. . . the vocabulary of the mental health professions does serve to render the alien familiar, and thus less fearsome. Rather than being seen as "the work of the devil" or as "frighteningly strange," for example, nonnormative activities are given standardized labels, signifying that they are indeed natural, fully anticipated, and long familiar to the sciences. (Gergen, 1994, p. 148)

A Brief History and Sociology of This View

The above characterization of talk-therapy (to some extent even mental talk in ordinary life) is, obviously, simplistic by virtue of being so narrow in its focus. Yet, in our opinion, it is not inaccurate as far as it goes.

The *pictorial* view of mental vocabulary and/or the validity of some or all diagnostics or mental descriptions has been severely critiqued directly and indirectly in psychological circles in recent years by Szasz and others following or influenced by him. Yet, in our opinion, the pictorial view typifies everyday clinical practice, as a brief history of the exponential growth of *both* the number of psychological helping professionals and the number of diagnostic descriptions of the clients, presented, for example, in *DSM-IV*, makes plain (Gergen, 1994). Simply put, there are more therapists (lay and credentialled) using many more scientific or pseudoscientific medicalized or quasi-medicalized pictorially based descriptions of many more clients than at any previous time in history. Psychological diagnostic description has permeated the broader culture and, we argue, with pernicious consequences.

The *pictorial* view of mental language has as well been seriously considered and critiqued this past half century by philosophically trained "philosophical psychologists." (Some of the earliest ones include Gilbert Ryle, *The Concept of Mind*; G.E.M. Anscombe, *Intention*; Stuart Hampshire, *Thought and Action*; H.L.A. Hart and A.M. Honoré, *Causation in the Law*; William A. Dray, *Laws and Explanation in History*, and most of the books in the series edited by R. F. Holland, *Studies in Philosophical Psychology*, including Anthony Kenny, *Action, Emotion and Will,* and A.I. Melden, *Free Action*.) A good deal of this criticism is properly and understandably associated with the writings and thought of the Austrian-born, Cambridge-trained philosopher, Ludwig Wittgenstein, most particularly with his later writings, for example, his *Philosophical Investigations*. In a more recent and, in our opinion, quite positive development, trained psychologists (and others with expertise in related practical fields) have come to study Wittgenstein more directly to explore nonpictorial approaches to psychological concerns and paradoxes (see Morss, 1992, 1993; Shotter, 1990, 1993a and b; Stenner, 1993).

As Van der Merwe and Voestermans put it in the abstract to their recent (and exceedingly valuable) article, "Wittgenstein's Legacy and the Challenge to Psychology," in *Theory & Psychology*: "The present resurgence of interest in Ludwig Wittgenstein is related to the growing concern in the philosophy and methodology of the behavioural sciences with the role played by conceptual frameworks, models and metaphors in the mediation of our experience of the world" (1995, p.27).

Wittgenstein's influence on the varied areas of psychology and social work grows by leaps and bounds. As such, it becomes increasingly important to ask *how* and, indeed, *whether* he is being understood. Van der Merwe and Voestermans think he is not being understood very well at all. They say: "Wittgenstein's message to psychologists is to *move about around things and events in the world*, [our italics] instead of trying to delineate essential features" (1995, p.38). And they immediately add in a section aptly called "Dilution of the Analysis of Forms of Life":

> Have psychologists gotten that message clearly? We are convinced they have not. One of the reasons for this is that Wittgenstein has been ambiguous himself about what it means to move about and around things and events. Wittgenstein himself provided an opportunity for escape from what he deemed as the prime task not just of philosophy but of all efforts at understanding, including psychological understanding. He has outlined two main routes. On the one hand, he introduces the notion of language-game. This notion 'brings into prominence the fact that the speaking of language is part of an activity or a form of life' (PI: §23). On the other hand, he remained preoccupied, one could say, with purifying strategies, that is, with attempts to employ philosophical analysis

for clarification of concepts. Along this latter strategic line the language-game approach has become an end in itself without much reference to or participation in the activity or the form of life of which language-use is a part. This second route has given ample opportunity for evasive moves like a defense of relativism or an overemphasis on the yoking relationship between concepts and the larger language-game frame. Psychologists in general have favoured this second route at the expense of really taking up the challenge of what it means 'to move around about things', that is to say, to come to grips with the role forms of life actually play. (1995, p. 39)

In an important sense this means going beyond the pragmatic view of language with which Wittgenstein is frequently associated. In *Lev Vygotsky: Revolutionary Scientist,* Newman and Holzman (1993a) propose that words surely are used within society in the manner of tools. (Following Vygotsky, we would call them "tools-for-results" in contrast to "tools-and-results.") And, no doubt, Wittgenstein is susceptible to being classified (if classification is your game) a pragmatist or instrumentalist in light of such remarks as "Look at the word or the sentence as an instrument and its meaning as its employment" (PI: §421). And perhaps even more for his oft-quoted remark, "For a large class of cases—though not for all—in which we employ the word 'meaning' it can be defined thus: The meaning of a word is its use in the language" (PI: §43).

Moreover, he is so classified by many philosophers in secondary sources. Yet, such classification can (and does) easily obscure Wittgenstein's "form-of-lifeism," not to mention his form of life. For while he uses the notion and language of "language-games" in several different ways, central to his understanding, we believe, are such provocative formulations as: " . . . the term 'language-game' is meant to bring into prominence the fact that the speaking of language is part of an activity, or of a form of life" (PI: § 23) and "Only in the stream of thought and life do words have meaning" (Z:§173).

The common overidentification of *words* and *language games* derives, we believe, from a deeper and commonplace confusion as to what *language-games* are. Not surprisingly, given Wittgenstein's anti-essentialism and anti-definitionalism there is no precise definition, in

Wittgenstein's writings, of what a *language-game* is. Different language games, like everything else, have only "family resemblances." But many psychologists (interested most particularly in issues of analytical metapsychology) have taken the meaning-use equation as a pragmatic frame of reference for understanding *language-games* as a philosophical/psychological technique for the analysis of mental vocabulary. This is surely one way in which Wittgenstein himself *uses* the term "language-game."

Merwe and Voestermans put it this way:

> It is almost a fad in psychological circles nowadays to accept Wittgenstein's criticism of psychology's conceptual confusion. 'Psychologists are prone to unclarity about everyday psychological concepts and the sophisticated experimental methods they employ fail to deal satisfactorily with the problems addressed,' Budd (1991, p.xii) wrote in his study of Wittgenstein's philosophy of psychology. (1995, p. 38)

But for Wittgenstein, we believe (following especially Baker, 1992), the meaning-use equation is not to be identified with understanding. For an equation (an identification) or, indeed, any analysis, does not *perform* the activity moving " . . . about around things and events" associated with the form of life and theory of meaning. An understanding of language games as a mere pragmatic tool of analysis is, we believe, no understanding at all. Understanding is not "delineating essential features" of either facts in the world (as in Wittgenstein's earlier *Tractatus*) or uses of concepts and language in society. It is a social activity; a performance, a moving " . . . about around things and events in the world." To understand and change meaning we must be historically active, that is, revolutionarily active, practically-critically active. We must change "the aspect" (the totality of things) by activity—moving about around things, changing our location—not via philosophical or psychological analysis. As Merwe and Voestermans put it: "Language and naming do not come out of the blue. Both originate in the forms of life to which practice, precisely in its bodily and emotionally structured form, belongs" (1995, p.42). They then quote Wittgenstein from *Culture and Value* thus:

> A philosopher says "Look at things like this"—but in the
> first place that doesn't ensure that people will look at things
> like that, and in the second place his admonition may come
> altogether too late; it is possible, moreover, that such an admo-
> nition can achieve nothing in any case and that the impetus for
> such a change in the way things are perceived has to originate
> somewhere else entirely. (1980, p. 61e)

And they comment on this typically practical-minded Wittgensteinian observation: "That is as much to say that change of aspect requires a change of life" (1995, p.43).

Indeed the issues of Wittgenstein's *form of life* and *form of thought* themselves (not just what he had to say about them) are, in our opinion, critical to the creation of a new psychology in general and a new clinical psychology in particular. For while a *pragmatic* understanding of the vocabulary of mental language in juxtaposition (and contradistinction) to a *pictorial* understanding of mental language is of substantial critical deconstructionist and social constructionist metapsychological value, it is "form of lifeism," we would suggest, which proves most vital in creating a new *social psychology* (Jost, 1995), a new developmental phenomenology (Van der Merwe and Voestermans, 1995) and a new domain of clinical practice (Gergen and Kaye, 1993; Newman and Holzman, 1993a and b).

WITTGENSTEIN'S FORM OF LIFE AND THOUGHT

Baker, one of the philosophical world's leading interpreters of Wittgenstein, looks at his form of (philosophical) thought and life as follows:

> I suggest scrupulous attention to Wittgenstein's overall
> therapeutic conception of his philosophical investigations . . .
> far from undertaking to give any general outline of the logical
> geography of our language . . . he always sought to address
> specific philosophical problems of definite individuals and to
> bring to light conceptual confusion which these individuals
> would acknowledge as a form of entanglement in their own
> rules . . . he operated as a general practitioner who treated the
> bumps that various individual patients had got by running

> their heads up against the limits of language . . . Wittgenstein's
> practice in philosophising is not less, but rather more, consis-
> tently therapeutic than we commonly recognize. (Baker, 1992,
> p. 129)

In the development of the social therapeutic group practice over the past two decades one of us (Newman) has sought to use the therapeutic Wittgenstein's practical-critical (unsystematic) "form of life," activity-theoretic understanding. In what does this consist? It must first be said that for practical purposes both the *pictorial* and the *pragmatic* "meta views on the vocabulary of mind" must be abandoned. For while the *pragmatic* view is surely both closer to life and closer to Wittgenstein, it is plainly not close enough. Why? Because both the *pictorial* and the *pragmatic* views are, at root, identity-theoretic; one, the *pictorial*, relative to "reality" so-called, the other, the *pragmatic*, relative to specific societal uses. The quite particular piece of space-time reality (the fact) named in the *pictorial* description and the equally particular societal use (the instrumental tool) named in the *pragmatic* description— obscures the prominence of relational activity, that is, ". . . that the speaking of language is part of an activity, or of a form of life."

Both a pictorial and a pragmatic theory of mental meaning give way to *relational activity* as the basis for social therapeutic approaches. Only in the *activity* of life in relations do words have meaning. And to alter the form of life is to alter the meaning of words and discourse.

The nagging practical/theoretic concern that this activity-theoretic approach somehow leaves out the "something" in "the mind" (or, in phenomenological terms, "the body") that cries out for expression or inclusion is well engaged by Vygotsky's radical activity-theoretic and dialectical view on thinking and speaking. He says:

> Thought is not expressed but completed in the word . . . .
> The structure of speech is not simply the mirror image of the
> structure of thought. It cannot, therefore, be placed on thought
> like clothes off a rack. Speech does not merely serve as the
> expression of developed thought. Thought is restructured as it
> is transformed into speech. It is not expressed but completed
> in the word. (Vygotsky, 1987, pp. 250–251)

So it is, we would argue, with all "mental states" or acts, not just thought or thinking. For Vygotsky's view is, it seems to us, a brilliant and useful critique of the concept of "expression," the companion piece to every and any dualistic, identity-based theory of mind, mental vocabulary and/or mental acts. The move to relational activity requires a full blown re-ontologizing away from the stuff of the mind and the stuff outside of the mind (a Cartesian mind/body-nature dualism) to a self/other unity. Only such an activity-theoretic ontology, it seems to us, can further mix with other elements of life and history to produce the forms of life which make meaning itself possible, on the one hand, and the transformation of life and its form, via the transformation of meaning, possible, on the other. This Vygotskian-Wittgensteinian activity-theoretic view of mental language and meaning is plainly a relational-theoretic, as opposed to an identity-theoretic Cartesian, viewpoint.

We may now be more able to approach the complex and disturbing issue of diagnostics in clinical work from a fresh (and less dualistic) point of view. Moreover, a more concrete discussion (of how social therapy does—performs—diagnosing) can, we hope, inform our "abstract" theoretical formulations.

ALL THAT SZASZ

For all that he has contributed to our thinking about such matters in the last quarter of a century, perhaps Szasz has done us a disservice. Not unlike the *pragmatization* of Wittgenstein (and, we would argue, the *instrumentalization* of Vygotsky by many American psychologists in the tradition of Dewey and Mead), Szasz has focused our attention so much on the myth of mental illness that he has diverted our critical eye somewhat from the myth of psychology. Perhaps our selves have become sufficiently saturated to point out that mental illness is painfully real but that psychology, ill-shapen by its identity-theoretic, antirelational, pseudoscientific pseudoparadigm, has become a haven for (and a proselytizer of) *forms of life* which are recognizably nondevelopmental. One such traditional therapeutic form of life is *diagnosing*.

Following Szasz, maybe we of a more critical persuasion have been much too easily taken in by endless trivial (though humorous) critiques of diagnostic descriptions (a form of psychological liberalism) without sufficiently looking at the diagnostic form(s) of life.

SOCIAL THERAPY: CHANGING THE FORM OF RELATIONAL LIFE

> "One does not cure neurosis, one changes a society which cannot do without it." (Lotringer, 1977)

The social therapeutic process is a collective moving about around things and events in the world. It is, more particularly, a moving about around emotional things and events in the world. Considering Wittgenstein's "retreat from essentialism," Van der Merwe and Voestermans state:

> What is 'a table,' a 'chair,' 'a game,' or an utterance like 'five red apples'? In order to solve that problem one should act, so to speak, and do things like using a table or a chair, or looking for communalities in games and go to a store and buy apples. By doing things such as these the fog will disappear. (1995, p. 38)

In social therapy, we seek to collectively move about around "depression," "anxiety," "three painful days," "I'm angry at you," etc. How do we move about around them? Surely not by analytically seeking to discover their essences. Definitely not by determining the truth value of judgments in which they are contained. And not even by cognitively uncovering the complex societal uses of such language. We do so by changing the form of relational life. In a word, we collectively and creatively *perform* (not act) our lives without the identity-based presuppositions of the existing form(s) of (our) society. And only as we create new forms of relational life, we would say, can we understand the existing forms of action. Only as we perform our lives together can we understand our lives as performance. Thus, the first and second and third person descriptions uttered by clients and therapists in individual and group therapy alike are not treated as referential, that is, as judgments either true or false, but as lines in a play (or, perhaps better still, a poem) that we are at once collectively creating and performing. The social therapist, as performer/director, helps to keep the activity performatory, that is, helps the group members to remember that they are in a play and not in "real life" where their descriptions and/or judgments are true or false. "Hey everybody," she or he might well say, "This is a play you're all improvising. It's the performance of your emotional lifetime. It's creating a new form of emotional life, new emotions, changing your life. Perform, per chance to grow, to develop. Keep moving about around emotional things and events. Keep moving. Change the form of your and our emotional life."

It is not easy to create such an environment. Even though, as Vygotsky teaches us, imitation and group performance (conjoint activity) are critical to growth, development and cultural adaptation in our earliest years (for example, in how we acquire language), by early adolescence for most of us our *performatory skills*, our capacity to be who we aren't, to be "a head taller" than we are, to do what we don't know how to do, are more and more related to pejoratively. Performing becomes either "acting out" or, for a few, expressing a special gift or talent to act. Thus, in social therapy, our ordinary childhood ability to perform must be reawakened and nurtured.

In such a radically performatory context the group members and especially the therapist are not, of course, knowers. Not merely because they do not know some or even most answers, but because there are no answers to be known. Yet the collective performance can grow, develop, deepen, etc. Will that be known? No. Nonetheless, it can both happen and be worked for as with any poem or performance, collective or otherwise. The group plays (in Vygotsky's sense) language games in all their infinite variety. It performs its own relational life. Indeed, it performs therapy and thereby creates psychology anew and continuously. In such an environment descriptions (or seeming descriptions, if you prefer) are like lines in a play or a poem in that they are, in a most important sense, not about anything at all. Poetic meaning, in many cases, self-consciously derives from the poem itself and not from what it is about. If in a play (perhaps a Sunday matinee) the performer utters the words "It is a dreary and dark day," it is unlikely that either other players or audience members will take issue on the grounds that it is 75 degrees and the sky is a perfectly cloudless blue outside.

In such a moving around about emotional things and events—changing the form of relational life, performatory environment—diagnoses themselves can be harmless and sometimes valuable. Despite all our sarcastic observation about the more absurdist characterizations in *DSM-IV*, it ain't funny. Why? Because in everyday pictorial, identity-theoretic therapy these descriptions (diagnoses) are usable as labels of stigmatization or at least social constraint. And we do not change that by any kind of analysis. We change that only by changing the diagnostic form of life. By opening up diagnosing to everyone, continuously though nonreferentially and nonjudgmentally. We all perform diagnosing together. Not to get it right. Not to have everyone get a chance. But to conjointly create/perform a zone of relational development (to vary slightly Vygotsky's zone of proximal development) in which we can together create new forms of life, new meanings, new lives. For the task of social therapy, following Wittgenstein, is to make the fog disappear, the mental mist vanish, to create an environment which doesn't require neurosis.

In the end, why must we accept the process of definition as a primary feature of therapy or consultation? Why must we join what is in place? The problem is not diagnosis but "joining what's in place," that is, the diagnostic form of life, the definitional form of description, the identificational form of discourse, the analytical form of therapy and emotive dialogue. If "diagnosing" is a problem (and indeed it is) let everyone do it in a radically democratic, performatory environment and it will no longer be a problem. For it is not the diagnosis but the authoritarian, patriarchal and private "truth" of it that does harm. People performing their emotional lives together includes the patient at least as much as an authoritarian pseudomedical, pseudoscientific diagnostic description.

◆   ◆   ◆

Please do not construe these remarks as a description of social therapy or an analysis of Wittgensteinian language games. They are—at least we hope they are—a small effort to change the form of life that is delivering papers at a professional conference.

REFERENCES

Baker, G.P. (1992). Some remarks on "language" and "grammar." *Grazer Philosophische Studien*, 42, 107–131.

Gergen, K. J. (1994). *Realities and relationships*. Cambridge, MA: Harvard University Press.

Gergen, K. J. (1995). Social construction and the transformation of identity politics. Presented at the New School for Social Research, New York City.

Gergen, K. J. and Kaye, J. (1993). Beyond narrative in the negotiation of therapeutic meaning. In S.M. McNamee and K.J. Gergen (Eds.) *Therapy as social construction*. London: Sage.

Jost, J.T. (1995). Toward a Wittgensteinian social psychology of human development. *Theory & Psychology*, 5(1), 5–25.

Lotringer, S. (1977). Libido unbound: The politics of 'schizophrenia.' *semiotexte*, 2(3).

Morss, J.R. (1992). Making waves: Deconstruction and developmental psychology. *Theory & Psychology, 2*, 443–465.

Morss, J.R. (1993). Spirited away: A consideration of the anti-developmental zeitgeist. *Practice, The Magazine of Psychology and Political Economy, 9,2*, 22-28.

Newman, F. and Holzman, L. (1993a). *Lev Vygotsky: Revolutionary scientist*. London: Routledge.

Newman, F. and Holzman, L. (1993b). A new method for our madness. *Practice, The Magazine of Psychology and Political Economy, 9(2)*, 1–21.

Shotter, J. (1990). Wittgenstein and psychology: On our 'hook up' to reality. In A. Phillips-Griffiths (Ed.), *Wittgenstein: Centenary essays* (pp.193-208). Cambridge: Cambridge University Press.

Shotter, J. (1993a). *Conversational realities: Constructing life through language*. London: Sage.

Shotter, J. (1993b). *Cultural politics of everyday life: Social constructionism, rhetoric and knowing of the third kind*. Milton Keynes and Toronto: Open University Press/Toronto University Press.

Stenner, P, (1993). Wittgenstein and the textuality of emotional experience. *Practice, The Magazine of Psychology and Political Economy, 9(2)*, 29–35.

van der Merwe, W. L. and Voestermans, P. P. (1995). Wittgenstein's legacy and the challenge to psychology. *Theory & Psychology, 5(1)* 27–48.

Vygotsky, L.S. (1987). *The collected works of L.S. Vygotsky,* Vol. 1. New York: Plenum.

Wittgenstein, L. (1953). *Philosophical investigations*, Oxford: Blackwell.

Wittgenstein, L. (1967). *Zettel*. Oxford: Blackwell.

Beyond Narrative to Performed Conversation
("In the Beginning" Comes Much Later)

FRED NEWMAN AND LOIS HOLZMAN

The ideas presented in this essay were developed in many conversational contexts between the summer of 1997 and the spring of
1998—from supervisory sessions with social therapists and therapists-
in-training to professional conferences of psychologists and face-to-
face and e-mail dialogues with narrative therapists and theorists. In
recent books and essays (e.g., Newman and Gergen, 1995, this volume
and Newman and Holzman, 1995; 1997), we had touched upon our
concern that many discussions of narrative lacked a philosophically
sophisticated engagement of the conceptions of truth and reality, and
presented themselves as methodological alternatives to more traditional interpretive and representationalist psychotherapy. During this time,
Newman had completed an essay entitled, "Does a Story Need a
Theory? (Some Thoughts on the Methodology of Narrative Therapy)"
which was to appear as a chapter in Pathology and the Postmodern:
Mental Illness as Discourse and Experience (Fee, in press). Building
upon our argument calling for "the end of knowing" in psychology and
psychotherapy (Newman and Holzman, 1997), Newman here speaks
not only of the methodological problems trying to account for or
explain (or theorize) narratives and stories, but also of the potential
dangers to clients. He concludes his argument with a supportive warning to fellow psychotherapists:

Much can be said about the practice of method (Holzman and Newman, 1979) that is narrative therapy and/or social therapy and/or other modes of postmodern therapies. But they require no theoretical backup. They must be true. If we do not recognize this, I fear that we will only be locking the people who come to us for help in their new stories in as problematic a manner as their having been locked into their old ones. The sign on the wall of the postmodern therapist's office must read: "Don't Explain." (Newman, in press)

In the present article, Newman and I examine some articulations of narrative therapy practice and expose their underlying commitment to explanation. (Earlier versions of this discussion were presented at the Annual Convention of the American Psychological Association in Chicago in August, 1997 and the Tenth Congress of Yugoslav Psychologists in Petrovac, Montenegro in September, 1997. It originally appeared in the Journal of Constructivist Psychology (1999, Vol. 12,1), *and is reprinted here with permission.—L.H.*

For the past several years, we (the authors) have been examining our own approach to human-social life—in particular, our clinical practice known as social therapy[1]—in light of recent postmodern and postscientific critiques of modern epistemology. In doing so, we have become more convinced that not only is a new nonepistemological mode of understanding desirable but that it is required for some of the new psychological practices, particularly those concerned with language. And yet, the hold of the epistemological paradigm—the identification of understanding with something to understand—is so strong that the radical and liberating potential of narrative, discursive and performative psychologies and psychotherapies (influenced in varying ways by postmodern thinking) may never, we fear, be realized. In our view, the strength of these approaches lies in their being postscientific—that is, they explain nothing (there is nothing to be explained) and themselves need neither explanation nor theory. Failing to either see this or realize it in practice, we believe, is to misunderstand both what science is as a modernist mode of understanding and what postscientific, postmodernist modes of understanding are and can be. For the emancipatory power of storytelling, narrative, performance, etc. comes from people discovering and transforming their life activity through creating a nonexplanatory understanding of the "story-ness," the cultural mythicality, the human authorship of consciousness.

The recent postmodern turn within psychology[2] has been valuable in raising doubts about objectivity (not only scientific objectivity but also whether there is an objective reality at all). Equally important are the things it raises about the relevance and validity of a knowing paradigm to human subjectivity, especially emotionality and its institutionalized treatment modality, psychotherapy (McNamee and Gergen, 1992). For nearly all approaches to (what is referred to as) psychopathology or mental illness—regardless of how they describe themselves, e. g., as helping, curing, healing or merely the relieving of symptoms—are based in cognitions (accountings, appraisals, understandings and interpretations that take the form of diagnoses, labels and identities). Treatment has been shaped by the modern epistemological paradigm (knowing) in which to understand something is to *know something about* something else.[3] In the case of human emotions, the "something else" typically takes one or another of the following forms: aggregated data concerning behaviors classified as either normal or abnormal; facts or memories about a person's childhood; a detailed family history; or quantitative data on brain functioning. The pseudo-scientific nature of these cognitively based methods of accounting—-classification, interpretation and explanation—has been written about extensively (for example, Dawes, 1994; Ingleby, 1980; Newman and Holzman, 1996; Szasz, 1961, 1996; Timpanero, 1976; Torrey, 1992). Yet, despite its highly questionable status as scientific investigation and its documented failure, the so-called objective study of the subjective still reigns supreme.

Postmodern critique and narrative and other practices influenced by it offer challenges and alternative ways of seeing. Perhaps therapeutic understanding is not understanding as we "know" it; perhaps it has little to do with science, diagnoses, cognition, mental states, inner realities or private worlds. This is the theme of several recent books on psychotherapy that emphasize the social construction of reality and the human capacity to make meaning (e.g., McLeod, 1997; McNamee and Gergen, 1992; Monk, Winslade, Crocket and Epston, 1997; Neimeyer and Mahoney, 1995; Rosen and Kuehlwein, 1996; White and Epston, 1990). However, few, if any, of these authors and practitioners are willing to entertain abandoning knowing altogether. Not only do they describe their goal as creating or expressing an alternative epistemology, they also presuppose much of the conceptual framework of modern epistemology even as they attempt to go beyond it. We will present instances of this later in the discussion.

It is not surprising, then, that our fellow critics of orthodox psychology tell us that our call for "the end of knowing" and a cultural-performatory (as opposed to scientific) understanding of human life is going too far (Newman and Holzman, 1996, 1997). Isn't it enough, they ask, to transform modern objectivist and individuated epistemology into a constructivist or a "social" epistemology and to posit "other ways of knowing"? And isn't it enough to perceive human life as cultural and proceed to explain, systematize, interpret and appraise it from that perspective? In what follows, we share some of our thinking about these issues, why we believe that such reforms are not enough and why psychology's foundation in epistemology needs to be eliminated.[4]

IS HUMAN SUBJECTIVE-SOCIAL LIFE STUDYABLE?

> And any theory not founded on the nature of being human is a lie and a betrayal of man. An inhuman theory will inevitably lead to inhuman consequences—if the therapist is consistent. Fortunately, many therapists have the gift of incon- sistency. This, however endearing, cannot be regarded as ideal. (Laing, 1967)

Laing's words are helpful in exposing the depth of the epistemo- logical bias. For if one believes that a scientific theory of human sub- jective-social life is an instance of a theory not grounded in "being human," then attempts to fit narrative and other postmodern approach- es into the scientific mode of understanding (to objectify, systematize and explain)—rather than seeing them as an alternatives to science—is a "betrayal" of man and woman.

One way narrative and other postmodern approaches "fit" the sci- entific paradigm is in their choice of a suitable postmodern object of study. As the scientific paradigm has evolved (or, if you prefer, as the grand-narrative has been written and spoken), a proper science requires the existence of some "naturally occurring" phenomenon which is the subject matter of theoretical statements about it. Unfortunately, most constructionist/constructivist, narrative and other approaches which take psychology to be an interpretive rather than an explanatory science (Bruner, 1984, 1993) do not successfully challenge this requirement. Whether conversation, discourse, narrative, story or text, the linguistic/semiotic/communicative/meaning-making unit is presuppositionally a "natural" (albeit social-cultural-historical) catego- ry, just as Chomsky's syntactic analysis of language (often criticized for being overly rational and idealist) depends on the presupposition that well-formed sentences are a natural category recognizable by so-called "native speakers" of a given "natural language," and just as the per- ception of moving physical objects and growing living objects by "native perceivers" was a presuppositional condition of modern physics and biology.

Some theorizing attempts to get around this requirement by insisting that reality is constructed (both collectively and individually) through our language. However, appealing to the "many realities thesis" is as much a fudge on the fundamental cognitive paradigm here in psychology as it has been in philosophy for many decades (e.g., Russell's different kinds of knowledge and Dray's different kinds of explanations). Perhaps some brief illustrations from contemporary psychotherapeutic authors will help make our point.

Epston, White and Murray (1992), for example, trace the fundamentality of stories in their approach (re-authoring therapy) to the philosophical position that an objective description of the world is not available to us; all we have is our lived experience of the world. "Given that what we know of the world we know through our experience of it," they ask, "What is the process by which we develop an understanding of our experience and give meaning to it?" (p. 96). Their answer is "stories": "It is through these stories that lived experiences is interpreted. We enter into stories; we are entered into stories by others; and we live our lives through these stories" (p. 97). They go on: "We cannot perform meaning in our lives without situating our experience in stories. Stories are, in the first place, given" (p. 100).

Besides the obvious problematic of the fundamentality of knowing in their formulation (their starting point is, after all, "what we know about the world"), they take stories as a naturally occurring phenomenon—"given" and essential to "performing meaning." Stories appear to be more fundamental than meaning or even than our experience; they "situate our experience" and enable us to "perform meaning." Anticipating our activity-theoretic perspective, we propose that it is more likely the case that we cannot situate our experience in stories *without performing (meaning)* than it is the case that "we cannot perform meaning . . . without situating our experience in stories!"

Another example comes from Rosen's (1996) overview of the foundations of constructivist and social constructionist psychotherapies. For Rosen, as for Epston, White and Murray, stories are the fundamental phenomena which shape and give meaning to our lives: "We are born into stories: the stories of our parents, our families, and our culture. These made meanings, which predate us and envelop us upon our arrival into the world, can be constraining, even imprisoning, or they can be freeing and liberating. . . . Born into the cradle of familial and cultural stories, we begin to construct personal narratives not long afterward, with all the idiosyncratic features that this may entail" (pp. 23–24). What we find particularly problematic is the essentialism and dualism of these formulations; substitute "environment" for stories and "personality" for "personal narratives" and you have a thoroughly modernist (replete with person-environment dualism) psychological claim about presumed naturally occurring phenomena.

Why is it so difficult to create a practice (or sustain a theoretical argument) coherent with the recognition that human subjective-social life is a qualitatively different sort of studyable thing than atoms, cells or the motion of the stars? Perhaps it has something to do with the paradoxicality of the human capacities for self-reflection and abstraction. We human beings regularly invoke and evoke assumed agreed-upon categorization as we live our lives—we seem to do things that fall naturally into categories (work, play, sleep, thinking, talking, singing and so on) whether or not we call attention to those categories. And we seem led to believe that the things we do (including understanding and experiencing the things we do) comprise "natural" categories (even if socially-culturally-historically constructed and thus different for different peoples). But precisely the opposite is the case. If stars and people "did things with each other" like we do with our neighbors, modern science would almost certainly have had a different history, if it evolved at all.

The claim we are making is that there are no naively reasonable and recognizable natural phenomena in the realm of human social life-as-lived; there is nothing that can reasonably be agreed upon as indubitably real. Attempts, then, to scientifically study human social life-as-lived wind up distorting the very phenomena that they aim to study by insisting that they occur naturally.

As countless philosophers and scientists have pointed out, human beings are, among other things, a self-consciously studying species; "our" phenomena do not exist apart from their being studied. Unlike our relationship to the stars, there is no "natural" (conceptual or even physical) distance between us and our own activity. In this respect, our relationship to ourselves (our species) is nothing like our relationship to the stars—it is, arguably, the very distance between the stars in the sky and human beings that makes the scientific study of stars possible—that makes it possible for human beings to have something to say about stars. And while twentieth century science has come to recognize significant and profound interactional effects of studying stars (witness, for example, relativity theory in all its variations), it is still the case that we do not—cannot—interact with them the way we do with each other.[5] We—at least some of us who are called poets or mad—may talk to the stars, but they appear not to hear us. Scientific study (logically and historically) requires that there be a conceptual distance (and, as such, an aboutness) between what is being studied and those who study. Perhaps the great distance (physical and conceptual) between human beings and the stars (some of the first objects of modern scientific investigation) was necessary for the emergence of science, indisputably one of humankind's greatest inventions. However, the self-conscious human condition (we are a studying species) is such that the distance required for our activity to be an object of scientific study *about which something can be said* does not exist.

As far as it has been determined, stars are impervious to being the object of human study, and astronomers and other scientists do not have to falsify what stars are in order to meet the criterion of objectivity. However, people are a different story—we are not impervious to being an object of study. When psychologists try to meet the scientific criterion of objectivity, they falsify human beings. Methodologically, studying behavior (or cognition or psychopathology) turns human beings into stars or, at least, makes us star-like.

If, as we are claiming, human life-as-lived is not studyable in the way that physical phenomena are, can we ever gain more understanding about it? If there is no "natural" object of study, is there anything to study? We think so, if we eliminate the distancing required to "do aboutness." Abandoning this modern epistemological requirement might liberate us from the constraints that force us to distort human activity so profoundly as to make it impossible to learn anything at all about human-social life. The myth of psychology—one hundred years of research that (as some critics, including ourselves, believe[6]) has taught us little about human beings—is that there is a natural object of study (behavior, consciousness, actions, conversations, discourse, narrative and so on) at the requisite distance which, therefore, makes psychology scientific.

In the unscientific psychology we propose, no method (scientific or otherwise) is applied. The methodology of activity entails the practice of method, not the application of method (Newman and Holzman, 1993, 1997). With regard to therapy, therapists and clients alike acknowledge that merely talking to another person about how one is feeling is often helpful. Perhaps it is the relational activity of the therapeutic modality *as activity* that is of value rather than the specific insights, interpretations, explanations, stories or narratives that grow out of the activity (due, presumably, to the application of a particular method). Perhaps it is the talking—not what is talked about—that is therapeutic. Perhaps "knowing emotionally" is not knowing at all (Newman and Holzman, 1996, p. 162; see also Shotter, 1993b). Perhaps people live their lives without applying any method at all— functioning, instead, on the basis of their attitudes and beliefs rather than on the basis of the kinds of objective standards, scientific methods, laws of deduction, and convictions of what is true or is really the case that philosophers and psychologists often posit as what makes people tick. Perhaps it is the case that, as Wittgenstein has said: "You can fight, hope and even believe without believing *scientifically*" (1980, p. 60).

One might think that the narrative perspective would be sympathetic to this *activity-theoretic* understanding of therapeutic discourse. However, from our readings, it does not appear to be the case. We turn again to Epston, White and Murray (1992) for illustration of what we take to be representative of the narrative therapy position, because the language these authors use makes the epistemological bias of the narrative approach very clear (at least to us!)—a bias that, we feel, limits the developmental and liberating potential of postmodern psychotherapy. In pointing out this problem, we also show the philosophical confusion the authors generate.

First, Epston, White and Murray reveal their thoroughly cognitive understanding of human experience: "In order to give meaning to our experience, we must organize it, frame it, or give pattern to it. To understand an aspect of our experience, we must be able to frame it within a pattern of experience that is known to us; we must be able to identify aspects of lived experience within the context of known patterns of experience" (p. 97)."

We take issue with the totality of their frame(work) and its idealist presupposition that human life is/must be/must be made/consistent, systematic, patterned and rational. While people can and do systematize and patternize, such abstraction and appraisal is clearly not a *necessary* part of the human understanding. But even the logic of Epston, White and Murray's argument escapes us. As far as we can tell, what is being said is the following: 'Human beings experience—without meaning. Then, we (somehow, without meaning) organize that experience, frame it and give pattern to it. We do that by identifying aspects of the experience in question with patterns of experience already known to us. Only then does this experience have meaning.' We wonder how, in this account, we are able to recognize this particular experience as an experience and, further, how those patterns of experience we are identifying the new experience with ever become known to us as experience (or at all). Empiricism's paradox remains intact.

This mentalistic accounting becomes even more confusing with the authors' addition of the role of stories in human life. They say, "a story can be defined as a unit of meaning that provides a frame for lived experience" (p. 97). Leaving aside the adherence to the modernist paradigm inherent in definition (another means of achieving "aboutness"), we want to pursue what the authors might be meaning by this statement, particularly what they might be saying about the relationship between "frame" and "lived experience." First, we have to assume that there is a person involved here, and that this person is both "framer" and "experiencer." Is the frame for lived experience (and, therefore, a story) itself lived experience, or is it something other than lived experience? If it is lived experience, then the authors' claim that lived experience needs a frame either cannot be the case or is an infinite regress and not of much analytic value. If it is *not* lived experience, then framing (stories) is a human action that has the strange characteristic of not being a lived experience. We have been presented with a theory in which people constructing stories is the centerpiece but which has as its two critical units of analysis a *disembodied* frame/story and an *un-understandable* lived experience! Rationalism's paradox remains intact.

Further, relating to stories as frames or organizers of life falsifies human life (including storytelling) by imposing upon it a paradigm of consistency. Therapists and researchers may choose if they wish to view a person's life as a rational narrative, but claiming that life is actually lived as a rational narrative is philosophically (and, we think, ethically) troublesome. All this confusion, we think, stems from the attempt to create a sufficient distance from human life-as-lived so that it can be an object of scientific study (that is, coherent with an epistemological paradigm). Perhaps there is clarity in searching for a *postscientific* object of study.

Another, perhaps more provocative, way to make our point is to consider, if only very briefly, the structure and function of stories. Within Western culture (and probably most other cultures as well), stories are a particular sort of account. Whether they stir or bore us, are funny or sad, are orally transmitted or written down, told by one's grandmother or a fiction writer, stories are accountings for things or events—specifically, accountings by way of offering up how things began. Structurally, stories are "in the-beginning-isms" and, in this sense, fundamentally religious. All that is well and good; we are neither saying stories shouldn't have these characteristics nor that they are not a very important part of human life. On the contrary, it is because they are such a prevalent cultural form that we feel the need to be mindful of the danger of getting caught up in the story and overidentifying it with life itself. For life is not lived in the manner of a story. Life (except for individual lives) has no beginning (or middle or end), but is continuous.

(Even with individual lives, there is a continuity of experience; living is more process in character than discrete and bounded.)

To the extent that narrative therapists focus on stories, it seems to us that they are vulnerable to overidentifying life with stories and imposing "in the beginning-ness" onto their clients' life activity. Through our own therapeutic experience, we have come to avoid this kind of overidentification by focusing on story making (the process) rather than on stories (the product of story making). For surely story making is closer to the activistic quality of life than a story is. For this reason, we suggest that it is more useful therapeutically in the work of transforming life process.

TOOLS, RESULTS, AND TOOLS-AND-RESULTS

Modernism has been, among other things, an extended period of transformation in the making and use of tools, both technological and conceptual. The historical catalyst for modern science was the ontological shift from stillness to motion as the fundamental ("natural") state of the physical world. Such a shift required a qualitative transformation in all kinds of tools, as the early scientists faced the great challenge of devising ways to study the things of the physical world. These objects of study—distanced from us—required new tools of analysis and technology. Studying the motion of the stars, for example, required the invention of physical tools (such as the telescope) and conceptual tools (such as areas of mathematics) by which they could be seen and studied. Postmodernism, we are repeatedly told, is a qualitatively different historical period—one marked by the fragmentation of subjectivity, the breakdown of grand narratives, the destruction not of appearances as during the modern era, but the destruction of meaning (for example, Baudrillard, 1968, 1987; Gergen, 1991; Lyotard, 1984, 1988). If we take these analyses seriously, it seems to us that we would need to question what the analogous postmodern (or post-postmodern) activity might be. How can we move ahead in a meaningless world? In our view, the activity analogous to the modern transformation of scientific *tools of study* is the postmodern revolutionary transformation of the *objects of study*. If postmodernism is to be something other than an extended period of paralysis, it must transform its object of study of human life from a pseudoscientific "natural" phenomenon into a post-postmodern, distinctly unscientific, "unnatural" one. *Unscientific study,* far from being a reversion to feudal, prescientific methodology is, as we see it, an advance over modern science.

Yet the questions remain. If we abandon aboutness, what can we do? Without it, are we doing anything other than "what we are doing"? If there are no human-social things which a study of subjective-social human life could be about, is there anything to study? If gaining understanding of ourselves as a species is not epistemological, what is it? Is there an object of study for such a nonepistemological activity? If there is, and it is not a "naturally occurring" phenomenon, then what is it?

If, as we and many of our narrative, social constructionist/constructivist colleagues believe, there is nothing social (-cultural-historical) independent of human beings creating it, then there can be nothing "natural" about how people participate with each other, nothing at a sufficient distance from us to "study." There is only what we create—not as product or result, but as simultaneously process-and-product, tool-and-result, as continuous, emergent activity. We are suggesting that the methodology needed to help narrative and other language-oriented and constructionist/constructivist approaches realize their potential is activity-theoretic as opposed to scientific (paradigmatically instrumentalist and dualistic).

It is not the use of language but the *activity* of language (speaking, conversing, storytelling, etc.) that is of activity-theoretic interest. Studying language activity requires that we self-consciously create some unnatural phenomena—*the performance of conversation (discourse, narrative, stories)*—so as to incorporate human self-reflexivity into our unscientific study at the outset. Moreover, the *study of the performance of conversation* is indistinguishable from the performance of conversation itself. Our argument in favor of performance and performed conversation as postmodern, postscientific objects of study is historically specific. The world in which we live is already filled with unnatural objects—economic commodities (obviously of a very different, antidevelopmental sort than the ones we are advocating). As Marx showed, economically and culturally commodified capitalism turns continuous social process into products. Economic commodities are anything but "natural" phenomena; they are artificially created objects produced for the purpose of sale (and exchange value) and, thereby, the maintaining of certain relations of power. We are becoming increasingly convinced that, given that we live in an alienated culture flooded with commodified objects, creating unnatural objects in support of human growth is necessary.

PERFORMED CONVERSATION

In our practice, we have found performance and performed conversations to be vital to the process of ongoing human development (developmental activity). We take performance to be a revolutionary activity in Marx's and Vygotsky's sense of the term—human activity that is fully self-reflexive, transformative of the totality, a tool-and-result rather than an instrumental tool for result, relative to nothing other than (outside) itself. Revolutionary activity is "all process," creatively and constantly emergent (Newman and Holzman, 1993).

Vygotsky's (1978, 1987, 1993) greatest contributions, in our opinion, were not so much as a cognitive or developmental psychologist, but as a methodologist. For him, human development was revolutionary activity—development (more properly, developing) is inseparable from creating environments for development. The social-cultural-historical process of creating what he called *zones of proximal development (zpds)* is the revolutionary activity of people jointly (collectively, socially) transforming totalities (Newman and Holzman, 1993, 1996). Zpds are not instrumental, means-ends tools for results, but "simultaneously prerequisite and product, tool and result" (1978, p. 65). They are where and how children perform "a head taller than they are" (Vygotsky, 1978, p. 102). In this way, human development is an "unnatural act"; we become who we "are" by continuously "being who we are not" as the tool-and-result of our activity.

Following Vygotsky, we take human development to be performatory, more theatrical and therapeutic than rational and epistemic. Vygotsky's zpd, in our opinion, is more a historical performance space or stage than a societal scaffold. His analysis of the zpd of the language-learning young child is suggestive of what we identify as the nonepistemological, performatory, revolutionary character of all human development (Newman and Holzman, 1997). It is the culturally sanctioned performed conversation.

We think Vygotsky pointed the way to the paradoxical nature and dialectical practice of human revolutionary activity-and-its-object-of-study. In the zpd—the performance space—where learning leads development, it is development that "comes first" (in the societal sense of being temporally prior). We can see learning leading development in the performance of conversations that very young children and their caregivers create. In the performance of conversation, the babbling baby's rudimentary speech is a *creative imitation* of the more developed speaker's speech. It is not, Vygotsky warns us, to be understood as the mimicry that some parrots and monkeys do. It is creative, revolutionary activity. It is what makes it possible for the child to do what she or he is not yet capable of. In imitating in the linguistic zpd, the child is *performing* (beyond her/himself) as a speaker.

Performance is, however, not a "solo act." The more developed speaker *completes* the child. Completion is among Vygotsky's most revolutionary—and postmodern—concepts (unfortunately, it has been ignored in the neo-Vygotskian literature; see Newman and Holzman, 1993; Holzman, 1997). Vygotsky posits that thinking/speaking are a dialectical unity in which speaking completes thinking: "The structure of speech is not a simple mirror image of the structure of thought. . . . Speech does not merely serve as the expression of developed thought. Thought is restructured as it is transformed into speech. It is not expressed but completed in the word" (1987, p. 251). This conception of completion challenges not only the representationalist view of language but, more importantly from a postmodern therapeutic vantage point, it challenges the expressionist view as well.

Mothers, fathers, grandparents, siblings and others immediately accept infants into the community of speakers (onto the performance stage). More experienced speakers neither tell infants that they are too young, give them a grammar book and dictionary to study, correct them, nor remain silent around them. Rather, they relate to infants and babies as capable of far more than they could possibly do "naturally"; they relate to them as fellow speakers, feelers, thinkers and makers of meaning.

Creative imitation and *completion* are the dominant activities in the zpd—the building activities that create the performance of conversation, the relational activities that *simultaneously* produce the environment in which learning leads development (creates the stage) *and* the learning that leads development (performance) simultaneously. Their "product" is nothing less than a new total environment of speakers. The significance of the zpd, as we see it, is that the capacity to speak and to make meaning is inextricably connected to transforming the total environment of speakers in the revolutionary activity of performing an ordinary "unnatural" act.

The lesson we might take from Vygotsky is this. A total environment in which very young children are related to by themselves and others as communicative social beings (in which they perform conversation) is how they get to be so. They say things—they babble, utter sounds, use words, make meaning—as an inseparable part of participating in social life. Clearly, something developmental happens in this ensemble performance of creating conversation.

This reading of Vygotsky is, admittedly, unorthodox. It is more *therapeutically developmental* than epistemic—rather like creating a performed conversation with Vygotsky instead of trying to understand what he is "really" saying. In this way, it shares important features with the later Wittgenstein's methodology (or, again, our reading of it). The *activity of philosophizing* was for Wittgenstein distinctly therapeutic—it can help prevent us from institutionalizing our words. He practiced philosophy as method (to do away with philosophy). Many have remarked that Wittgenstein's approach in his later writings was more clinical and therapeutic than analytic (see, for example, Baker, 1992; Baker and Hacker, 1980; Newman and Holzman, 1996; Peterman, 1992; Shotter, 1993a and b; and van der Merwe and Voestermans,

1995). To Wittgenstein, our "illness," or "presenting problem," is the way we speak and think about speaking, thinking and other so-called mental processes. It obscures, he says, the activity of language. But language-games—performed conversations—can clear away the confusion: "When we look at such simple forms of language the mental mist which seems to enshroud our ordinary use of language disappears. We see activities, reactions, which are clear-cut and transparent" (Wittgenstein, 1965, BBB, p. 17). Playing language-games "bring[s] into prominence the fact that the *speaking* of language is part of an activity, or of a form of life" (Wittgenstein, 1953, *PI*, 23).

Wittgenstein had no love for the scientific method (no less modern epistemology), especially as it is applied to human-social phenomena. Language-games were the centerpiece of his therapeutic method for better understanding the unsystematic, unexplainable activity that is language in use.[7] Vygotsky rejected (although not completely) the instrumentalist, tool for result method of science in favor of a dialectical tool-and-result methodology in order to better understand human development as a cultural phenomenon. These two late modernist thinkers, in our view, set the stage for postmodern psychology.

PERFORMATORY SOCIAL THERAPY

Vygotsky and Wittgenstein have also greatly informed our practice, performatory social therapy. Our therapeutic concern is how to create, in Vygotsky's completive sense, with what clients bring to therapy. (Unlike many narrative therapists, we do not believe that clients come into therapy with stories; we believe they come in with emotional pain.) Our developmental concern leads us to help clients transform their life activity through reinitiating their capacity to perform, specifically, their capacity to perform conversation. This developmental, performatory perspective has implications for the role of the therapist in relation to stories and narratives.

According to McLeod (1997), the narrative approach involves listening for stories, although different therapists listen for different reasons. Psychodynamic and constructivist therapists influenced by narrative ideas listen in order to gain access to what is, supposedly, behind the story. In contrast, narrative therapists "are interested in the story for itself" (p. 117). Among the reasons for this kind of interest is the possibility of therapist and client deconstructing the story, a process White (1992) describes as "procedures that subvert taken-for-granted realities and practices, those so-called truths that are split off from the conditions and the context of their production" (p. 121).

We are sympathetic to this procedure; however, we understand the potential value of deconstruction quite differently from the way narrative therapists understand it. For their focus is indeed on "the story for itself" and not the activity. For some, the therapeutic value of the narrative approach is that it results in an alternative—and better—story (e.g., "enabling stories" that are alternatives to the "problem" story the client came into therapy with, Drewery and Winslade, 1997). Others, seeing "truth" sneaking in the back door here, merely emphasize the support clients get from the realization that there are endless possibilities for creating their life-narrative (e.g., Gonçalves, 1994) or claim that creating new stories changes one's life ("New futures result from developing narratives that give new meanings and understandings to one's life and enable different agency," Anderson and Goolishian, 1992, p. 37).

Our view is closer to that of Gergen and Kaye (1992), who also believe that we must go beyond narrative construction to realize the potentials of postmodernism. They, too, are uncomfortable with the all too common "commitment to narrative," that is, the belief that "the individual lives within the narrative as a system of understanding" (p. 179). Building on Gergen and Kaye's criticism, what is important to us is not the result of deconstruction, but the *activity of* deconstructing. Deconstructing stories (creating a performed conversation) is a changed and changing life activity. It is the process of transforming one's life, not the process of transforming meaning. With Vygotsky and Wittgenstein, we believe that meaning is transformed through transforming life activity, not the other way around. As we see it, performed conversation is an approach that is in keeping with Gergen and Kaye's urging that postmodern therapy work to *transcend* meaning, not to transform it (1992, p. 175).

Epistemology is a socio-cultural phenomenon that has dominated Western civilization from the Greeks until the current century. Science, its most important product, is and, no doubt, will continue to be a lasting contribution to civilization. But like all cultural developments, it is not universal in its usefulness. Indeed, when imposed on areas to which it has no relevance, it has effectively paralyzed human development. Modern psychology embodies this paralysis.

Our "emotional states of mind" in late capitalist culture are alienated, individuated and truth-referential commodifications. The being of them and the understanding of them are inextricably connected, not dialectically, but by fast-drying (calcified) ideological cement. Whereas knowledge of physical truths (also alienated) employs an aboutness that at a minimum captures a scintilla of the "real" relationship between an observer and a distantly observed inanimate star, the crude application of this physicalistic scientific-epistemic model to human-to-human activity fundamentally distorts the particular, self-referential (paradoxical), relational, activistic dimension of life-as-lived. It is these cemented, truth-referential, alienated and individuated so-called expressions of so-called inner life (emotional, cognitive and attitudinal states of mind) that we must move about around in creating a new, socially completed form of emotive relational life.

Performed activity is a creatively varied and continuous movement around the rigid, alienated events (states) of emotional life in our scientifically psychologized culture. In performing, we dealienate (to the extent possible, given the overall societal environment) our individuated selves and re-establish our social relationality *in practice*, in *socially completed activity* (Newman and Holzman, 1996).

It is in this way that narrative, social constructionist/constructivist, performative and other postmodern approaches to human subjective-social life can liberate us. They have the capacity to expose the limitations of the modern understanding of conscious human activity in general and the painful constraints of modernistically overdefined emotionality in particular. Like Vygotsky's zpd and Wittgenstein's language-games, the creating and telling of stories and narratives and the performing of conversations produce *in their activity* a sensuous understanding of the individualistic fly bottle in which human beings reside. It is the tool-and-result activity of postmodern storytelling—not a new story or the realization that there are unlimited stories—that we believe is therapeutically developmental.

NOTES

1. For academically oriented discussions of social therapy and a cultural-performatory psychology, see Holzman (1996, 1997); Holzman and Newman (1979); Newman (1991, in press); Newman and Holzman (1993, 1996, 1997), and the series of articles in Holzman and Polk (1988). See also Newman's books for a general audience (1994, 1996).
2. Even the recent literature is too vast to list here. Among the more interesting and most cited are the writings of Kenneth Gergen, John Shotter, Mary Gergen, Erica Burman, Rom Harre, and Ian Parker.
3. We are aware of the many delineations of various types of knowing in the philosophical literature, which we take as unsuccessful attempts to escape the cognitive bias.
4. See Newman and Holzman (1997) and Newman (in press) for fuller discussion of some of these issues.
5. While scientific constructs such as electrons and magnetic fields may be attempts to configure a reality that does not reveal itself in obvious ways, it is still the case that such constructs impute an ontic reality.
6. Critiques of psychology abound. We call it a myth (Newman, 1991; Newman and Holzman, 1996). See also the historical and social-cultural critical analyses of psychology of Burman (1994); Danziger (1993, 1997); Dawes (1994); Morss (1990); and Torrey (1992).
7. Other recent works discussing the relevance of Wittgenstein's writings to psychology include Bakhurst (1995); Chapman and Dixon (1987); Gergen (1994); Jost (1995); Jost and Hardin (1996); Parker (1996); and Shotter (1991, 1993a, b, 1995).

REFERENCES

Anderson, H. and Goolishian, H. (1992). The client is the expert: a not-knowing approach to therapy. In S. McNamee and K. J. Gergen 2(Eds.), *Therapy as social construction*. London: Sage, pp. 25–39.

Baker, G. P. (1992). Some remarks on "language" and "grammar." *Grazer Philosophische Studien, 42*, 107–131.

Baker, G. P. and Hacker, P. M. S. (1980). *Wittgenstein: Understanding and meaning*. Oxford: Blackwell.

Bakhurst, D. (1995). Wittgenstein and social being. In D. Bakhurst and C. Sypnowich (Eds.), *The social self* (pp. 30–46). London: Sage.

Baudrillard, J. (1968). *Le système des objets*. Paris: Denoel-Gonthier.

Baudrillard, J. (1987). *Forget Foucault*. New York: Semiotexte.

Bruner, J. S. (1984). Narrative and paradigmatic modes of thought. Invited address, American Psychological Association, Toronto.

Bruner, J. (1993). Explaining and interpreting: Two ways of using mind. In G. Harman (Ed.), *Conceptions of the human mind: Essays in honor of George Miller*. Hillsdale, NJ: Lawrence Erlbaum.

Burman, E. (1994). *Deconstructing developmental psychology*. London: Routledge.

Chapman, M. and Dixon, R. A. (Eds.) (1987). *Meaning and the growth of understanding: Wittgenstein's significance for developmental psychology*. Berlin: Springer.

Danziger, K. (1993). *Constructing the subject: Historical origins of psychological research*. Cambridge: Cambridge University Press.

Danziger, K. (1997). *Naming the mind: How psychology found its language*. London: Sage.

Dawes, R. M. (1994). *House of cards: Psychology and psychotherapy built on myth*. New York: The Free Press.

Drewery, W. and Winslade, J. (1997). The theoretical story of narrative therapy. In G. Monk, J. Winslade, K. Crocket and D. Epston (Eds.), *Narrative therapy in practice: The archaeology of hope*. San Francisco: Jossey-Bass, pp. 32–52.

Epston, D., White, M. and Murray, K. (1992). A proposal for re-authoring therapy: Rose's revisioning of her life and a commentary. In S. McNamee and K. J. Gergen (Eds.), *Therapy as social construction*. London: Sage, pp, 96–115.

Gergen, K. J. (1991). *The saturated self: Dilemmas of identity in contemporary life*. New York: Basic Books.

Gergen, K. J. (1994). *Realities and relationships: Soundings in social construction*. Cambridge, MA: Harvard University Press.

Gergen, K. J. and Kaye, J. (1992). Beyond narrative in the negotiation of therapeutic meaning. In S. McNamee and K. J. Gergen (Eds.), *Therapy as social construction*. London: Sage, pp. 166–185.

Gonçalves, O. F. (1994). Cogntive narrative psychotherapy: The hermenetic construction of alternative meanings. *Journal of Cognitive Psychotherapy: An International Quarterly, 8,* 105–125.

Holzman, L. (1996). How Newman's practice of method completes Vygotsky. In I. Parker and R. Spears (Eds.), *Psychology and society: Radical theory and practice*. London: Pluto, pp. 128–38.

Holzman, L. (1997). S*chools for growth: Radical alternatives to current educational models*. Mahwah, NJ: Lawrence Erlbaum.

Holzman, L. and Newman, F. (1979). *The practice of method: An introduction to the foundations of social therapy*. New York: NY Institute for Social Therapy and Research.

Holzman, L. and Polk, H. (Eds.) (1988). *History is the cure: A social therapy reader*. New York: Practice Press.

Ingleby, D. (Ed.) (1980). *Critical psychiatry: The politics of mental health*. New York: Pantheon Books.

Jost, J. (1995). Toward a Wittgensteinian social psychology of human development. *Theory & Psychology, 5(1),* 5–25.

Jost, J. T. and Hardin, C. D. (1996). The practical turn in psychology: Marx and Wittgenstein as social materialists. *Theory & Psychology, 6(3),* 385–393.

Laing, R. D. (1967). *The politics of experience*. New York: Ballantine Books.

Lyotard, J-F. (1984). *The postmodern condition: A report on knowledge*. Minneapolis: University of Minnesota Press.

Lyotard, J-F. (1988a). *The differend: Phrases in dispute*. Minneapolis: University of Minnesota Press.

McLeod, J. (1997). *Narrative and psychotherapy.* London: Sage.

McNamee, S. and Gergen, K. J. (Eds.), (1992). *Therapy as social construction.* London: Sage.

Monk, G., Winslade, J., Crocket, K. and Epston, D. (Eds.) (1997). *Narrative therapy in practice: The archaeology of hope.* San Francisco: Jossey-Bass.

Morss, J. (1990). *The biologising of childhood: Developmental psychology and the Darwinian myth.* East Sussex: Lawrence Erlbaum Associates Ltd.

Neimeyer, R. A. and Mahoney, M. J. (Eds.) (1995). *Constructivism in psychotherapy.* Washington, DC: American Psychological Association.

Newman, F. (1991). *The myth of psychology.* New York: Castillo International.

Newman, F. (1994). *Let's develop! A guide to continuous personal growth.* New York: Castillo International.

Newman, F. (1996). *Performance of a lifetime: A practical-philosophical guide to the joyous life.* New York: Castillo International.

Newman, F. (in press). Does a story need a theory? (Understanding the methodology of narrative therapy). In D. Fee (Ed.), *Pathology and the postmodern: Mental illness as discourse and experience.* London: Sage.

Newman, F. and Holzman, L. (1993). *Lev Vygotsky: Revolutionary scientist.* London: Routledge.

Newman, F. and Holzman, L. (1996). *Unscientific psychology: A cultural-performatory approach to understanding human life.* Westport, CT: Praeger.

Newman, F. and Holzman, L. (1997). *The end of knowing: A new developmental way of learning.* London: Routledge.

Parker, I. (1996). Against Wittgenstein: Materialist reflections on language in psychology. *Theory & Psychology, 6(3),* 363–384.

Peterman, J. F. (1992). *Philosophy as therapy: An interpretation and defense of Wittgenstein's later philosophical project.* Albany: SUNY Press.

Rosen, H. (1996). Meaning-making narratives: Foundations for constructivist and social constructionist psychotherapies. In H. Rosen and K. T. Kuehlwein (Eds.), *Constructing realities: Meaning-making perspectives for psychotherapists.* San Francisco: Jossey-Bass, pp. 3–51.

Rosen, H. and Kuehlwein, K. T. (Eds.) (1996). *Constructing realities: Meaning-making perspectives for psychotherapists.* San Francisco: Jossey-Bass.

Shotter, J. (1991). Wittgenstein and psychology: On our 'hook up' to reality. In A. Phillips-Griffiths (Ed.), *Wittgenstein: Centenary essays* (pp. 193–208). Cambridge: Cambridge University Press.

Shotter, J. (1993a). *Conversational realities: Studies in social constructionism.* London: Sage.

Shotter, J. (1993b). *Cultural politics of everyday life: Social constructionism, rhetoric and knowing of the third kind.* Toronto: University of Toronto Press.

Shotter, J. (1995) In conversation: Joint action, shared intentionality and ethics. *Theory & Psychology, 5(1)*, 49–73.

Szasz, T. (1961). *The myth of mental illness*. New York: Harper & Row.

Szasz, T. (1996). *The meaning of mind*. Westport, CT: Praeger.

Timpanero, S. (1976). *The Freudian slip: Psychoanalysis and textual criticism*. London: Verso.

Torrey, E. F. (1992). *Freudian fraud*. New York: HarperCollins.

van der Merwe, W. L. and Voestermans, P. P. (1995). Wittgenstein's legacy and the challenge to psychology. *Theory & Psychology, 5(1)*, 27–48.

Vygotsky, L.S. (1978). *Mind in society*. Cambridge, MA: Harvard University Press.

Vygotsky, L. S. (1987). *The collected works of L. S. Vygotsky*, Vol. 1. New York: Plenum.

White, M. (1992). Deconstruction and therapy. In D. Epston and M. White (Eds.), *Experience, contradiction, narrative and imagination*. Adelaide, South Australia: Dulwich Centre Publications, pp. 109–152.

White, M. and Epston, D. (1990). *Narrative means to therapeutic ends*. New York: W.W. Norton.

Wittgenstein, L. (1953). *Philosophical investigations*. Oxford: Blackwell.

Wittgenstein, L. (1965). *The blue and brown books*. New York: Harper Torchbooks.

Wittgenstein, L. (1980). *Culture and value*. Oxford: Blackwell.

A Therapeutic Deconstruction of the Illusion of Self

In this presentation—the opening session of the 1998 Spring Training Institute of the East Side Institute for Short Term Psychotherapy—Newman gives a personal account of his thirty-year "search for method" as a psychotherapist. In sharing the origins and methodological turning points in the development of social therapy, he tells the story of how and why language became the subject of intense intellectual debate during this century. He revisits the birth, substance, achievements and limitations of positivism, analytic philosophy and ordinary language philosophy. More a dramatization than a formal lecture, Newman plays multiple roles, including Descartes, Wittgenstein and Vygotsky, while always performing himself. In editing Newman's presentation for this volume, I have made minimal changes so as to preserve the informal narrative.—L.H.

I'm a little intimidated by my own title which rings rather academic. But coming up with that title has been of value to me, because it's made me think about some things that I haven't thought about in this particular way for a long time. So let me share with you what the title is about and maybe, if we can comprehend the title together, we'll have made some kind of step forward.

There is something of a contradiction in our talking about this, however, since the point that I'm eager to make is that any kind of serious deconstruction of the illusion of self is going to be a therapeutic deconstruction and, since we're not doing therapy together, one might reasonably ask, "Well, how could you possibly do what it is that the title suggests you're going to do?" And the answer is, I can't.

As some of you know, I was formally trained in philosophy, not in psychology. I started out in philosophy in the 1950s in what's called analytic philosophy at a moment when it was just coming into being. In some respects, analytic philosophy was doing what's now called deconstruction long before there was any concept of deconstruction. Postmodernism was really not yet around, and everyone then thought about themselves as modernists (insofar as people thought about this at all) — it was kind of "cool" to be modern. In my lifetime things have gone from being cool to be modern to being a disgrace to be modern.

Philosophy has gone through a profound transformation in the course of the twentieth century. For centuries, it was the study of "great ideas" and "big questions"—conceptions like "the good," "knowing," "life" and "meaning." Then, at the end of the nineteenth century, due to the work of many different people in philosophy and other fields (especially linguistics, anthropology and sociology), there emerged a shift in what studying and learning in general were all about. As a part of that, there occurred a significant shift in what philosophy was about. The centuries-old notion that somehow ideas could be abstractly studied or abstractly understood—in a sense, the very essence of philosophy— came under severe critique.

This shift encompassed many different movements which, for lack of a better term, we could call positivism. Both its late-nineteenth-century and twentieth-century versions (which was known as logical positivism) opened up the question of whether the study of ideas by this abstract method, which has been part of a Western heritage (and in some respects an Eastern heritage as well) for two thousand years, was worthless, was fruitless, was ridiculous, was—to use the term that was most used by these positivists—meaningless. Stated in its most extreme form, the positivistic critique went something like this: Philosophy may be nothing more than a certain grouping of human beings called Philosophers who, while on the payroll of universities and colleges throughout the world, utter certain words. These words they utter when they are doing philosophy are essentially empty, abstract and meaningless. They are, in effect, nonsensical, but they have the illusion of meaning something (at least amongst the "chosen," that is, the Philosophers). Positivism raised the question of whether philosophy—thousands of years of activity, trillions and trillions of words—ultimately meant nothing at all.

From the very outset of my training in philosophy I had always been a little suspicious of philosophy, so I was somewhat sympathetic to the positivists' argument, even though I was learning this trade and becoming a Philosopher. I had come out of a relatively poor, working-class background. No one in my family had ever graduated high school, much less graduated college, much less gotten a Ph.D. I had apprenticed as a machinist when I was a young man, and was headed for a lifetime of work in machine shops. Then, for a variety of reasons, including the opportunity opened up by the G.I. Bill, I managed to get into college and started taking courses. And it occurred to me that if I was going to go to college then the thing I wanted most of all was to find a subject which was as utterly and completely impractical as possible. If my journey at the time was getting away from the practicality of machine shops and that kind of difficult, laboring work, I thought I should find something that had nothing to do with machine-work, that had nothing to do with anything even close to machine-work, indeed, that had nothing to do with reality and the world at all. I was looking to *get away from it all.* I went to undergraduate school at City College and spent three and a half years trying to find the way to do absolutely nothing and get paid for it, and philosophy turned out to be that way of life.

I went to graduate school at Stanford just at the time when some very high-powered people had been hired (who have since become some of the dominant American philosophers of the latter part of this century) and the university was becoming a primary center of analytic philosophy. I actually associate this shift with a specific moment in time, the strange way we identify a phenomenon of this sort with a certain date, like one might say, "War broke out July 3rd" in spite of the fact that these kinds of things happen gradually. But that wasn't my experience. Between the time I finished at City College in December, 1959 and drove out to California over the course of a month to start at Stanford, my experience was that everyone suddenly stopped studying philosophy and started studying language. I sort of have the feeling that there was this mass meeting that I didn't attend while I was driving to California, where everyone made an agreement to change the subject matter. So when I got to California, it no longer seemed as if I was studying the same thing that I'd been studying those years at City College. I had originally gone to Stanford to study Eastern philosophy with David Nivison, a leading scholar in Asian Studies, on the recommendation of one of my City College professors. Over the summer, Nivison had decided to abandon Asian philosophy altogether and start doing analytic philosophy. So I get out there, and he says, "I'm glad you came, but I'm going to do analytic philosophy." And so, having virtually no mind of my own, I went with him.

This was a revolutionary moment within philosophy. Now, philosophy has always been a very narrow field, so it wasn't as if this revolution got much coverage in the press. But internally, it was gigantic. An entire subject matter was being transformed. In the middle of a world in which truly profound and meaningful things were happening, philosophy was having its own little revolution.

It turns out that there was indeed something to study, the analytic philosophers said—even if ideas were not reasonable subjects for study because they were too slippery, they were too abstract, they had no grounding or, insofar as they were grounded, they were best studied by science and not by an abstract method. The thing that could be studied, that could yield some worthwhile results (as opposed to the metaphysical meaninglessness of traditional philosophy), said the analytic philosophers, was *language*.

The major shift toward language that has occurred over this century didn't just happen in philosophy, but in all areas of study. Arguably though, it began—and obtained a substantial foothold—within philosophy itself. If we couldn't study ideas, we could at least study *the language that we used in articulating these ideas*; that was sufficiently palpable, sufficiently identifiable. We could develop methods for the study of the language that we use to talk about the good, the bad, the evil, the right, the wrong, the worthy, the known, the unknown, the mysterious, the real, etc. We could take a harder look at what it is that was happening when people were talking about ideas, even if the ideas themselves were not meaningful.

Because surely, people were talking about them. Even if it's the case that not a word that any philosopher since Plato had ever said was meaningful, analytical philosophy pointed out, it was still the case that people had said lots of words. People were engaging in certain kinds of discourse; it wasn't just philosophers who engaged in discourse. Ordinary people say things like, "This is a good thing"; "This is the right way to behave"; "This is a bad thing"; "This I know to be true"; "This is reality"; "This is not reality." They might not say it in the pompous way that philosophers do, but they do speak that language in appropriate, ordinary kinds of ways. They speak these conceptions—to use a conception that came out following Wittgenstein—in *ordinary language*. Indeed, a whole school of philosophy emerged, also out of Wittgenstein but associated with a British philosopher named J. L. Austin, called the ordinary language school of philosophy, which attended to what it is that ordinary people meant when they said things like, "This is the right thing to do." Simple things like that. Terms like "right" come up again and again. What do they mean? The ordinary language people, as a kind of a subdivision of analytic philosophy, would study what ordinary people meant, and philosophers, then, would study not only what ordinary people meant but what philosophers themselves meant in the use of this language.

So the study of language suddenly blossomed. It was like this unbelievable thing happened: Suddenly, overnight, almost everyone in philosophy was studying language. In my opinion, this study of language was inseparable from what is now identified by postmodernists as deconstruction. So, again, not to take pride in philosophers getting there first—I don't want to do a whole philosophical, chauvinist thing—but I do think that philosophers have been into the business of doing deconstruction long before some of the people in different fields, including psychology, have come on board. Philosophers have been looking at language, and attempting to figure out how language meant, what it meant, when it meant, if it meant, etc., for quite awhile.

So here I was in the midst of this kind of revolution. Part of what began to happen with this discovery of analytic philosophy—the study of language and the study of the language of philosophy—was that many people (and nearly everyone at Stanford) was taking a look at the entire history of philosophy and traditional philosophical thought from the vantage point of the new analytic approach. People were into discovering which of the traditional philosophical works were utterly and completely metaphysical, utterly and completely meaningless, and which you could somehow salvage something from by studying the language of their philosophical argumentation.

They started looking at some of the traditional philosophical figures, and some of what seemed to be the great ideas (particularly the great philosophical ideas of Western thought). One of those ideas, one of the real glorious, classical philosophical arguments that people started to look at was the argumentation of Descartes, the French philosopher of the 1600s. Descartes, as probably many of you know, was something of a genius; he was a great mathematician, one of the discoverers of analytic geometry, and wrote in many other fields. He is well known even outside of philosophical circles for his argument, known by its full name in Latin: the *cogito ergo sum*. *Cogito ergo sum* is roughly translatable as "I think, therefore I am."

This was Descartes' effort to try to find a method to discover some indubitable building blocks for modern science. Back in the seventeenth century, the abandonment, at least philosophically, of the belief in faith and the religious method and the move to a more scientific method led to the attempt to discover if there were some truths which were so transparently certain that they are indubitable (could not be questioned).

Descartes was working to discover a method and a process by which he could identify indubitable truths—and what he came to was, *I think, therefore I am*. Part of what he was dealing with was the engagement of a popular skeptical argument of that moment in history, the argument from illusion: that it is possible to imagine that all kinds of things could be illusory. For example, I could be looking at Tom here, but maybe I'm suffering from a delusion or an illusion; maybe he's not there at all, maybe it's a complex trick with mirrors, maybe it's my bad eyesight. That is, illusion is forever possible. The argument from illusion had been around for a very long time in Western thought—at least since the Greeks and Heraclitus. But this notion of illusion became more significant as things became increasingly empirical. For illusion is not a problem for religious thought, for fairly obvious reasons—in a religious model, the most important objects are not to be seriously seen anyhow, so illusion is not problematic. But when you're starting to evolve a mode of thought in which empirics play more and more of a role, then the *concept* of illusion becomes more troublesome. Because then people can more and more question the certitude of what you're claiming, empirically or observationally, by saying, "Wait a second, how do you know that for sure? Maybe that's a misperception. Maybe that's not really what you're seeing."

There were, after all, the beginnings in this period of some discoveries which revealed that things *weren't* as they seemed. Copernicus is pointing out that the world is round, not flat as it might have seemed to the naked eye. People are inventing new approaches with magnifying glasses and telescopes. People are starting to see all kinds of things that are different from what was apparent to the naked eye. So this notion of illusion is a very very powerful conception which cries out for critical analysis in the 1600s and 1700s, the early moments of the Enlightenment and modern science.

So Descartes is saying, "Wait a second, illusion is always possible. In purely empirical terms, anything could be an illusion." He grants that point. "But," says Descartes, in developing the *cogito*, "Even if it's the case that what I'm thinking is illusory or delusory, even if what I'm thinking is all wrong, even if the object of my thought is completely mistaken, what can be established by the fact that I'm thinking something is that *there is a thinker*."

Let's try this out with perception for just a moment, to get the feel for it. I might be thinking that I'm perceiving Tom. I say, "I know Tom, I see him every week, he's someone I know very well, I'm sure that's Tom," and it might turn out that it's a mannequin of Tom. "Oh my god, I wasn't seeing Tom at all." But, I was at least seeing a mannequin of Tom, I was at least seeing what was the illusory phenomenon that I took to be Tom. So there was something that was certain in that, argues Descartes, namely, that there was someone who was doing the seeing or the thinking or the perceiving, even if there was complete delusion taking place.

Descartes goes through this intensive method and discovers this as a basic truth, *cogito/I think, ergo sum/therefore I am*, which becomes one of the most famous philosophical arguments and one which contributed very substantially to the development of modern science. It becomes a foundational claim of what has come down to us as rationalism; that it is rational to realize that though we might be incorrect in all of our empirical perceptions, it's at least the case that we can count on the certitude that something is going on by someone when they're making what may perhaps be endless mistakes. *Cogito ergo sum. I think, therefore I am.* There is a thinker. Maybe the thinker is fooled consistently, but there is a thinker.

The engagement of this conception by analytic philosophy was fascinating to me. Thousands of things were written about this and I couldn't possibly summarize all of them; but I want to talk just a little bit about the general approach to this classical argument in the hands of the analytic philosophers. Here's what they said:

If you look at *I think, therefore I am* linguistically, it's a very strange and perhaps fundamentally specious argument. Why? Well, some of them said (I won't even cite names here, this is a combination of literally hundreds of people who wrote about this), *I think therefore I am* is no more valid as an argument form than is the argument, *I'm having a ham sandwich, therefore I am*. After all, from the vantage point of what language means, if you're having a ham sandwich, there must be someone who's having a ham sandwich. The argument of the form *I think therefore I am* is true not by virtue of some extraordinary feature of thinking but simply by the linguistic form of that kind of statement, and therefore you could substitute for "I think, therefore I am," "I'm having a ham sandwich, therefore I am," "I'm sitting in my room, therefore I am," "I'm smelling, therefore I am," "I'm foul, therefore I am," or whatever.

The analytic philosophers argued that a linguistic statement of that form entails that someone is doing something, because that's what the statement means. One could say, perhaps, that that linguistic form establishes something, but what it establishes is something about the nature of *language*, not about the nature of reality. Reality still remains outside, and Descartes' notion that he had established something about reality is mistaken. What he really came upon, unself-consciously, was a certain feature of so-called subject-predicate language.

Articles after article in journal after journal were written about this. And then many people started to develop reactions to that form of argument and the analytical critique of the *cogito* itself started to get critiqued. This critique (of the analytic philosophy argument) looked something like this.

So wait a second, perhaps it's true that *cogito ergo sum, I think, therefore I am* is linguistically similar to "I'm having a ham sandwich, therefore I am." But there is something quite special, these philosophers argued, about the language, if not the concept, of thinking. There's something conceptually interesting about thinking and the language of thinking, indeed, about mental language in general (including emotive language, perceptual language, cognitive language, attitudinal language), for example, "I'm having a thought"; "I have an idea"; "I have a conception"; "I have a feeling"; "I have pain." While it might not be the case that it is profoundly different in one way from "I'm having a ham sandwich, therefore I am," it is the case that if you look at mental language you will come to see that it does entail an "I." Even if the mental experience you're having is itself an illusion, it does require an "I" to be having the illusion. You think you see something, or think you know something, or think you understand something, or think you believe something—you could be wrong about all those things. A man could be having a nightmare and scream, "I believe that Antarctica is floating over my head!" and in a more sane moment when he wakes up he could say, "No, I guess Antarctica was not floating over my head, but I did, in that experience, believe that."

But that believing, so this counter-argument went, does require an "I." There must be an I because of the nature of how emotive or cognitive or mental language works. If mental language can be completely in error vis à vis the object, if you understand and study and look at it, it seems to at least entail that there is a subject which has a certain relationship to the object. And so while Descartes might have not been quite accurate (after all he was living, some of these analytic philosophers said, a very long time ago and he wasn't hip to language), it is the case that there does seem to be something special about mental language, and that special thing is that the I, or the self, has to exist for us to make any sense out of it at all. You see, if you throw out the self, if you reject the I, it becomes impossible to use mental language at all in a way that is comprehensible.

This is an argument that attracts many people. Indeed, my guess is that in some form or another, most people in this room (indeed, most people in the world) would find this argument terribly compelling. There's an ongoing history of this kind of argumentation, but for the moment I don't want to continue that history, because I want to make a shift to another history right now.

Wittgenstein was one of the founders of analytic philosophy. He himself wanted no schools. but many different schools emerged out of Wittgenstein's later work. He didn't set them up and he didn't particularly care for them, but they did emerge nevertheless. Wittgenstein addressed mental language, particularly in his later writings which were published only posthumously, and most particularly in a volume that has come to be known to us as *Philosophical Investigations*. Some of the most important things he wrote about mental language had to do with a very interesting conception—something called "private languages." He raised this very interesting question: "Is it possible that you could have a language that no one understood except the person who made it up? A language that was purely private. It wasn't a language to communicate with others, it was just a language by which, for lack of a better formulation, you communicated with yourself. Is it possible to have such a language?"

It was an esoteric topic, but it turns out to be not quite as esoteric as it might appear at first glance. What Wittgenstein was pointing to was that the commonsensical position is that there are private languages. Even if they don't use the language of private language, most people do tend to think that their purpose in speaking is to give expression to what it is that's going on in their heads. And though we might find public forms of communicating them (saying "I'm having this idea, I'm having this belief, I have this feeling, I have pain," etc.), we do endorse the concept of private languages because, says Wittgenstein, we fundamentally endorse the conception of thinking to ourselves. Most people would say, "Well of course I think to myself, I walk around, I think about things, I have ideas, I have beliefs, I have feelings, I have attitudes, I have intentions, I have desires. These things all go on long before I ever attempt to communicate them or share them. These things all go on in a place called my head, my mind, my will, somewhere or other."

Some people would even say something like, "As a matter of fact, I have pictures in my head. I think about something, and I actually see a picture, then I give expression to it by using certain language. I have feelings, perhaps they're not in my head, perhaps they're in my heart, perhaps they're in my stomach, perhaps they're in my soul, but there are things that go on *inside* of me. Perhaps I use the appropriate social terms for the purposes of communication, but I can make up new ones. I can make up a handful or a whole new set of terms. Instead of calling a certain intention to go to the park tomorrow *going to the park tomorrow* I could call it *Someone eats banana peels on Thursday*, and give that the name of that intention. So that when I refer to it myself, no one would know what I was talking about. Not only could you have a private language, in a certain way we all have the capacity for private language, and we all have the ability to create private language, and the only reason that we don't *just* engage in private language creation is that we wish to use language to communicate with others, and so there are societal conventions which accomplish that. But surely we have the capacity for private languages, we *think* things, we *feel* things, we *believe* things, we *intend* things, *we have an inner life*."

Wittgenstein wants to explore whether we really do have an inner life. He wants to explore not just the language we use in talking about our so-called inner life, but the language of inner life itself. Is there a self? Is there a place where we think these thoughts, feel these feelings, have these beliefs? If so, where is it? How does it work? How does the language work? Is it useful to understand this whole phenomenon as us having thoughts, feelings, pains, intentions, beliefs, desires, the whole litany of mental life? Is it best to understand us as having them somewhere inside of us and then, in the process of communicating, giving "expression" to them? Is it the case that when I'm saying something to someone what I'm doing is expressing what I already have or know or understand or has somehow or another gone on inside my head? That something, at some level, in some way, has gone on in here, and now I'm somehow finding a way to communicate that by a process called expression? And that you could and will and do express yourself in return? Is "We express ourselves to each other" a sensible way of understanding—asks Wittgenstein—this whole phenomenon of communication? This whole phenomenon of language?

Are we expressors? And if we are expressors, doesn't it seem to follow that Descartes and the analytic philosophers of that tradition who said that there must be a self were right? Because if we are fundamentally people who express what is going on inside, then the self could be understood as that inside, if you will, or at least that something inside which gives expression to what it is that's inside. There has to be an active, internal agent, so the argument goes, to carry out this internal work. For lack of a better word one could call that self. So, says Wittgenstein, this picture that has been around for hundreds and hundreds of years of the human being as an expressor seems to fit hand in glove with the notion of a self.

Then Wittgenstein goes on to challenge that picture. He says that it's a faulty picture. He goes into endless detail and exquisite and fascinating analytic argumentation to show that this is a defective picture. In much the way that the picture of the earth as the center of the universe did at one point in history, this picture—of an inner life, an outer world and an expressionistic relationship between the two such that people give expression to what is happening in their inner lives—dominates our way of talking, thinking and understanding. Other people hear that and are able to identify with it because, so the picture goes, they have an inner life which is not so dramatically different from yours, so they can relate to and identify with those words. Wittgenstein says—with endless analysis—why he thinks that picture is faulty.

What Wittgenstein doesn't do, at least so far as I can see, is to suggest an alternative picture. He makes a blistering critique of that expressionistic picture. But he doesn't offer, it seems to me, a positive conception or positive picture which is not—let me use a term here which is a traditional philosophical conception—*dualistic* in a particular way. By dualistic what we mean here is that there is an inner world and an outer world, divided from each other and bridgeable by a number of different things, but most particularly bridgeable by something called communication. And this dualistic picture suggests a very complex inner life for each of us which—typically through language—we give expression to, so that others know what it is that is going on for us. And by virtue of that, we can reach communities of agreement sometimes, we can communicate with our children sometimes, we can communicate with other countries and other cultures sometimes or, at the least, we do something which, everyone would agree, sometimes, is communication.

We think of ourselves as communicators. "Oh, I just had a talk with so-and-so. She said *this*. I said *this*. She said that." "Oh, you understood each other, it sounds like you understand each other." "Oh yeah, we communicate pretty good." What does that mean, "We communicate pretty good"? Well, according to the picture that Wittgenstein was critiquing, it means that I was able to find language which gave expression to what was going on for me in my head so that my friend over there could identify with it sufficiently to say, "Oh yeah, I got that. Let me tell you what's going on for me. Blah blah, . . . " and I said, "Oh, yeah, and . . . ." We did this process and we communicated with each other, and we can tell we communicated with each other because we wound up at the same restaurant. There's the pragmatic evidence that we communicated. If we hadn't communicated, she would have gone here and I would have gone there. Indeed we do, very frequently, wind up at the same restaurant. Some days are worse than others, and we don't, but most days we manage to get to the same restaurant. That is an argument for this kind of communication, and for this expressionistic model that Wittgenstein is critiquing, but as I said, he never offers a positive picture, an alternative picture.

Which is what I was looking for. I had abandoned philosophy and, as some of you know, taken up the practice of therapy. There are hundreds of different schools of therapy and, within them, different therapists do different things. But still, it seemed to me that most therapeutic approaches bought in on this expressionistic dualism and, therefore, the conception of self. Most bought in on the notion that the therapeutic work, while it might be done in a zillion different ways, was to be understood in terms of getting to the bottom of what was going on for the other person or persons with whom you were working; that there was something "deeper" and that therapy could be profoundly useful if you could discover the deeper thing that was going on. With some of the more contemporary therapists, you could even help to *reconstruct* the concept of self. You could help people to understand better what it was that was going on underlying what they took to be going on. The therapeutic process, somehow or other, was designed to do just that—to get more deeply into the inside, to get more deeply into the self. Again, I don't want to stereotype that because there are endless techniques for doing and formulating that. But it seemed to me, at least, that people were buying into that overriding picture.

I was not the least bit comfortable with that picture. So when I started doing therapeutic work, some thirty years ago, I did so as an explicit effort to be of help to people with the usual things that they bring to a therapist's office, but to not invoke that conception of an inner self which I was going to help them get more deeply into and therefore deal with all the accoutrements that traditionally guide therapy (for example, the "resistance" that people have to getting to this "inner self"). I was not going to attend to those kinds of things, as best as I could avoid them. But it's very hard to avoid, in part because it's such a dominant picture and ordinary conception that clients bring it in, even if you don't happen to feel comfortable with it.

So I began to search for a method—to find a way of helping people which did not rely on what I took to be the foolish and unhelpful notion that there was this inner life, which was going to or trying to gain expression, and that my job as therapist was to help people get more deeply into their selves.

I've been working for thirty years now, and I think I've made some headway on this, although in the earliest years it was very hard. I didn't feel the least bit comfortable that I was succeeding. I would find myself constantly reverting to that language, getting self-seduced into talking about things in that way, and then wondering if I wasn't just fooling myself. "Maybe it's just a theoretical belief which really doesn't have applicability, because I find it hard, myself, to *not talk* that way. I don't know how to talk to a person because the underlying subtext of communication is something I'm challenging, but the other person isn't challenging it, so it becomes very hard to talk." The underlying subtext is part of what makes it possible for us to communicate, it seemed to me, and if this person is talking with *this* conception underlying what language is, and I'm doing another thing, well then, it's very hard to talk.

I did get somewhat better at it over the years. Then I discovered someone who actually gave me a conception that I felt very close to in terms of my therapeutic work, but that I had never seen formulated before. It was transformative for me to finally discover an alternative, positive new picture. The person who gave me this new picture was the Soviet psychologist Lev Vygotsky. Vygotsky was not a clinician; in fact you could make out a case that he was very traditional and conservative in the area of clinical psychology, as were most of the Soviets at the time, in my opinion. He was a developmentalist, an experimentalist, a cultural psychologist. But he was profoundly concerned with method. Vygotsky says that the study of method is not just something that one does in advance of engaging in psychological activity; it is the very core of psychological activity. The notion that there is a fixed method, and then what one does in doing psychology is simply to apply that method, as, for example, one does in the physical sciences or in the natural sciences, is a fundamental misunderstanding of human life. There must be a *dialectical methodology*, Vygotsky says, a new kind of methodology which is continuously being created off the psychological interactions.

People, as opposed to stars, have reactions to the process of being studied. Stars respond to all kinds of natural phenomena but, so far as we can tell, they don't respond—in our ordinary way of understanding 'respond'—to being studied. They stay relatively the same even as they're being studied. People are constantly responding to the very activity of their being studied. But it's not a *problem* that people respond to being studied, it's a *characteristic* that people have. It's not as if, "Oh, wouldn't we be better off if we could simply follow the advice of behaviorists, and pay no attention at all to being studied, and just continue to behave in this kind of way and that kind of way." Insofar as one reproduces that kind of situation in a laboratory, it is a profound source of error; because what it does is to fundamentally transform what human beings are like in the effort to study them, and if you change the subject matter of what you're studying, in order for it to be studied, that is, says Vygotsky, by definition a lousy study. It's not a study of how people actually are, it's a study of how you can get people to be, in order for them to get studied. So, Vygotsky says, psychology has to create a method which is sensitive to this fundamental feature of human beings—that we are responsive and continuously responsive to what is going on, and therefore continuously involved in the activity of changing what's going on.

Vygotsky introduces this rather extraordinary methodological distinction having to do with tools. One kind of tool is the tool *for* a result. It's the kind of tool we understand very well. We use a hammer to produce a certain kind of result; we use a lathe to produce a certain kind of result; we use conceptual tools to bring about certain results. There are all kinds of instrumental tools like this in psychology, in the social sciences, in engineering, in life.

But, says Vygotsky, there is another kind of tool—not a tool *for* a result, but a tool and a result. That is, a tool which is sensitive to the fact that you cannot separate the tool itself from the result the tool is going to produce, because they are inextricably bound together. For Vygotsky, the psychological tool is best understood developmentally as a tool-and-result in which the process of using the tool to understand another person impacts profoundly on the other person which impacts profoundly on what the tool is. The tool is transformed in tool-and-result methodology; the tool is transformed by the process of the resulting phenomenon that comes from the study itself. In our efforts to understand, to help, to study, to advise, to teach, to therapize, etc., other human beings, we have to create a methodology which understands that extraordinary relationship. The method must not be simply the use of tools which create the illusion that they can be abstracted from their use; it must be the creation of tools which are made in such as a way as to recognize that in *using* them they will bring about results which will *transform* them in the very process of using them. This is an extraordinary distinction. I was very moved by that. I remember when I first read Vygotsky I was literally blown away by it. But the best was yet to come.

Vygotsky actually comes up with a new picture to replace expressionism (the problem I'd been having for thirty years of never finding a useful alternative characterization). I'm reading Vygotsky and suddenly come upon words to this effect: *"The relationship between thinking and speaking is not the relationship of one being the expression of the other."* I stopped. He's talking explicitly to this issue, what is he going to say? Am I finally going to find this new picture? "When you speak," says Vygotsky—and you can extend this to writing, but here he's talking about speaking—"when you speak, you are not expressing what it was that you were thinking, you're *completing* it." I sat there—I don't want to be over-dramatic about this—but I literally was stunned. "You're completing it." The speaking is not in a *separate world* from the thinking. There is no *separate* world. The speaking is a completion, the completion of what is traditionally identified as this inner process. Speaking/thinking is one complex dialectical unity. They're not two separate kinds of things which must be somehow joined societally. It's one thing. It's not as if in the movement of my arm, for example, the part when I'm doing this is one kind of thing, and the part when I'm doing that is another kind of thing. What we have is a process by which the movement goes from here to there. Such is the relationship between inner life and outer life, between thinking and speaking. There are not two separate worlds, with what we call expression connecting them. There's only one thing. It goes through complex transformations, and goes interactively back and forth.

Suddenly I had a clearer understanding of some therapeutic things that I wanted desperately to do and began to do. Because one of the immediate implications that I drew from this extraordinary new picture was that if speaking is the completing of thinking, if what we have here is a *building* process, which has different looks and different dimensions and different forms at different moments, but is all part of a continuous process of building, then this undermines the notion that the only allowable "completer" is the same person who's doing the thinking. For, if the process is completive, then it seemed to me what we're looking at is language—and this goes back to Wittgenstein—not simply as a way of giving expression to what it is that's going on for us "in our heads" but language as an activity of building. That is, what is happening when speaking or writing, when we are participating in a dialogue, discussion or conversation, is that we are not simply saying what is going on but are *creating* what is going on. We are not looking simply to passively discover what is inside, we are looking to create what is neither inside nor outside but what is socially available to be created. We are builders, we are creators, we become poets! And we understand each other—on this picture, as I understand it now—by virtue of engaging in that shared creative activity. And even though the traditional picture of language suggests that human beings are utterly and completely isolated, attempting to somehow or another get together by giving pictures of our inner selves, in my opinion, we are indeed not isolated in that way.

Some ten or so years ago, I began, more self-consciously than I ever had before, to work with people therapeutically to do what I call—and this is, again, my own strange philosophical orientation—pulling the referential rug out of dialogue. Could we find a way of talking and communicating with each other that is our building something by our very use of language in our talking and communicating? Could we do that, as opposed to becoming endlessly caught up in the notion of referentiality: "Is what you're saying true? Are you right? Am I right?" Could we somehow pull that referential rug out and find a way of using language poetically and creatively?

And so we started what was a very hard therapeutic process, not just for my clients but for me as well, to see what it would mean to try to get rid of truth, to try to get rid of reference, to try to get rid of self, and to work in ways that dialogue or discourse itself was creative. I started looking for ways to do that, and started learning from people I was working with who were profoundly helpful in teaching me what it would mean to create that. People who, for example, would undertake to complete what other people were saying—not to tell them what they took them to mean, or what they thought they really meant, or what the deeper meaning was, or what they identified with (so as to change the topic to be talking about themselves). No, not to do any of that, but to take whatever was said as part of an ongoing, collective, creative process, so that what wound up being the case at the end of a therapy group is that we had created something together. I found myself searching for a term for what we had created together. I didn't know where to look and I kept searching.

And then it hit me over the head. I had, almost independent of this process, started to work in theatre sometime during the 1980s. I was doing theater over here in this part of our loft, and doing this thing called social therapy in the other part. At some point it got through to me that there was a profound connection between the theatre and the therapy I was doing. I was able to discover what it was that we were creating in therapy by this process, flawed as it was, troublesome as it was, difficult as it was. What we were creating in therapy, having pulled out the referential rug, was *performance*. People were creating a play. They were creating a performance. And that performance was of wonderful, developmental, therapeutic value. People were learning how to perform—going back to Vygotsky's language—people were learning how to perform *beyond themselves*. They were breaking out of the habit of simply *being* themselves to discovering not who they were but *who they were not*. It kind of hit me like a lightning bolt that that's how we learn as children. Vygotsky showed us that if children simply learned who they were on the basis of being who they were, they would never go anywhere, they would simply stay fixed. In the process of creative imitation that children go through, they are related to as performers in the language speaking community before they have the foggiest idea how to speak.

This performatory ability to continuously create with language doesn't limit us to that underlying deeper person, or to truth, or to giving expression to who we really are, but is a continuous process of creating who we are. As I've come to understand it, this is what human development is about. And it's what it is, for me, to help people develop. I'm convinced that therapy is of minimal value, unless it is developmental. I agree that there is some value in people simply sharing their pain and I think therapy therefore is worthwhile if it does nothing more than that. But if therapy is to be truly useful, in my opinion, it must be developmental. I think there is some kind of development that takes place in the process of ensemble, collective performance, not just of someone else's play, but *performance of our own discourse with each other.* Our very human interaction—our talking to each other, our touching each other, our feeling with each other, our loving each other, our teaching each other, our being with each other in all the myriad number of ways in which we do that—is fundamentally a creative process. It's not simply a process which is rooted in our giving expression to who we are as if that was some sort of fixed phenomenon.

So when I speak of therapy as engaging and deconstructing the illusion of self, this is what I'm talking about. It's this notion of self as a fixed inner necessity to be able to be the *cogito* of the *cogito ergo sum*, an inner necessity in any of the ways that we've been talking about it today. There is, in my opinion, no inner necessity for self, nor is there an outer necessity. This is not in any way to deny individuality. I firmly believe in individuality. But if individuality, as a conception, is designed to keep us permanently separated from each other, I find that not only morally troublesome, I find it fundamentally mistaken. Because we are not, in my opinion, separated from each other. We begin as social, we live as social, we end as social. This doesn't minimize my or your individuality. The marvelous feature of the creativity of being who we're not, in my experience, is that in being who we're not, we actually come to be more of who we are and show what is most unique about us. I think nothing is less unique than "giving expression" to the so-called inner or deepest self. The process of looking for our deepest self is a nondevelopmental process and a painfully frustrating one. Agreeing with Wittgenstein and many others, I think it's a search that is never realized, because—to put it straightforwardly—there ain't nothing there. Though there ain't nothing there, what there is is our capacity to continuously create something.

So, if you want to do a balance sheet of what you gain and what you lose from all this, you lose the self, and you gain the capacity to continuously create, collectively and in ensemble. I think you gain a deeper and deeper sense of collective human development and creativity. Some people, including people who are in therapy with me or study with me, frequently complain to me about this loss of self. "Don't you understand, it's a terrible thing! The self is the most important thing I have! I can't give up my self, I spent years trying to find myself! How can you ask this of me? I'm going to report you to the APA."

Well, I'm not concerned to help people to discover self. I'm concerned to help people discover life. When people come to me for therapeutic help with problems, with terrible pain, I'm not interested in getting more deeply into who they are so as to identify the roots of their problem or their pain and therefore to somehow ameliorate it. My concern is to help them to live. Now, that raises an interestingly question which I've been asked frequently: "Well, Fred, in your approach do you ever create an entirely new self?" And my response is that I'm interested in your getting rid of the old self, not creating a new one. I'm not interested in creating any identity, or any self. I'm interested in helping people to grow developmentally through a process of better under-standing—in a practical and activistic sense—their capacity to create. If we help people to create in the way in which I'm discussing, we have, at least in my experience, our best chance of helping people deal with the terrible pain that they frequently bring into therapy. That is what I mean by that funny title, *A Therapeutic Deconstruction of the Illusion of Self.*

Science Can Do Better than Sokal:
A Commentary on the So-called Science Wars

FRED NEWMAN

For some years I've been troubled by an apparent decline in the standards of rigor in certain precincts of the academic humanities. But I'm a mere physicist. If I find myself unable to make heads or tails of jouissance *and* difference, *perhaps that just reflects my own inadequacy.*

So, to test the prevailing intellectual standards, I decided to try a modest (though admittedly uncontrolled) experiment. Would a leading North American journal of cultural studies— whose editorial board collective includes such luminaries as Frederic Jameson and Andrew Ross—publish an article liberally salted with nonsense if a) it sounded good and b) it flattered the editors' ideological preconceptions?

The answer, unfortunately, is yes. Interested readers can find my article, "Transgressing the Boundaries: Toward a Transformative Hermeneutics of Quantum Gravity," in the Spring/Summer 1996 issues of Social Text. *It appears in a special number of the magazine devoted to the "Science Wars." (Alan Sokal, "A Physicist Experiments with Cultural Studies,"* Lingua Franca, *1996, p. 62)*

With these words, Alan Sokal (a professor of physics at New York University) explains what motivated him to submit an article to cultural studies journal Social Text *and, after it was accepted and published, reveal that it was a parody. Responses to Sokal's hoax appeared in mainstream newspapers and magazines as well as nearly every left-liberal and intellectual publication (e.g.,* The Nation, Village Voice, In These Times, Dissent, Times Literary Supplement [UK], *and* The New York Review of Books). *Much of the dialogue, however, didn't really go anywhere, as both sides took a defensive posture. Sokal continued to show the "silliness" of the postmodern "Masters," especially their fuzzy thinking, and insist that the Science Wars, characterized as a fight picked by conservatives against postmodernists, feminists and left intellectuals, was not really a war because many of the scientists who were against postmodernism (he cited himself) were politically pro-gressive.* Social Text *retaliated by pointing out Sokal's poor scholar-ship (for example, his errors in describing the members of* Social Text's *editorial board deconstructionists) and by trying to distinguish post-modern deconstruction from science studies. As for substantive issues, Sokal kept arguing for the existence of material reality; his critics for the acceptance that scientific laws are social constructions.*

In the Spring of 1997, at a two-day conference on Postmodernism and the Social Sciences: Human Agency, Self and Culture, sponsored by the New School for Social Research in New York City, one of seven panel discussions was devoted to "Postmodern Ethics: What the Social Text Affair Does and Does Not Prove." Sokal presented a paper with this title; he was followed by three discussants: Linda Nicholson from SUNY Albany, Kenneth Gergen from Swarthmore College, and Fred Newman.

Newman's contribution was the following essay, in which he brings conceptions and arguments from the philosophy of language to bear on the Science Wars. He attempts to break through the terms of the debate to raise the issue that the critique made by postmodernism is more appropriately directed at the application of the scientific paradigm where it doesn't belong, and not at science. He calls for a coming together (a united front) of science and postmodernism.—L. H.

What does the *Social Text* affair prove? Well, "prove" is a touchy word in a dialogue so concerned with parody. But we can certainly speak of our subjective response to the whole business and, more generally, to the "science wars." To me, the affair is a further indication of the extraordinary extent to which the science establishment has been threatened by the nearly three-decades-long offensive of postmodernism. To be sure, the current response of the science establishment is partially due to political/economic factors, i.e., the concern that opportunistic forces (usually identified as on the right) will use postmodernist, antiscientific analysis to support cutbacks for science dollars in an already shrinking education budget. No doubt. After all, politics may not be everything but everything is political. Pragmatically speaking, science has every reason to be up in arms. However, not surprisingly, science does not wish to make its case against postmodernism on vulgarly pragmatic grounds. Instead, it seeks to show the "truth" of the matter and to expose the absurdity of a good deal—the *essence*—of postmodernism.

Science has a strong position in this war. But science's tactical difficulty—characteristic of any incumbent in these times—is that while it holds the office (and the franking privileges!) many do not trust the pompous, smug employment by science of its own criteria to debate the issue of science's validity, just as many are cynical that the Democrats and Republicans—the two party monopoly—will ever legislate serious campaign reform. Science's posture looks too self-serving. It looks too much like what the logical positivists (in defense of science) used to say about nineteenth-century Hegelian-style metaphysics, viz. it's irrefutable. Or long before that, how the Church argued the case against Galileo—God is on our side.

Even though I am a strong supporter of science and its astounding accomplishments, am formally trained in philosophy of science (nowadays viewed by Professor Sokal and many other scientists in the "science wars" as potential allies), and I disagree with the obvious silliness of some postmodernism, and even with much of its serious work (I think it fails to go far enough), I too am extremely mistrustful of science's self-defense. Indeed, to me Professor Sokal's response does more to illustrate postmodernism's proper concern than all or most of what the postmodernists have said or written. And why wouldn't it? Postmodernism is first and foremost a provocation.

First, let me make some rather obvious observations. The issue cannot be whether there are or aren't external objects, but what is meant by making such kinds of claims. Sokal's appeals to various forms of handwaving realism are, in my opinion, philosophically empty. The world might have come first (i.e., before scientists) but, at least on some accounts, meaning didn't. Nor, for that matter, did truth. Nor language, etc. The claim that there is a book on the table may well be a proposition about one external object's location on another external object, but what this *aboutness* claim means—what correspondence and, therefore, truth, mean—still remains, according to many, to be discovered. Some contemporary philosophers (e.g., Rorty, 1982) consider this longtime philosophical issue worth abandoning. Others do not. Still, it is not only postmodernists but friends of science who consider this a fundamental issue of significance.

It seems to me that Sokal and other science defenders moving so quickly to this vulgarly "ontological" issue is a serious mistake, defensive and/or disingenuous. Scholasticism no more denied an external world than did modern science affirm it. The bizarre appeal to common sense denies, at least as I have come to understand it, the extraordinary discovery that was and is modern science, viz. a way of *describing, explaining* and *characterizing* what is going on in the physical world (using mathematical and empirically verifiable conceptions) which yields predictive and retrodictive accountings (explanations) of marvelous value.

Sokal's kind of defense seems to me, ironically, antiscientific. In his hurry to show science to be commonsensical and postmodernism to be absurd, he might well be throwing out the beautiful mathematical-empirical model baby with the realist-idealist bathwater. For, if you feel compelled to laugh off the possibility that science is, in a most important sense, a manmade myth, then you also throw out that it is one of the most useful myths ever created by our species. Therein lies its strength and, in my opinion, its progressivism. The strongest claim in support of science is not that, together with its close historical companions, capitalism and modern technology, it *had* to prevail (It's simply how the world is!), but that it *did* prevail. Such, as I understand it, was Kuhn's (1962) proscience thesis in *The Structure of Scientific Revolutions*. Nowadays, Kuhn is hailed by many scientists in the war against postmodernism but not so, in my experience, back then when his book first appeared.

Back in the 1950s and 1960s when I was more a full-time philosopher of science, I did not notice too many physicists or, more generally, hard scientists attending very much or very seriously to the responsible and, in my opinion, insightful critique of science by philosophers of science. On the contrary, my experience was that philosophy of science was taken as anywhere from irrelevant to frivolous by the science establishment. Postmodernism, by contrast, has gotten the scientists' attention. For all the nonsense (identified by Sokol and others, e.g., Gross and Levitt, 1994; the authors in Gross, Levitt and Lewis, 1996)—indeed, perhaps in part because of the provocative nonsense—postmodernism has impacted to an extent that analytically oriented philosophers of science did not. More credit to them!

It was, after all, the quite respectable W. V. O. Quine, not some "postmodern nitwit," who wrote in his seminal essay "Two Dogmas of Empiricism":

> As an empiricist I continue to think of the conceptual scheme of science as a tool, ultimately, for predicting future experience in the light of past experience. Physical objects are conceptually imported into the situation as convenient intermediaries—not by definition in terms of experience, but simply as irreducible posits comparable, epistemologically, to the gods of Homer. For my part I do, qua lay physicist, believe in physical objects and not in Homer's gods; and I consider it a scientific error to believe otherwise. But in point of epistemological footing the physical objects and the gods differ only in degree and not in kind. Both sorts of entities enter our conception only as cultural posits. The myth of physical objects is epistemologically superior to most in that it has proved more efficacious than other myths as a device for working a manageable structure into the flux of experience. (Quine, 1963, p.44)

A defense of science based on a denial of the claim that physical objects are not myths but reality is not, in my opinion, a defense of science at all, but a mistaken and misguided effort to turn science into some kind of secular religion or all-purpose paradigm of understanding. And that is precisely what some postmodernists (and I number myself among them) find so objectionable.

I am not suggesting that we should turn this most important debate (the so-called science wars) into a moral discussion about whether philosophers of science were properly treated back in the 1960s by a science establishment which now seeks them as allies in the battle against postmodernism. So what? Even if true it wouldn't be the first ethically questionable reconsideration of friends and foes. It is, however, worth mentioning because it exposes an unnecessarily defensive posture of contemporary science and thereby makes more difficult a new and progressive development which, in my opinion, could be actualized by a *coming together* of science and postmodernism.

The emergence of science, technology and capitalism in the 1600s and 1700s, as I understand it, was specific to deep-rooted conceptual (philosophical) military, navigational, economic and technological concerns. To be sure, there are serious disagreements among historians of science as to which factors contributed more or less. The point of general methodological agreement, however, is that science did not emerge as the consequence of a search for a new paradigm. Rather, the scientific paradigm emerged over many, many decades from the effectiveness of a loosely identified set of practical solutions to practical problems guided in varying ways and to varying degrees by mathematical and empirical *ways of looking* at the presenting problems and the physical contexts in which they appear. Surely it was not an effort to assure the existence of physical objects. Nor, indeed, was it an effort to create a new paradigm.

As Chomsky (in Horgan, 1996) so eloquently—as always—put the matter: The emergence of science as a paradigm of understanding is almost surely unexplainable using the scientific paradigm. And it is the *specificity* of science (technology and capitalism) and its ensuing emergence as a paradigm which must be kept in focus in our efforts to bring peace to the science wars. For it is the extraordinary paradigm that emerged lawfully, if unfathomably, out of the historical specifics of the sixteenth, seventeenth and eighteenth centuries that is now being questioned here in the late twentieth century. Science need not and should not reject either its almost unbelievable practical accomplishment nor the emergence of the scientific paradigm. It can take credit for the former (its accomplishments) and probably has little or nothing to do with the latter (its emergence as a paradigm of understanding).

Here in the late twentieth century, presenting problems specific to this historical conceptual moment quite reasonably raise the question of whether the science paradigm has the capacity to generate good answers to these new questions. Social, psychological, political and economic questions of our day and the scientifically determined submodels typically appealed to in order to answer them (sociology, psychology, political science and economics) seem to many sufficiently troublesome and unsuccessful as to justify a critique—not of science but of the applicability of the scientific paradigm.

Philosophers of science have played as bad a role in establishing the science paradigm and in insisting on its applicability to everything as anyone. No less brilliant philosophers than Carl Hempel (1965) and Donald Davidson (1980) urge that the causal, deductive model of explanation as it has paradigmatically emerged from the practical-critical specificity of hard science and technology must, to use Hempel's metaphor, "cover" the soft sciences and history. But when Hempel starts to put down on paper the covering laws "governing" Cortez's invasion of Mexico, we are forced to laugh in much the way many of us do in reading *DSM-IV.* The language and the language-game of history and psychology are not the mathematically and empirically shaped language game of physics. Unlike with physics, the infinitude of ordinary language descriptions of historical and psychological events and the virtual absence of *any* criteria of identity for different descriptions produces the giggles accompanying a reading of the clinical psychology manual.

The deductivist paradigm of knowing that has been thoroughly shaped by Aristotelian logic and, over the last several hundred years, by modern science may well have little or nothing to do with helping people deal with their depression. This is hardly an attack on science. Indeed, science might prove helpful in dealing with the problem without the science paradigm playing any role at all. As one example, Lev Vygotsky's work (1978, 1987, 1993) seems to me a good example of science's great value in a cultural nonscientific approach (see Newman and Holzman, 1993, 1996, 1997).

What I am urging, in broad political terms, is a united front of postmodernism and science. Over the last hundred or so years the gross misapplication of the deductive paradigm to critical areas of human concern has contributed, in my opinion, much more to the problem than to the solution. Four of the most vulgar products of this kind of mistake are psychology, economics, political science and Marxism. Our world needs, among other things, a humane (unscientific) psychology; an economics not so plainly based on class biases; and a new progressive public philosophy. Perhaps a united front of progressive scientists and postmodernists could further stimulate work in these critical areas. A world in crisis demands such efforts. A fantasy? Perhaps. But not a parody.

REFERENCES

Davidson, D. (1980). *Essays on actions and events.* Oxford: Oxford University Press.

Gross, P. R. and Levitt, N. (1994). *Higher superstition: The academic left and its quarrels with science.* Baltimore: Johns Hopkins University Press.

Gross, P. R., Levitt, N. and Lewis, M. W. (Eds.) (1996). *The flight from science and reason.* New York: New York Academy of Sciences.

Hempel, C. (1965). *Aspects of scientific explanation and other essays in the philosophy of science.* New York: The Free Press.

Horgan, J. (1996). *The end of science: Facing the limits of knowledge in the twilight of the scientific age.* Reading, MA: Addison-Wesley.

Kuhn, T. (1962). *The structure of scientific revolutions.* Chicago: University of Chicago Press.

Newman, F. and Holzman, L. (1993). *Lev Vygotsky: Revolutionary scientist.* London: Routledge.

Newman, F. and Holzman, L. (1996). *Unscientific psychology: A cultural performatory approach to understanding human life.* Westport, CT: Praeger.

Newman, F. and Holzman, L. (1997). *The end of knowing: A new developmental way of learning.* London: Routledge.

Quine, W. V. O. (1963). *From a logical point of view.* New York: Harper & Row.

Rorty, R. (1982). *Consequences of pragmatism.* Minneapolis: University of Minnesota Press.

Vygotsky, L.S. (1978). *Mind in society.* Cambridge, MA: MIT Press.

Vygotsky, L.S. (1987). *The collected works of L. S. Vygotsky,* Vol. 1. New York: Plenum.

Vygotsky, L. S. (1993). *The collected works of L. S. Vygotsky,* Vol. 2. New York: Plenum.

The Story of Truth (A Whodunit)
or Philosophie dans la Théâtre

FRED NEWMAN

A*fter reading the script Newman had written for the third con-secutive convention of the American Psychological Association, I told him that "The Story of Truth (A Whodunit) or Philosophie dans la Théâtre" might well be the most unenlightening play ever written. Newman, of course, took that as the compliment I intended. Like some essays in this volume (e.g., "Science Can Do Better than Sokal: A Commentary on the So-Called Science Wars"), "The Story of Truth" examines foundational philosophical issues of psychology, the scientific paradigm and science itself. To me, the play is a performance of absur-dity—the intellectual absurdity of the way in which the postmodernism vs. science debate is often carried out and the existential absurdity of being "permanently in the fly bottle" of reality.—L. H.*

"The Story of Truth" was performed live at the 106th Annual Convention of the American Psychological Association in San Francisco in August 1998.

Characters

(in order of appearance)

Chairwoman
Umbeck
Agent Fall
Umbeck 2
Agent Fall 2
Pomo
Sikko
Narrator
Mime

Care should be taken in dressing the stage to set it up for an actual lecture, not a play.

The stage is set for a lecture presentation at the annual convention of the American Psychological Association. There is a lectern onstage and two people sit on chairs stage left. One, a woman, is the chairwoman of the session. The other, a man, is the guest speaker. The CHAIRWOMAN waits until the audience gets seated and calmed down, then goes to lectern.

CHAIRWOMAN: Okay, if everyone could please take your seats. We're about ready to begin. *(She waits until people sit. Perhaps she encourages people further. She pauses, then turns to her notes.)* Today's speaker is a most distinguished scholar. He has written many well-known books. I'm sure that most members of our audience have read at least one of them. His most famous work, *Quantum Leaps in the Psychology of the Mind*, received the 1989 Wilson Award for best research on interdisciplinary subject matter. For the last 10 years he has been Distinguished Professor of Physics at Case Western Reserve University. He has served as special consultant to three different presidents. We are proud to have him today as the Hilgaard Distinguished Service lecturer. He will speak to us this morning (afternoon/evening) about varieties of truth. Ladies and gentlemen, let me introduce Dr. Herman Umbeck.

(She turns to DR. UMBECK to welcome him to the podium and leads the applause as he comes to the lectern.)

UMBECK: Thank you, Madame Chairwoman. I'm delighted to have this opportunity. As many of you know, my academic interests have ranged far and wide with the particular focus on philosophy, physics and psychology. For the past decade I have been concerned to meet the challenge of postmodernism by formulating a conception of truth that has equal applicability to the three fields that I have devoted my intellectual energies to. For it seems not unreasonable to me that if such diverse enterprises as philosophy, physics and psychology had a common conception of truth, this conception would reasonably apply to virtually everything. I am pleased to report to you here today that I have indeed found such a conception, tested it—analytically, empirically, practically, and found it to be in all ways unwanting. To be sure, the effort to articulate a theory of truth has been a feature of western thought from Plato to Tarski. But we can thank postmodernism for so stimulating those of us who believe deeply in science and its method to begin a renewed effort to discover the meaning of truth. Perhaps the best way . . .

(From a seat ten rows into the audience AGENT FALL rises, interrupting the talk.)

FALL: Dr. Umbeck, Dr. Herman Umbeck, of 2335 University Place in Cleveland, Ohio? Is that your address, sir? *(UMBECK doesn't answer.)* Dr. Umbeck, Dr. Herman Umbeck, of 2335 University Place in Cleveland, Ohio? Is that your address, sir?

UMBECK: *(Turns to CHAIRWOMAN)* Madame Chairwoman, can you do something about this interruption?

(She comes to the podium.)

CHAIRWOMAN: Sir, there will be time for questions after Dr. Umbeck's presentation.

FALL: I'm sorry, I can't wait. I'm Agent Frank Fall with the Federal Bureau of Investigation. And Professor Umbeck is under arrest.

CHAIRWOMAN: Under arrest? What are you talking about? Is this some kind of a joke?

FALL: No, ma'am, I'm afraid not. Professor Umbeck is being indicted on charges of fraud.

UMBECK: Indicted? Fraud? By whom? For what? What are you talking about?

FALL: *(Starting toward the stage)* It's a federal indictment, by the Federal Bureau of Investigation, sir. Your research is totally fraudulent. The statistics you have given in your study are all made up. The theoretical analysis is, under scrutiny, meaningless. Moreover, the research was done on a federal grant and therefore represents fraud against the United States government. I must warn you that anything you say can and will be held against you. *(FALL has by now reached the stage.)* And you have the right to a lawyer, sir. I would seriously recommend that you say nothing until you have obtained one.

UMBECK: Are you crazy? What is this? This isn't Russia, or China, or some communist country. This is America. I'm free to obtain whatever results I choose. We have a Constitution here. Who are you? This must be some kind of joke. You must be some kind of postmodernist.

FALL: *(Shows his badge to UMBECK)* No, Professor Umbeck, I am with the FBI. We've been following your work for any number of years now. I've been following you about for the last four years myself. Waiting for the moment when you would publicly announce this so-called theory of truth. Now that you have done so, you have committed criminal fraud. And, I'm afraid you are under arrest.

UMBECK: *(Breaking the mood of the scene and speaking directly to the audience)* What do you make of this scene? Am I really under arrest? That is, is Umbeck really under arrest? Or is all this a part of my (or his) lecture on varieties of truth? How are we to know? Does it make a difference?

FALL: *(Staying in character and "in the scene")* Nice try, Dr. Umbeck. But I'm afraid it won't work. This arrest is not a part of your lecture. It's real. Again, I remind you, anything you say or do can be held against you.

UMBECK: Well, exactly how real is it? I'm playing a character Herman Umbeck—who you say is under arrest. Are you a character, too? If so, on what authority are you arresting me? Surely not the FBI's. Presumably, they do not give authority to actors to arrest people—even (or especially) fictitious people.

FALL: But I am not a character in a performance. I am a special investigator working with the Federal Bureau of Investigation. And you are under arrest.

UMBECK: Who is under arrest? There is no such person as Herman Umbeck. The author of this play made up this character. I am simply saying those words. As are you.

FALL: But this *is* a meeting of the American Psychological Association and you were introduced as a distinguished scholar. Isn't that so?

UMBECK: Yes.

FALL: Well, that's fraud.

UMBECK: No, that's theatre.

FALL: But theatre unidentified as theatre is fraud. This is a hoax.

UMBECK: No. This is a play. Perhaps it is a play about a hoax or a play about a fraud. But the play is not a fraud or a hoax.

FALL: You'll have a chance to explain that to a judge, Dr. Umbeck. But you're under arrest.

UMBECK: But am I really under arrest or simply under arrest in the play?

FALL: I'm not in a play.

UMBECK: Then you are a fraud. Because you are not really with the FBI.

CHAIRWOMAN: *(Interrupts dialogue)* Ladies and gentlemen, it is relatively easy to get into this predicament—what might be called a "reality predicament." Human beings have the capacity to create fictitious or imaginary characters and as well to ascribe actual characteristics to those imaginary characters. In most cases, the institutionalized context will effectively determine what's really going on and prevent the reality predicament from getting out of hand. But the strength of our imaginative skills does make it possible to even challenge the institutional arrangement. So that some in this room might well be confused as to whether Dr. Umbeck really is or really isn't under arrest. Indeed, some might be confused as to whether Dr. Umbeck really is or isn't. Some might reasonably see the entirety of this performance as illustrating certain characteristics of truth and reality and therefore as a performatory dimension of Umbeck's speech or as a performatory statement by the author of this play about truth, reality or whatever else. But our concern today is not with how easy it is for us to get into this predicament but how virtually impossible it is to get out of it.

FALL: *(Interrupts)* Madame, I am not exactly sure I know who you are, but I have a sense that you are aiding and abetting Dr. Umbeck in the perpetration of his fraud. If you say anything more, I'm afraid I'll have to put you under arrest also.

CHAIRWOMAN: *(To audience)* You see what I mean?

UMBECK: *(To FALL)* How long are you going to persist in this fiction that you are with the Federal Bureau of Investigation? If you keep it up much longer, I'm going to call a cop and have him arrest you.

FALL: And what would he arrest me for?

UMBECK: For impersonating an FBI agent.

FALL: But I thought you said that I couldn't arrest you for impersonating a distinguished scholar.

UMBECK: So then you admit that you're not an FBI agent?

FALL: I admit no such thing; I just want to expose to this audience the fraudulence of your position and the hoax of your position.

CHAIRWOMAN: How do we get out of this?

UMBECK: Why do you want to get out of it? Why do we have to get out of it? Indeed the paradoxicality of truth and reality seems to be a permanent feature of human culture. There appears to be no way out of it. Modernism is both correct and incorrect on this matter, but then again so is postmodernism.

CHAIRWOMAN: *(Motions for UMBECK and FALL to come off to the side with her; she speaks to the audience)* Give us just a moment to work this thing out. *(They go off and whisper furiously for 20 seconds. Then the CHAIRWOMAN returns to the microphone.)* Ladies and gentlemen, Dr. Umbeck is correct. It is harder to get out of this predicament than to get into it, so what we've decided to do is to start all over again. Give us just a moment. Thank you.

(The actor who was playing UMBECK goes out into the audience and sits in FALL'S seat, and the actor who was playing FALL sits where UMBECK was sitting on stage. The CHAIRWOMAN goes to the lectern and introduces UMBECK, now being played by the actor who was playing FALL, with exactly the same words that opened the play.)

CHAIRWOMAN: Today's speaker is a most distinguished scholar. He has written many well-known books. I'm sure that most members of our audience have read at least one of them. His most famous work, *Quantum Leaps in the Psychology of the Mind*, received the 1989 Wilson Award for best research on interdisciplinary subject matter. For the last 10 years he has been Distinguished Professor of Physics at Case Western Reserve University. He has served as special consultant to three different presidents. We are proud to have him today as the Hilgaard Distinguished Service lecturer. He will speak to us this morning (afternoon/evening) about varieties of truth. Ladies and gentlemen, let me introduce Dr. Herman Umbeck.

(She turns to DR. UMBECK 2 to welcome him to the podium and leads the applause as he comes to the lectern.)

UMBECK 2: Thank you, Madame Chairwoman. I'm delighted to have this opportunity. As many of you know, my academic interests have ranged far and wide with the particular focus on philosophy, physics and psychology. For the past decade I have been concerned to meet the challenge of postmodernism by formulating a conception of truth that has equal applicability to the three fields that I have devoted my intellectual energies to. For it seems not unreasonable to me that if such diverse enterprises as philosophy, physics and psychology had a common conception of truth, this conception would reasonably apply to virtually everything. I am pleased to report to you here today that I have indeed found such a conception, tested it—analytically, empirically, practically, and found it to be in all ways unwanting. To be sure, the effort to articulate a theory of truth has been a feature of western thought from Plato to Tarski. But we can thank postmodernism for so stimulating those of us who believe deeply in science and its method to begin a renewed effort to discover the meaning of truth. Perhaps the best way . . .

(From a seat ten rows into the audience AGENT FALL 2, played by the actor who originally played UMBECK, rises, interrupting the talk.)

FALL 2: Dr. Umbeck, Dr. Herman Umbeck, of 2335 University Place in Cleveland, Ohio? Is that your address, sir? (Umbeck 2 doesn't answer.) Dr. Umbeck, Dr. Herman Umbeck, of 2335 University Place in Cleveland, Ohio? Is that your address, sir?

UMBECK 2: *(Turns to CHAIRWOMAN)* Madame Chairwoman, can you do something about this interruption?

(She comes to the podium.)

CHAIRWOMAN: Sir, there will be time for questions after Dr. Umbeck's presentation.

FALL 2: I'm sorry, I can't wait. I'm Agent Frank Fall with the Federal Bureau of Investigation. And Professor Umbeck is under arrest.

CHAIRWOMAN: Under arrest? What are you talking about? Is this some kind of a joke?

FALL 2: No, ma'am, I'm afraid not. Professor Umbeck is being indicted on charges of fraud.

UMBECK 2: Indicted? Fraud? By whom? For what? What are you talking about?

FALL 2: *(Starting toward the stage)* It's a federal indictment, by the Federal Bureau of Investigation, sir. Your research is totally fraudulent. The statistics you have given in your study are all made up. The theoretical analysis is, under scrutiny, meaningless. Moreover, the research was done on a federal grant and therefore represents fraud against the United States government. I must warn you that anything you say can and will be held against you. *(FALL 2 has by now reached the stage.)* And you have the right to a lawyer, sir. I would seriously recommend that you say nothing until you have obtained one.

CHAIRWOMAN: *(Stands and goes to lectern)* Gentlemen, this is exactly what we did the last time. We're in the same predicament.

FALL 2: Oh no, the difference is that this time he's under arrest, not me.

CHAIRWOMAN: Act II. By now most of you have heard at least a little about the affair in which Alan Sokal, a physicist at NYU, submitted an essay to the left cultural/philosophical journal, *Social Text*, which they then reviewed and decided to publish. Sokal subsequently revealed his essay to be a parody designed to reveal the bankruptcy of postmodernist (pomo) ideas. There followed a relative avalanche of articles ridiculing *Social Text* in the *New York Times*, the *Wall Street Journal*, many local mainstream papers throughout the country, plus the *Village Voice, The Nation, In These Times*, and so on.

(As she is making these remarks the two actors put on oversize head masks. Two people hold up a curtain across the stage as in a puppet show

so that only the head masks appear to the audience. At the same time the Chairwoman turns on Punch and Judy/French-sounding music on a boom box.

Unlike Act I, Acts II and III are played in a self-consciously performatory manner.)

CHAIRWOMAN: (Continues) Today, we continue this great debate between postmodernism and science. Let me introduce our debaters. First, Professor Andre Pomo *(She motions to the head that is POMO.)* Professor Pomo teaches and does research at the Institute for Anabaptist Liturgy at the Sorbonne. His opponent in today's debate is Assistant Professor Alan D. Sikko. Dr. Sikko is assistant professor at New York University and author of the popular teaching aid, Theoretical Physics for Theoretical Students. Professor Pomo will speak first. *(The CHAIRWOMAN sits down.)*

POMO: *(With a French accent)* These efforts to discredit postmodernism are very flattering. They show that the sacred cow of science is having much difficulty under the ongoing assault of the many varieties of postmodern thought. For 500 years the basic paradigm of science was uncontested. The Enlightenment claim that science and rationality (defined by it) could and would produce a universal knowledge of everything seemed untouchable. But now all that has changed. For while science has been able to make brilliant and extraordinary discoveries (all too many in the area of how human beings can best destroy each other) the extension of the scientific paradigm to the social sciences has been found substantially wanting. What does postmodernism have to say about science? In essence, we critique science's self-serving claim that it is a universal paradigm of knowing. Science is a social myth. No doubt a most valuable myth. But still not an eternal truth. Indeed, there are no eternal truths. And there is no unquestionable reality. For science like all other human-made products is profoundly fallible.

SIKKO: *(Interrupting and speaking in a very youthful American accent)* Professor Pomo, maybe this is a good point for me to break in. Science, you see, is not like everything else. It does not take an Einstein to figure out that in the last several hundred years science and the scientific method have successfully uncovered truths about the nature of reality that absolutely distinguish it from other methods. To be sure, it is a manmade product. But so is a boat and a chewing gum wrapper. But presumably you would not choose to sail the Atlantic Ocean on a chewing gum wrapper. Science is not just another manmade product. It is that particular product which has shown its capacity to uniquely distinguish fact from fiction, truth from illusion.

POMO: But "distinguish truth from illusion"—on whose criteria? Fifty years ago, the scientists and their philosophical friends, the logical positivists, complained bitterly about Hegelian metaphysics on the grounds that the criteria by which it asserted its truths was itself metaphysical. Now science does the same thing. Science insists that not only does it have the truth, but that the criteria by which we determine what is true must be scientific criteria.

SIKKO: But science has every right to use its own criteria. Scientific criteria based on detailed empirical measurement and mathematico-logico analysis has proven successful beyond belief. Even if we fully accept that science is manmade, why wouldn't we recognize that what man has made in this case is a standard for determining truth and reality, rather than just another myth like, for example, astrology, which historically has totally failed to do so.

POMO: But what of science and mathematics' own discoveries— like quantum physics, relativity theory, Gödel's incompleteness theorem, etc., which explicitly show the indeterminacy of science and the limits of rationality?

SIKKO: There you go again. Using scientific terms out of context and, thereby, misunderstanding what they really mean.

POMO: *(Angrily)* Good grief, Sikko, What makes you think that scientific terms aren't usable "out of context" as much as any other terms. Poetry, my friend, is nothing but using terms out of context. You scientists make it seem as if no one used the terms "truth" and "reality" until science came along. But philosophy, poetry, religion, and just plain ordinary people were conversing about truth and reality before science was even a twinkle in theology's eye.

SIKKO: *(Now he's getting angry)* Pomo, you are nothing but a metphysician. In relativizing everything you do not see the progress that human beings have made. You do not see science as one of the great progressive human discoveries.

POMO: *(Angrily responds)* No, my friend, I see progress. It is you and your scientific dogmatists who project science as the end of progress. The varieties of human truth are infinite and the application of so-called scientific truth to inappropriate matters is as destructive and distortive as the application of religious truth to inappropriate matters. Even your distinguished American scholar Herman Umbeck recognizes that.

SIKKO: *(Pulls off his mask and comes out from behind the curtain)* Umbeck? Umbeck? Umbeck is a fraud! He makes a parody of science. He should be put in prison.

POMO: *(Pulls off his mask and comes out)* You have a lot of nerve condemning parody makers, Sikko. Your mentor and colleague Sokal is an admitted parody maker.

SIKKO: But Sokal makes parodies in the name of truth and science.

POMO: No, Sikko, he makes parodies for the same reason that everybody else does, namely to publish. Indeed, Professor Sikko, life is a parody. Test that in your scientific laboratory. *(He laughs maniacally.)* Life is a parody. And there is no way out. Science pretends to be a heaven on earth. But there is no heaven on earth. You and I are just people wearing different masks.

SIKKO: But ours come off.

POMO: A mask is no less a mask for never coming off.

CHAIRWOMAN: *(Enters what has now become a heated fight)* Gentlemen, I think we've reached a stalemate once again. Do you have a third act? Still another beginning? If we cannot resolve this, can we at least go on?

POMO AND SIKKO: *(In unison)* Oh, yes. We can go on forever.

(They return to their seats and put down their head masks. The CHAIRWOMAN turns to the audience.)

CHAIRWOMAN: Our final act.

(The two men set up the stage with the chairs next to each other so they form a bench. One of them, the NARRATOR, comes to the podium. He reads the "epistemological machine" story and mimes the Mad Doctor, as the MIME performs the story in mime as it is read. The chairwoman puts on new music, a version of "Walking Through the Park One Day.")

NARRATOR: Imagine someone walking down the street being approached by another person who offers him $100 for about a half hour's worth of work. Mr. A agrees to this arrangement and is taken to a sub-sub-basement laboratory. He is placed on an operating table and attached by a complex set of cables to a computerized mechanism. It is explained to him by the presiding attendant (presumably a physician) that all of his nerve endings can be stimulated by this attachment and that the nature of the experiment in which he has agreed to participate will consist of stimulating the nerve endings in such a way as to produce a variety of "virtual reality"-type experiences. He is further assured that none of these experiences will be painful and that the entire experiment should last no more than a half hour or 45 minutes.

After the attachments are complete Mr. A is asked to relax. The next experience that Mr. A has is of himself sitting around a campfire in a heavily wooded area eating a hot dog. This experience lasts for a minute or two, whereupon Mr. A is returned to the laboratory and hears the attending physician ask him how that was. He nods, indicating that it was fine. His next felt experience is that of being on a boat sailing down a river under a pleasantly warm sun. This also lasts for a few minutes, whereupon he is asked by the attending physician if that was satisfactory to him. He agrees that it was. Immediately he comes to experience himself in a single-engine airplane gliding peacefully across what appears to be a midwestern sky. After a few more minutes he is once again spoken to by the attending physician, who this time thanks him, takes a few minutes to unhook the cables, hands him a crisp $100 bill and leads him to the door. Mr. A opens the door to the sub-basement in order to exit to the street. But his next experience is that of sailing in the basket of a hot air balloon over a deep blue lake; this lasts for a minute or so. Then he sees the attending physician, who apologizes for this additional experience and thanks Mr. A again for his help. Once more the cables are taken off and Mr. A heads to the door, opens it into the sub-basement from which he expects to exit to the street, but instead experiences himself swimming in a peaceful pool in what seems to be a suburban area of Los Angeles.

Perhaps what this piece of science fiction shows best of all is that once we are locked into epistemology, there is no obvious conceptual, nonperformatory way out. We are permanently in the fly-bottle. Wittgenstein teaches us that we can only end philosophy by doing something else. We must perform otherwise. The same is true of psychology.

MIME: *(Now standing next to him, hesitantly)* Well, then, tell me how many angels can dance on the head of a pin?

NARRATOR: *(Thinks deeply for a moment)* I don't know. Perhaps we should start the music and see.

(CHAIRWOMAN starts the third piece of music, a waltz, to which NARRATOR and MIME dance. They exit the stage waltzing with CHAIRWOMAN behind them.)

Twenty-Two Weeks of Pointless Conversation

DAN FRIEDMAN

This essay by Newman's longtime colleague Dan Friedman provides an opportunity to relook at Newman's methodology from an
entirely different vantage point—the theatre. Having examined, in previous essays, the practice of developmental performance as manifest in
social therapy, we now examine it as developmental theatre. This discussion is particularly timely, as more and more psychologists, psychotherapists and educators become involved in efforts to synthesize
theatre and psychology.

Friedman is a theatre historian and playwright whose knowledge of
the field of psychology has come from working with Newman, myself
and our colleagues. Thus, he sees Newman's challenges to Western culture's core conceptions, such as the individual, the self, identity, referentiality, truth, reality, etc., as exposing of the conservatism of the
institution of theatre. He tells us how the building blocks of both traditional theatre and political theatre—plot, character, audience and their
relationship—rely on these same core conceptions. Schooled in orthodox Marxist political and cultural analysis and its accompanying
modes of activism, Friedman is able to share the intellectual and emotional conflicts developmental theatre poses as he chronicles the twen-
ty-two-week conversation he and Newman created with a class of thirty
students/colleagues. Among other things, their collective activity gives
new meaning to "performance studies."—L.H.

PROLOGUE

Between October 1996 and May 1997 Fred Newman and I conducted a series of classes on developmental theatre. These hour and a half gatherings of some thirty people met once a week for twenty-two weeks over three trimesters under the auspices of the Center for Developmental Learning, a project of the East Side Institute for Short Term Psychotherapy. While there were some shifts in enrollment between trimesters, a core of about twenty remained constant. Most of those who took part in what evolved into an ongoing performatory dialogue work with Newman and me in various capacities at the Castillo Theatre in New York City, where Newman is the artistic director and I am the dramaturg. Others are (or had been) clients of Newman's at the East Side Center for Social Therapy and/or have been involved with him in one of the numerous community-empowerment projects he has led over the years.

Thus the classes were, to a large extent, conversations among colleagues, people who had worked together for years in the creation of what they have come to call "developmental theatre." They met in this relatively formal setting to reflect upon, explore and deepen their understanding of what they had created. What Newman, I and the thirty-some others involved constructed over twenty-two weeks turned out to be not as much *about* developmental theatre as it *was* developmental theatre. By examining in detail what happened over these weeks, we will, at the same time, be looking at the activity of developmental theatre itself.

First, by way of introduction: Fred Newman is a philosopher of science and language by training who has for 30 years worked as a political organizer and innovative psychotherapist. He is perhaps best known as the founder of social therapy, a nonpsychological, cultural-performatory approach to emotional development. He came to theatre through his political organizing, having helped to found the Castillo Culture Center in New York City in 1983 as a means of culturally empowering ordinary non-artists. Newman became actively involved with Castillo as a director and playwright in the late 1980s. He has since written some twenty full-length plays, directed scores of productions of his own work and that of other experimental and progressive playwrights, and has functioned as the artistic director of the Castillo Theatre since 1989.

My background in the theatre is more formal. I hold a doctorate in theatre history and dramatic theory from the University of Wisconsin and have performed in and directed community, trade union and political theatres since 1969. I began writing plays in high school and long considered myself an artistic disciple of Bertolt Brecht. I share with Newman intensely humanistic/political concerns and was among those who helped establish the Castillo Center and its theatre company.

Newman has written of himself as a playwright: "My attitude is revolutionary, not theatrical. My world view is philosophical, not dramaturgical. My craftsmanship is that of the organizer, not the director" (Newman, 1998, p. xxvii). His lack of formal theatrical training has, in my estimation, been his greatest strength as a theatre innovator. Unlike me and other progressive (and not-so-progressive) theatre people he is not of any theatrical tradition (be it Brecht's Epic Theatre, street theatre's agit-prop, or "socialist realism" and its liberal cousins) and so he has not been restrained or confined by any tradition. Not aware of the right way of doing things on stage, he was able to see new ways of doing things.

The ongoing dialogue between trained theatre artists such as myself and Newman has been a central feature of Castillo's evolution and the emergence of developmental theatre.[1] This fifteen-year-long (and counting) conversation might be characterized as an encounter between philosophy and theatre. Although Newman is far more sophisticated as a philosopher than most of his Castillo colleagues have been as theatre artists, their joint activity of building the Castillo Theatre has resulted in the creation of an environment from which has emerged a performatory activity that is artistically innovative, politically progressive, philosophically subversive, and, those of us involved in its creation believe, useful to continued human development.

The 22 weeks of class are most usefully viewed in the context of this ongoing dialogue; they were self-consciously set up as a means of continuing and deepening that conversation.

The first trimester was constructed as a conversation between Newman and me on the key concepts of development theatre. This was the most pedagogically conventional of the three trimesters. I would start each class with a brief talk (somewhere between 20 and 40 minutes) on a particular aspect of developmental theatre as I, at that point in the process, understood it. This introductory lecture attempted to place developmental theatre in the larger context of theatre history, and was, of course, influenced by my background as both a trained (orthodox) theatre scholar and an orthodox (trained) Marxist. Newman (unorthodox on both counts) would then respectfully contest (in most cases) and build on (in all cases) what I had said to deepen our understanding of the subject under discussion. These two presentations would then invariably open up into a discussion involving the whole class, most often taking the form of a question and answer session, with Newman (and to a lesser extent myself) responding to questions from the class. During the eight weeks of the first trimester we achieved a collective articulation of what developmental theatre is/is becoming relative to the institution of the theatre and its 2,500-year history. It provided those involved with a common vocabulary and a springboard for the more activistic and explicitly performatory work that was to follow in the second and third trimesters.

The second trimester consisted of what, in conventional terms, might be called a practicum. A play that I had been writing, *Tales of the Baal Shem Tov*—a conventional Brechtian parable—was read by the class and, over the course of eight weeks, deconstructed and transformed into a developmental script (if such a term can be used). This transformation consisted primarily of pulling the rug of referentiality out from under the play and of working collectively to make the script a dynamic element in a performatory process instead of a polished, self-contained, artful commodity. This transformation involved the members of the class writing and improvising scenes, as well as directing, performing and discussing them. In the course of this work the script changed, but more to the point, members of the class grappled in practice with many of the concepts dialogued about in the first trimester.

The third trimester (six weeks long) began with me interviewing

Newman about directing developmental theatre and evolved into a series of interview/performances by members of the class of each other on all sorts of subjects. The creation of these interviews brought with it an exploration of conversation as a developmental activity and an examination of its centrality in the creation of developmental theatre. It also brought to the fore many of the resistances to and fears of performance to be found among this group of people who have committed a good deal of their creative lives to the activity. Among the issues raised and dialogued on in the course of the trimester were a number that go to the heart of a new postmodern culture of the mind, including the inability to accept contradiction, the need to know, the fear of humiliation, the nature of the "self," and the difficulty of remaining fully aware (in the show) at all times.

From an essentially two-way dialogue on the nature of developmental theatre the course, through its own internal logic, transformed into an ongoing and constantly evolving performance of developmental theatre. The deconstruction of that arc from aboutness to nonreferential performatory activity is the subject of this paper.

◆　◆　◆

To understand the unfolding of the first trimester it is necessary to understand the shared experience and language that both "teachers" and "students" brought to the dialogue. Newman and most of the other builders of the Castillo Theatre came to the theatre as political organizers. Our approach to culture is anthropological in the sense that for us culture is a way of life rather than a set of privileged aesthetic objects. For Castillo, culture refers to the perceptual frames, symbolic structures and narrative conventions that human beings have constructed in the course of their social/historical activity. To that extent, this approach is solidly within the current mainstream of anthropology and cultural studies, particularly as they have been impacted upon over the last two decades by social constructionism.

Within this general orientation, those involved in Castillo have come to view the theatre as a social/historical construct, and, more specifically, as an institution of social control in the sense that it has played a major role (as its prodigy, film and television, continue to do) in constructing and propagating the grand-narratives by which a society understands itself and the world. This concept of theatre has it roots in Marx's analysis of the dynamic between the "superstructure" and "base" of a society. The superstructure, according to Marx, consists of the cultural, religious, legal, pedagogical and political institutions which evolve in relation to the needs of the economic base, that is, in relation to the basic economic relations (including power relations) by which a society produces and reproduces itself.[2]

Castillo's understanding of the theatre is indebted in particular to George Thomson, an obscure British Marxist classicist who in 1941 published *Aeschylus and Athens*, a book which traces in detail the relationship between the emergence of classes in ancient Greece, the rise of the Athenian state, and the coming into being of the theatre as an institution of social control (Thompson, 1969). This is not to say that Newman and the others building Castillo do what they do because they had read Thomson's book; most, in fact, haven't. Rather, Newman and Castillo do what they do—engage the institution of the theatre by creating theatre—informed by Marx's methodology. Thomson made his analysis of the institution of the theatre using his reading of Marx's methodology and, it turns out, this analysis has proven helpful to Castillo's activists in understanding what it is we are doing.

Another concept necessary for understanding Castillo's work and for following the dialogue/activity that unfolded over the 22 weeks under examination here, is *alienation*. Alienation, like the notions of superstructure and economic base, has its roots in Marx. The term has become part of mainstream sociological, cultural and psychological discourse, although it is often used today with a primarily psychological denotation/connotation (that is, as a description of a subjective emotional state) which Marx might have trouble recognizing.

For Marx, alienation is not a state of mind or an emotion; it is an actuality of social life under capitalism. It is the result of the fact that under capitalist economic relations the bulk of humanity (the working class) is not directly connected to the product of their labor. Instead of creating for use (or for immediate exchange) workers create products which belong to others. Work is no longer, for the most part, connected to the product it creates or to the life of the producer. In Marx's words, work under capitalism, ". . . is not the satisfaction of a need, but only a *means* for satisfying other needs" (Marx, 1966, p. 98). People work to "make a living," that is, they sell their labor power as a commodity (an item of exchange). Their labor power creates other commodities to which they have no connection, except, perhaps, as consumers, in which case they must buy back what they have (collectively) built, as in the case, for example, of the auto worker who buys a car.

As Newman, writing as a psychotherapist, put it in a 1983 essay, ". . . as Marxists, we don't take the notion of alienation to be psychological. We take it to be sociological. What we mean by that is that alienation is not simply a state of mind; it's not how people feel. Rather, it's how people *are*. And people get to be that way by virtue of how the entire system and activity of production (which influences more than simply the narrow acts of industry, but rather influences the total process of human production and human life in our society) creates a fundamentally alienated society" (Newman, 1991, p. 30).

Of course, the actuality of alienation has profound effects on the psychology of the alienated individual (not to mention on the emotionality of the alienated society as a whole). Newman, in his work as a social therapist, is quite familiar with the painful emotional byproducts of alienated culture. But for people concerned with transforming our "fundamentally alienated society," the question is: Given that alienation is part and parcel of a particular organization of activity, what *other* activity is needed to make it possible to break through/transform alienation's deadening effects? If no such activity/tool is available to us then qualitative change (development) would indeed, as the general consensus now holds, be impossible. Any serious cultural transformation, Newman has long argued, must include finding a way to break through (break up, transform, destroy) alienation. The late twentieth century alienated individual has become a passive object (as distinct from an active subject) in our social narrative. S/he behaves (and feels) within the context of a ready-made discursive setting, a setting that by its very nature is in the service of those in power.

Newman and his colleagues found the means for challenging alien-ation in the work of Lev Vygotsky, a developmental psychologist in the Soviet Union in the 1920s and early 1930s, who brought Marxist methodology to the study of early childhood development. Among his many important discoveries, Vygotsky noted that infants and young children develop by performing. They learn language and all the other social skills that constitute being human by creatively imitating the adults and older children around them; in Vygotsky's words they per-form "a head taller than they are" (Vygotsky, 1978, p. 102).

The built-in irony of socialization is that as we perform our way into cultural and societal adaptation we perform our way *out* of perfor-mance. As soon as we learn how to perform as men and women in ways appropriate to our gender, class and ethnicity we are pressured (by the very caretakers who at first encouraged performance, indeed who per-formed with us) to stop playing/performing. We are told to "act our age," to "grow up," to "act like a young lady," etc. Except for the tiny handful who become professional actors, most of us stop performing, and hence stop developing, by early adolescence. (Actors are supposed to only perform on stage; off-stage their behavior is as prescribed as anyone else's.)

"A lot of what we have learned (through performance) becomes routinized and rigidified into behavior," writes Holzman, a develop-mental psychologist and a close colleague of Newman's. "We become so skilled at acting out roles that we no longer keep creating new per-formances of ourselves. We develop an identity as 'this kind of per-son'—someone who does certain things and feels certain ways" (Holzman, 1997, p. 33). The kind of people we become are, among other things, alienated individuals within a social framework upon which we apparently have no significant impact—most of us never even question that the world we function in might, indeed, be change-able.

Noting that both small children and grown actors have the ability to perform—that is, to be both "who they are" and "someone else" at the same time—and seeing people with whom he worked consistently growing (performing) into tasks and roles that initially seemed far beyond them, Newman became convinced that performance was a human developmental capacity that could be reignited at any point in life. Thus for Newman and many others working with the Castillo Theatre, performance is not understood primarily as an artistic activity (though surely it can be artful); it is a basic human capacity without which we could neither become socialized nor transform and transcend the limitations of our socialization. Indeed, at the present point in history performance throughout life and in every aspect of (everyday) life has become an absolute necessity if we are to move beyond the developmental dead end of late capitalism. Performance, Newman has come to argue, is the activity by which we can break through alienation and create something new.

"For in a world so totally alienated as ours, doing anything even approaching living requires that we perform," Newman wrote in 1989. "To be natural in bourgeois society is to be dead-in-life. Unnaturalness is required if we are to live at all" (Newman, 1989, p. 6).

Newman's nonaesthetic understanding of performance has something in common with anthropologist Victor Turner's view of performance as a "liminal" activity, that is, activity on the threshold, activity which allows for innovation and change. Newman also shares with Nicolas Evreinoff, the early Soviet director, the conviction that performance need not be confined to the theatre or other ritualized moments, and that as an everyday activity performance ". . . is one of the mainsprings of our existence, of that which we call progress, of change, evolution and development in all departments of life" (Evreinoff, 1927, pp. 22–23). Yet Newman's understanding of performance is more activistic than either Turner's or Evreinoff's. It should be noted that neither of them were a direct influence on Castillo's work.

These, then, are the shared concepts of culture, theatre, alienation and performance which the participants in the developmental theatre class brought to their dialogues. Taken together, they can be considered the conceptual starting point of the 22 weeks of conversation and performance which followed.

ACT I

My opening remarks in the first class of the first trimester outlined the historical origins of theatre in ancient Greece, India, China and Japan, and argued (following Thomson) that the theatre came into being in cultures transitioning from tribal to class society as a means of providing ritualized/performatory resolutions to new social contradictions which were irreconcilable in the actuality of class-divided society. In tribal society the theatricalized/performed aspects of life made no distinction between actor and audience. The performance (dance, chanting, ritualized role playing, etc.) was done collectively by the tribe as a whole or by a tribal subdivision for the good of the tribe as a whole, i.e., to influence the hunt or the fertility of the crop or to assure victory in war or to make possible a transition in the life cycle of an individual.

Once societies divided into slave and master, serf and landlord, and so on, this collective performance became impossible (not to mention dangerous to those in power) and in its place the institution of the theatre was constructed. The theatre separated actor from the audience and divided performance from daily life. Instead of collective activity for the common good, performance was transformed into an art done by specialists who enacted social conflicts and presented fictional resolutions (for the most part on terms favorable to the status quo) to actual social conflicts.

In short, I concluded, theatre as an institution was not about development. How then, could we speak of "developmental theatre"? Indeed, why would people, such as ourselves, who are concerned with human development, have anything to do with theatre?

The discussion which followed focused on what it is that makes theatre an institution, and how an activity, such as performance, gets institutionalized. Newman argued that the institutionalness (and conservatism) of the theatre could best be located not in its presentation of resolutions on stage, but in the fact that it presented "plays" at all. Resolution is not only in the content of the theatre, it is in the very separation of "a play" from play. *The play* conservatizes because it separates performance/play/liminal activity from the general community. The development, progress, survival of the theatre will not come from the imposition of a new set of ideas, or resolutions (or anti-resolutions), or new performance techniques, or new whatevers on the theatre. Such impositions are what progressives and revolutionaries attempted in relation to theatre throughout most of the twentieth century. What they missed completely is that the theatre as a conservatizing and stabilizing institution is replicated and re-enforced in the very presentation of a play, no matter how "progressive" its content.

The way to engage the institution of theatre, therefore, is not to present plays, but to use theatre as an arena for adult play. Newman uses "play" in the Vygotskyian sense of early childhood play, play without predetermined rules, play as liminal, experimental activity, play as doing what you don't know how to do, play as a performance activity.

This is not to say that Castillo doesn't present plays, it does. In engaging the institution of theatre we can't do away with plays all at once, Newman points out, any more than he can, in his engagement of the institution of psychology, immediately do away with therapy, or at least clients' expectations of therapy. People come to the theatre to see plays—there are 2,500 years of expectation, habit, and cultural practice in that expectation. But the experience of attending a play at Castillo is calculated to, at the very least, begin the process of making performance and play accessible to the audience member. Unlike a director whose primary concerns are aesthetic, and who presumably would like an audience member to leave the theatre thinking, "That was beautiful and amazing; I could never do that," Newman has often said that his ideal audience member leaves the theatre thinking, "That looks easy; I could do that, I could perform."

During the first class, Newman concentrated on the key role of pointlessness in both subverting the play and for introducing the activity of play. Plays are traditionally about resolutions, and resolutions obviously contain a "point." However, even where no explicit resolution is offered, "aboutness" is itself a resolution. Pointedness is a frame of reference for Western civilization; pointedness itself re-enforces the status quo. However, play in the creative, child-like sense has no point. Its very pointlessness is part of what allows it to be creative and transformative. At Castillo, Newman said, we try not to make a point, but to play.

In the second week we continued the discussion of the relationship between the institution of the theatre and the activity of performance. My introductory talk traced the history of performance within the theatre, from ancient times through contemporary realism, and returned to the question of how performance could be "liberated" from the theatre.

Newman responded that this task could not be seriously approached as long as the fiction, the myth, the social construct, called "theatre" (or for that matter the one called "real life') were accepted. Postmodern thinkers have shown that the entire theatre/real life dichotomy is bogus. Postmodernism's insight is not that the theatre is artificial (we all knew that all along) but that so-called "natural" or "real" life is neither natural nor real. Reality itself, according to the social constructionists and postmodernists, is a social/historical construct consisting of (among other things) perceptions, emotions, attitudes, ways of interacting, etc.

Very much a part of that ongoing construction are conventions of social behavior. Daily life is filled with ritual, filled with prescribed ways of talking, walking, moving our faces, holding our hands, etc. Our everyday lives are vastly more codified than anything we have seen on stage. In fact, this codification is how we can understand each other at all. Both theatre and "natural life" are social/historical constructs; the wall between them (fourth or otherwise) is an illusion created out of the needs of a society divided into antagonistic classes. Creative performance and play are reserved for the stage and screen where they can be controlled and manipulated, while conventional behavior is demanded/needed for coming to terms with "reality."

It's not simply that theatre (film, television) is used to propagate certain values and concepts (though it surely is), but that theatre itself is core propaganda. That is, its very existence as an institution propagates and perpetuates the separation of performance from life. Its monopolization of performance (as a skill attainable only by the "talented" and permissible only in strictly prescribed circumstances) works to disempower the mass of the population, by denying them access to the developmental species activity of performance.

One of the results of this is the passivity of the audience. The audience comes to the theatre to be acted upon, not to act. It is as alienated from the enactment of social conflict on stage or screen as it is from any other commodity. The theatre assumes an audience that is increasingly alienated from performance, in Newman's words, "increasingly dead."

"It is with rage at that presumption of deadness that I come to work in the theatre," Newman told the class. "Developmental theatre is theatre which doesn't encourage or accept that deadness. It engages the assumption of deadness both on the part of theatre artists and by the audience itself. Developmental theatre is not a new type of theatre, but theatre which recognizes the performatory dimension of human life."

Castillo's discovery, Newman maintained, is not about the theatre. (There isn't much left to discover about the theatre qua theatre). Our discovery is about the relationship between theatre and everyday life. Developmental theatre is therefore primarily an organizing, not an aesthetic activity; it is the activity of engaging the relationship between the complex social construction known as theatre and the even more complex social construction known as everyday life.

Over the next three weeks we looked at Newman's plays as produced at the Castillo Theatre to explore the ways in which they attempted to negotiate this engagement. We did so by examining Newman's scripts in relation to the traditional craft elements of dramaturgy: dramatic structure, character development, and language. Many in the class were familiar with the body of Newman's work as a playwright—indeed many had performed in and/or designed them—and the discussion ranged freely over some 20 play scripts and productions. Here I will attempt to summarize these three weeks of discussion in such a way that knowledge of the scripts is not necessary.[3]

Dramatic structure is the way in which conflict unfolds on stage. In Western (and most Eastern) theatre the conflict is organized into a story, a plot, a narrative. One of the most striking characteristics of Newman's plays is their apparent indifference to plot. Some have them, most do not. It's not that they are phantasmagorical or absurd; they are conversations among recognizably (at least initially) real characters. It's just that these conversations usually don't *go* anywhere, narratively speaking. Sometimes, as in *Billie & Malcolm: A Demonstration* (1993) and *Risky Revolutionary* (1996), characters just sit around and talk about things that have happened to them. At other times, as in *Stealin' Home*, (1996) and *Satchel (A Requiem for Racism)* (1998), scenes in which very little happens are strung together, unified primarily by the fact that the same set of characters, talking about/around the same set of subjects, appear in them. In other cases, such as in *What Is To Be Dead?* (1997), two philosophical conversations, one in Russia in the late nineteenth century, the other in the United States in the late twentieth century, interweave, but no story ever evolves. Even in the few plays which appear to have conventional plots, such as *Left of the Moon* (1994) and *Coming of Age in Korea* (1996), the story is told more than once, in so doing undermining the authority of its own narrative.

The dramatic tension in Newman's plays (to the extent that there is any) therefore comes not from the plot per se (since there often is none) but from the conflict *between* the various versions or fragments of the narrative. In this sense it may be helpful to approach Newman's dramatic structure as a theatrical equivalent of cubism. Like cubism, his plays give up single-point perspective (and the moralism implied in the "correct" way of seeing things) to show the same thing/story/character/concept from a variety of perspectives at the same time. However, the analogy to cubism is limited (and perhaps misleading) to the extent that it implies that the point of Newman's plays is to make many perspectives available to the audience. There is no point to Newman's plays, and their pointlessness is connected to their plotlessness.

"A big breakthrough of postmodernism is the recognition that these are all stories," Newman told the class, "as opposed to the insistence that there is one special story called 'reality.' I think that's an advance, but I don't think it's going far enough. I'm trying to get beyond stories altogether."

Why? Because in Western culture, at least since the Greeks, we have looked at and understood ourselves, individually and collectively, as stories. Stories have predetermined shapes, outcomes, resolutions and implicit meanings which are historically constructed within a particular social-cultural continuum and they almost always support the world-as-it-is. Even a plot in which the protagonists rebel against the world-as-it-is supports the conservatizing narrative framework. Plots/stories/narratives, no matter what their content, limit our possibilities for development. The propagandistic element of the theatre, in the formal, not just substantive sense, is that it re-enforces this sense of our lives as stories.

"Narrative is what keeps us from performing creatively," says Newman. "It keeps us as characters in somebody else's story."

Instead of offering the audience new narratives (that is, new role possibilities), developmental theatre offers the possibility of life without narrative, a possibility that demands constructing our lives in a more active, creative, that is, performatory, way.

If there is no narrative, no story, what exactly is performed? Conversation.

Conversation, for Newman, ". . . is that existential moment when human beings, who have been on their individual paths, touch one another . . . It can create new meanings—meanings rooted in the performatory, relational activity of collectively creating more and more differing and new forms of life." Forms of life, a phrase adopted from the philosopher Ludwig Wittgenstein, implies for Newman the creation of new (nonnarrative) ways of organizing experience.

Unlike a plot, a conversation need have no point. It is an open-ended social activity with the potential to go somewhere or to dissipate or fracture or spin or transform in any number of ways. Newman describes his plays, as well as the process of creating them, as attempts at holding interesting conversations without trying to identify in advance what to do with the conversations.

"There is no story in developmental theatre," Newman told the class. "What there is instead is conversation, which in my scripts is often a playing around with time and identity. That's the corresponding structural element to narrative, that's what gives them interest on stage."

Developmental theatre, at its most effective, is performed conversation and therefore makes no qualitative distinction between scripted and improvised conversations. The classes at which all this was being discussed were, in this sense, as much developmental theatre (that is, performed conversations) as is a Newman play produced on Castillo's stage—perhaps more so in that the classes, as off-stage performances, were more explicit engagements of the relationship between so-called theatre and so-called real life.

Newman's dramatic language is, not surprisingly, highly conversational. It is perhaps this relaxed "everyday" quality of the language that has made his rather weird plays accessible to a public acculturated to realism. The major influences on Newman with regard to language come from Vygotsky and Wittgenstein, who, in different but compatible ways emphasized the *activity* of language (as opposed to its pictorial or pragmatic functions). For Newman, it is not so much the *what* of speaking which is significant, but *that* we speak to each other. It is through the activity of language-making that we collectively and continuously create and re-create all sorts of things, including relationships, identities, narratives, decisions and ourselves.

Among the things created by Newman's scripted conversations are characters. Yet many of the characters in Newman's plays so fundamentally violate what it means to be a "character" that they might well be called something else—although just what is not clear.

The fifth week of the trimester began with me briefly tracing the development of character in the theatre from Aeschylus, the first playwright whose scripts have survived, through contemporary realism. While approaches to character have varied tremendously in terms of psychological complexity and realistic verisimilitude over the millenia, the theatre has always assumed that a character is an individuated, stable, clearly defined unit. Many cultural historians, in fact, identify the beginning of theatre with the moment when Thespis (the first actor) stepped out of the chorus and, as an individual, addressed the chorus from which he had just emerged.[4] The collective mimetic ritual of tribal unity was thus shattered and in its place came theatre, that is, the ritualized performance of individuated characters enacting social conflict. This assumption of character has become fundamental to the theatre, which has approached character in various ways but has never, until the very recent emergence of postmodernism, questioned that the basic unit of dramatic action is the individual, the character.[5]

In Newman's plays the boundaries of character are rarely clear. In *Carmen's Community* (1987) Carmen is one personality in two different bodies. In *Outing Wittgenstein* (1994) we find one character (Wittgenstein) in two bodies with two different personalities. In *Mr. Hirsch Died Yesterday* (1986) we meet two different people—one white, male, Jewish and straight, and the other Black, female and lesbian—with the same history. In *Stealin' Home* (1997), we have one character who lives two different lives. In *What Is To Be Dead?* (1996) two sets of characters with different histories wind up being the same people, even though they are separated by culture and a hundred years.

Character, for Newman, is rarely a stable, clearly defined entity.[6] The perimeters between you and him and her and me are fluid, porous and constantly shifting. While the audience comes to the theatre wanting and expecting to identify with the characters, identification is extremely difficult because the characters are not ontologically stable; they disappear and re-emerge and transform. Instead of providing role models, Newman's developmental theatre suggests that there are no permanent roles. Stated in more philosophical—less theatrical—language, there are no particulars. His *character as other-than-a-specific-one* challenges not only a fundamental assumption of the theatre, but a core (dualistic) belief of Western culture, particularly pronounced over the last 500 years—that the individual is distinct from society, that the fundamental ontological units are discrete particulars which, taken together, make up the totality. For Newman and many other postmodernists, the individual (not to mention the dramatic character) is a very powerful socially constructed myth.

If Newman's characters are not self-contained individuals, not particulars, what are they? One useful way to approach them is as emerging elements in the unfolding social activity of the group. It is the group/the totality that Newman is interested in exploring on stage, as elsewhere.

After my overview, Newman began his discussion of character by talking about Sigmund Freud. Newman proposed that although Freud's psychoanalytic theory is marginal today, his worldview has come to dominate twentieth century culture, including the theatre. One of

Freud's basic political/cultural assumptions (which, of course, didn't originate with him) is that in the (assumed) group/individual dichotomy it is the group which is irrational, unintelligent, reactionary, bestial. Lacking ego, the group is, on the one hand, easily manipulated and, on the other, always on the verge of getting out of control. It is the individual, according to Freud, that is progressive, creative, rational.

"I think exactly the opposite," said Newman. "The conservatizing structure on human social behavior is the imposition of the individual on our culture. The individual is fundamentally conservative; it holds onto itself. The social construction of the 'individual' is all about establishing legal justification for ownership by the few of much social wealth. What's progressive, creative and developmental about humanity grows from the group. We are, after all, a social species. Everything we've created and built we've done socially. The group can give birth to the individual, but the individual can't stop the ongoing creative process of the group."

Developmental theatre is not based on the assumption of particulars (including particular individuals) and therefore the plays don't contain characters in the usual sense. Instead Newman's plays focus on the social/creative process of the group.

This disavowal of character, some in the class said, contradicted their perception of strong characters in numerous Newman plays— Thomas Jefferson in *Sally and Tom (The American Way)* (1995), V. I. Lenin in *Lenin's Breakdown* (1994), Malcolm X in *Billy and Malcolm: A Demonstration* (1993), were three of those mentioned.

Noting that he liked to "evoke the weight and heaviness of individuality" in challenging it, Newman said that he often chose to write about the "big shots"—those in our culture who are usually considered the makers of history—in order to expose them, instead, as the *products* of history. Jefferson, the individual, is just as much a *product* of the social activity called the American Revolution as the Constitution of the United States is.

"*Sally and Tom* is not about Thomas Jefferson," said Newman. "It is about the process of the creation of Thomas Jefferson. . . . The individual is an alienated product of social process. Development comes through social process; the alienated product holds it back . . . The interaction, not the product of that interaction, is the core of my plays. I focus on the conversation, not who's doing the talking. I work to make emergence—not the individual—the hero."

This focus on social process instead of on the individuated, alienated product of that process, puts a demand on an audience used to seeing/relating to/identifying with the product. Developmental theatre, Newman argued, has to generate another way of seeing, because "it can't be seen in the usual way, it's just not visible that way."

It also puts a demand on actors for another way of performing. Given that many in the class had performed in Newman's plays at the Castillo Theatre, it's not surprising that how to act in developmental theatre became a topic to explore.

Acting in the theatre has consisted, since that first actor stepped from the chorus, of the performance of an individuated, stable character. In the West since Konstantin Stanislavsky and Freud, acting has become psychologized, that is, approaching the performance of a character has come to mean understanding/creating the "inner life" and "emotional memory" of the imaginary character.[7] These tools, so useful to the actor in contemporary psychological realism, are not particularly helpful in the performance of developmental theatre.

Newman approached the discussion of acting in developmental theatre by comparing Freud and Marx, the two most influential thinkers of twentieth-century society.

"Freud thinks the social world is how it is because of how the mind works. If you look at the world, says Freud, you see the human mind. Marx thinks that the workings of the mind are a result of how society is structured. As a materialist, Marx understands everything, including the human mind, as the product of social interaction and organization," said Newman.

"At first glance, they may appear to be opposites, but their methodology is actually the same. In the 1960s and 1970s there were attempts to synthesize Marx and Freud, but they can't be synthesized because their method is already the same. Both work to 'get deeper,' to 'get to the bottom of things.' For Freud this means getting to the bottom of the mind, where he finds the id, the ego and the superego. For Marx it means getting to the bottom of society, where he finds classes and the means of production. Their common mode of understanding is reductionistic—to get to the root causes, to take the whole apart and find out what it's made of, to discover the basic building blocks."

Modernist theatre shares this basic methodological commitment to getting to the bottom of things, to finding the inner workings. With regard to performing, that means finding the inner workings of the character, her/his emotional underpinnings and motivations. Developmental theatre, essentially a postmodernist development, has no concern with getting to the bottom of anything—whether it be the story or the character—because it doesn't accept that there is a bottom to get to. To the postmodernist, understanding has to do with discovering the interconnectedness of things, the various ways in which phenomena interact and connect, not with what is going on under the surface, since it is not at all clear that anything is going on under the surface (or, for that matter, what the surface is as distinct from what is "over" or "under" it).

Given Marx's obvious influence on Newman's work in psychology, politics and theatre, it is worth noting that this postmodernist understanding of understanding is not inconsistent with dialectics, the interactive method developed (in modern times) by Hegel and the early Marx. That Marx himself did not consistently apply this method (in which tool and result and process and product are unified) in his own theoretical and practical work, does not alter the influence of his activity theory on Newman and other postmodernist thinkers. For example, the distinction between economic base and superstructure discussed earlier was turned by the later Marx and his orthodox followers into an instrumentalist relationship in which the economic base determines/causes the shape/nature of the superstructure. For Newman and other postmodernists who are building on, or, perhaps more accurately, *completing* the early Marx, the base and superstructure—to the extent that they are useful categories at all—are parts of the same totality. There is no surface and no core, no cause and effect. Base and superstructure are a complex of interconnections which interpenetrate and shape each other. The theatre, for example, is not a reflection of reality, as is usually maintained;

it is, instead, an active shaper of that complex of social constructs called reality.

"Developmental theatre embodies a rejection of modernist methodology," Newman maintained. "It rejects psychology and it rejects a materialism that assumes a distinction between surface and core, superstructure and base, activity and motivation."

It is not the task of the actor in developmental theatre to find the "inner truth" of a character, but to create the "outer connections" between characters. The acting activity in developmental theatre is not an inner journey into a closed entity (either the character's or the actor's psyche); it is, instead, a social (interactive) journey into transformation. When asked what kind of actor he liked to work with, Newman replied, "An actor who has no need for the character as a crutch."

One of the relationships explored (and exposed and performed) in developmental theatre is the relationship between the actor and the character. In all theatre there is a dialectic between the actor as actor and the actor as character. One of the things that distinguishes developmental from traditional theatre is that in developmental theatre that dialogue is not covered over. Instead, it is actively brought to the fore and performed along with the other relationships being created on stage. The class talked about the special excitement of the rehearsal process, the period in a production when the dialogue between actor and character tends to be most obvious and creative. In traditional theatre, the goal of the rehearsal process is, among other things, to cover over that dialogue by opening night so that the actor has, as far as the audience can tell, "become" the character. In developmental theatre, the director and actors work to keep the dialogue open and obvious to the audience throughout the run of the play.

This concentration on developing and exposing the relationship between the actor and the character is also one of the ways in which developmental theatre works to blur (eventually obliterate?) the distinction between the theatre and everyday life. It is to be hoped, said Newman, that the audience member, through this dialogue, this creative tension between actor and character, can come to identify performance not with a set of acting conventions and skills, but with the activity of showing people who you are and who you are not at the same time, an activity which anyone (regardless of talent) can do anywhere.

All of this discussion brought the group, in its final class of the trimester, back to the question of the relationship between community and theatre. The historic emergence of theatre out of the needs of a community in ancient Greece was re-examined in relation to the emergence of theatre within the political movement and development community which Newman has led for a quarter of a century.

Newman pointed out that the distinction between theatre and the rest of the development community's activity is not at all clearly defined. In this respect, the community's relationship with performance is closer to "pre-history," that is, to tribal society, than to later societies in which the theatre has become a distinct institution. This porousness between theatre and daily life is, at this point, part of a deliberate effort to bring performance into everyday life. However, as many in the class recalled, the development community had not started out with a clear notion of performance as a developmental activity. In fact, it didn't even start out with a clear notion of community.

Castillo's (and the community's) earliest plays were not very distinct from its other organizing activities. Performed May Day celebrations in the mid-1980s involved groups of people dressing in costumes of progressive movements from around the world and throughout history—for example, the Black Panthers, the Sandinistas, the Industrial Workers of the World, and so on. After a rally in full costume at New York City's Union Square, historically a gathering spot for the Left, the performers/demonstrators would march to Castillo where activists dressed as historical figures such as Albert Parsons, Rosa Luxemburg, and Ho Chi Minh, would give speeches and everyone would party. *A Demonstration: Common Women, the Uncommon Lives of Ordinary Women* (1986), the first "play" ever directed by Newman, was, as its title indicates, as much a demonstration as play, featuring a confrontation between two groups of protestors—radical lesbians (mostly white) and welfare activists (mostly Black)—in the middle of a large public space, surrounded by skits, film clips and songs. The audience, which stood and milled around during the event, took part, to various degrees, in most of these performatory activities. Radical lesbians and welfare organizers had been among the earliest builders of what would become the development community and their ritualized encounter in the middle of Castillo's black-box theatre was less than a razor's edge away from "real life." *From Gold to Platinum* (1986) was a full-length play which emerged from a series of discussions held by members of different organizations in the community about what a second American revolution might look like. While it was performed on a stage (Symphony Space on Manhattan's Upper West Side) before hundreds of people, its cast of 40-some was made up entirely of political activists, most of whom had never been on a stage before.

Unlike earlier attempts at progressive theatre, Newman pointed out, "We were never theatre people trying to bring art to the people; we were, and are, community builders and our theatre-like activity has emerged from that organizing process."

Thus, theatre within the development community has never become a distinct, closed institution. As a performatory extension of other organizing activities, it remains open to all. This situation has led to many of the perspectives and activities discussed in these pages. Most importantly, it led to the (re)discovery that performance can be a developmental activity in everyday life. Using nonactors in these early performance pieces and continuing to do so in the later plays has made it clear that performance is something anyone can do, and, further, that it should not be confused with the specific set of conventions and skills called acting. When the activity of performing began to be consciously employed in other organizing environments (most especially social therapy), we found that performance—being who you are and who you are becoming—could, when liberated from the conventions and confines of the theatre, be a very growthful activity.

As Castillo's and Newman's work has grown more theatrically sophisticated, there has been a conscious effort to make sure that the connection, the open border, between community building/organizing and theatre is maintained. This has been done in a many ways, perhaps most significantly in Castillo's insistence on using both professional and amateur performers in its shows. This mix, which has been vital to emergence of developmental theatre from the beginning, allows for the activity of liberating performance from the theatre to be embodied in each production. The audience member is confronted through this mix with the actuality that she or he could do what the people on stage are doing—perform.

"When you try to understand developmental theatre, you can't just look at its appearance," Newman concluded. "It may look like other theatre, or it may look like weird theatre or bad theatre or whatnot. But what something is is inseparable from its history. Our history is that of community building. Whatever we can, and have, said about it as theatre is primarily metaphor. The actuality is that it's an organizing process."

Act II

For the second trimester, Newman and I agreed that a more profound understanding of developmental theatre could best be achieved by intensifying the performatory-ness of the class. Newman suggested that we could ask the class to perform as developmental playwrights, taking a play that I had been writing for over a year called *Tales of the Baal Shem Tov*, which was essentially a Brechtian-type fable, and reworking it into a script more appropriate to a developmental production. Continuing the class as a practicum which brought experienced playwrights together with people who had never written a scene in their lives was fully consistent with developmental theatre's method of mixing amateurs and professionals in an environment in which they both are encouraged to perform beyond themselves. Since I was (and am continuing to) struggle with the limitations I had placed on my dramaturgy by my early (and stubbornly dogmatic) commitment to Brecht, I was particularly eager to see what could come out of this engagement of my latest script.

The first class of the second trimester began with my giving the participants some background on the script and how I had come to write it. The play, I explained, is based on Jewish folktales of Israel ben Eliezer, called the Baal Shem Tov, Master of the Many Names of God, the founder of the Hasidic movement. While the remnants of the Hasidic movement today, concentrated in parts of Brooklyn and Jerusalem, are known primarily for clinging to their semi-medieval ways, the origins of the Hasidic movement are progressive. Arising in Eastern Europe at the end of the seventeenth century when the Jewish world had been devastated by a wave of pogroms (half the Jews of the Ukraine, for example, were wiped out within a few years) and two false messianic movements, the Hasidic movement was, in my estimation, a progressive reinvention of Judaism through the development of a new form of community.[8]

In the script, I projected parallels between the early Hasidic movement and the contemporary developmental community led by Newman. To this end, I made use of the parable in the Brechtian tradition, with each scene, idea and character meant to stand for a contemporary idea, event and person. The play, not incidentally, is meant to be performed primarily by puppets, a Brechtian "distancing" effect, designed to discourage the audience from identifying with the characters, and thus allowing them to think critically about the events depicted in the play.

The script had first been read during Castillo's 1995 New Plays for New Days Festival, at which new plays are showcased each summer. At that point, Newman had asked why I had written a play about a conservative figure. Instead of seeing the Baal Shem Tov as a proto-revolutionary, as I did, Newman saw him as someone who had found a way to preserve a backward-looking tradition. In an attempt to answer (or at least grapple with) his question, I inserted into the play three "interludes" in which a character called "The Author," drinking coffee at a donut shop in contemporary New York City, talks with three old men with white beards—Walt Whitman, Karl Marx and eventually Israel ben Eliezer himself—about why he is searching for the Baal Shem Tov.

After this introduction, the class of 30 read aloud Act I and Interlude I of *Tales of the Baal Shem Tov*. We then began a discussion of the script, which consisted mostly of a critique of what people in the class perceived as the conservative content of the play. Newman quickly shifted the focus of the discussion by saying that he thought the conservatism of the play was more to be found in its form than in its content. First of all, the language, which was highly poetic, forced us to look at it as a thing-in-itself, as an artistic element, and therefore took us away from the conversation. Language is a tool or an artifact, while conversation is an *activity*. Conversation creates meaning, while language per se encapsulates (petrifies) meaning. When the tool (language) dominates over the activity (conversation), it is difficult—perhaps impossible—for the result to be developmental.

In addition, Newman continued, the parable form is inherently conservative because it demands a predetermined structure which works toward a predetermined end. If you know where you're going, there's nothing developmental in getting there. Relative to the characters, Newman argued that if the characters all represent something else, then what you've created are characters who define (and predetermine) the conversation, instead of letting the conversation create the characters. Finally, the "aboutness" of parable, not to mention most of other theatre, is inherently supportive of the status quo because what can it be about other than what we already know? Referentiality, which is the underpinning of *Tales of the Baal Shem Tov,* ties us to "reality," the conservative social construct of late capitalist society. What else could referentiality be referring to?

Based on the conversation in the first class, Newman suggested that the class take on the task of "pulling the rug of referentiality out from under *Tales of the Baal Shem Tov.*" The liberating/developmental thing about the theatre, he said, is that it doesn't have to be about anything. We assigned the class the task of writing scenes inspired by, or growing out of, the Baal Shem Tov script—but scenes which were about nothing.

The second week some people, a small minority of the class, came in with scenes, which were then turned over to volunteer actors (fellow classmates) who performed them. These first scenes were interesting for a number of reasons. First of all, everyone who wrote a scene, without exception, took off from the Interlude sections of the play, which were set in the twentieth-century coffee shop, rather than from the body of the script, which was set in Eastern Europe in the seventeenth century. What clearly interested the class was what the Baal Shem Tov had to say to the late twentieth century and/or why I, an atheist and radical political activist, was interested in such a character. The Baal Shem Tov, Dan and the Waitress (who, in the original, is only implied, she never speaks, or even appears) were present in most of the first scenes—and remained the main characters in the scenes that were written and performed through the trimester.

At the same time, what we discovered was that the pull to be about something was very strong. Different scenes had different takes on the play's meaning—for some it was about the Baal Shem Tov's misleadership, for some it was about challenging the concept of heroism, for others it was about the sociability of coffee shops (a theme, I might add, that is very close to my heart), for still others it was about creating the environments in which these odd meetings could occur. Yet, they all remained about something. In fact, a good deal of time in all the scenes was taken up in explaining who the Baal Shem Tov was/is. There was a felt need by each of the playwright/participants to explain to the audience who they were watching and why. This, the class concluded, was because most of us, at that point, remained committed to the play being *about* the Baal Shem Tov.

So while the restraints of the Brechtian parable had been loosened somewhat, and the showiness of the language toned down, the play's referentiality (its aboutness) remained intact. These first scenes were, as Newman put it, "still being overdetermined by the product, or the desire to produce a product, a play about the Baal Shem Tov." We talked about the creative tension that always exists between building on what we have and not getting locked into and conservatized by what we already have. The class was still stuck in the aboutness of the original script. The task before us, we decided, was to discipline ourselves *not* to too quickly discipline ourselves.

To help accomplish that goal, Newman gave a second assignment—to write a scene which started with the Baal Shem Tov, the answer-giver of the original script, declaring, "I want some answers!" These new scenes could build on the ones written this week or be completely new. This assignment was meant to accomplish two things. First, by casting the answer-giver of the original script as someone seeking answers, it gave the writers license to ask questions rather than feel obliged to provide explanations and answers. Secondly, it set up the new scenes with a desire to discover something. The drive to explain is likely to lead to lectures; the desire to discover is more likely to produce conversations.

In the third week we made a great deal of progress in overcoming aboutness. The scenes that were written (and with each passing week more and more of the participants took on the task of playwriting) for the most part did not refer explicitly back to the original script. Unlike the first round of scenes, they didn't attempt to explain who the Baal Shem Tov was/is and what his religious and philosophical views were/are. For the most part they stopped trying to connect him conceptually to the late twentieth century. In some cases the Baal Shem Tov wasn't even a character in the scene. Not surprisingly, given the line, "I want some answers!" with which each of the new scenes began, the theme or the activity of searching for answers, for meanings, came to the fore.

However, what remained in almost all the scenes was a particularly stubborn kind of referentiality known in theatre as exposition (background information), that is, the scenes attempted to explain themselves. The class playwrights were concerned to let the audience in on what (supposedly) had happened before the performance began. They assumed that a conversation could not be understood or appreciated without explanation or referentiality. While the scenes were no longer referring explicitly to the original script, they remained referential to "reality," to causality, to the activity of explaining, and, through all of these, to traditional theatrical convention. The scenes remained about something—in this case they were about themselves.

We discussed how this aboutness continued to get in the way of development. If the activity of a scene is explaining itself, then the conversation can't really go anywhere except backwards, if you will, to the imagined origin of the imagined conversation. Exposition assumes that the world proceeds linearly from the past to the present and hence gives the past power to determine the future. The internal aboutness of the scenes (and their implicit cause-and-effect linearity) also impacted on character development. Instead of letting the characters emerge from what they said and did, what they were saying and doing was being determined by a preconceived notion of who they were and what they had done. In that sense, these new scenes were not so very different from the original script in which what the characters said and did was predetermined by the point I wanted to make through them.

To break free of the pull of this deep-rooted referentiality, Newman set up a series of improvisations in which three people at a time went to the center of the room and attempted to have a conversation that started in the middle and that made no reference to what came before. As you might imagine, this was not easy. We did about five such improvs, stopping and starting again if the conversation began to include exposition. In the discussions after the improvisations, Newman said that a good rule-of-thumb for writing conversations developmentally is to never let the audience or reader know what's going on until it's absolutely necessary. With this piece of advice in mind, the class was given the assignment of writing scenes (either building on ones already written, or improvised, or completely new ones) that began in the middle and contained no exposition, no internal or causal referentiality.

In the fourth week something truly remarkable happened. Nine people brought in scenes that did exactly what we had asked them to. There were nine nonreferential, nonexpository scenes, each of which was an interesting conversation, contained intriguing characters, and was well written. Reading through the scenes once, we then cast the characters (the same characters appeared in many of the scenes), hastily put them together in an arbitrary order, and performed them back to back. A theatrical piece had been created which reflected upon, and at the same time extended/liberated, the original *Tales of the Baal Shem Tov*.

We were quite impressed with ourselves. In the space of four weeks (12, if you include the previous trimester) we had succeeded in creating a developmental environment in which people could perform beyond themselves: Nine people who had never written anything for the theatre before had written exciting theatrical scenes.

Beyond patting ourselves on the back, we discovered, through the performance of these new scenes, some interesting things about *Tales of the Baal Shem Tov.* First of all, we discovered that the Baal Shem Tov is a "doofus." Taken together, the Baal Shem Tov (the class had begun to refer to him as Mr. Tov) who emerged in these scenes was likeable and good-natured, as well as distracted and ineffectual. We also discovered that the play contains a searching, a quest. The Baal Shem Tov is searching for answers, Dan is searching for the Baal Shem Tov, and various other characters are searching for ways of coping with loss, for connections to other people, and so on. We learned that the play was gentle; the characters, all ordinary people (including "Mr. Tov," now an odd old man walking into coffee shops and bodegas asking for answers), had been bruised and buffeted by the world but were basically supportive of each other. There were no villains and little anger in this play. Finally, the experience of seeing the scenes performed in a quickly chosen order demonstrated that the play needed neither plot nor sequentiality to hold together as a theatrical experience.

These discoveries were possible, Newman claimed, not because we had known what the play was about. In fact it was by freeing the play, and ourselves as authors and directors, from aboutness that we were able to learn anything useful about the play. This was a clear case, we agreed, of how it is *not knowing* that provides the possibility of creativity and development. As Newman put it, "To the extent that we know what a play is *about*, we don't know what it *is*."

The fifth week was used to reflect on what had happened and in dialogue on where to go from here. I gave a summary of the first four weeks, and proposed that what we had done was to deconstruct the play. I recalled that years earlier when I had asked Newman for his definition of creativity, he had called it the reorganization of what is. Nothing comes from nothing; we all start with something—the cultural heritage we find ourselves a part of, our personal experiences, a script, whatever—and we reorganize it into something qualitatively new. That new totality is then material for further reorganization. Since Newman and I had first had that conversation, the social constructionists and postmodernists had given that reorganizing process a name—deconstruction—and provided some insight into how it is done. Deconstruction has come to refer to the process of creatively taking apart what exists.

Our development community and others had added what many post-modernists only imply, the concept of "reconstruction," that is, the process of putting together something qualitatively new.

The process of deconstruction/reconstruction, I proposed, is at the heart of developmental theatre. As a developmental director you take what is—which includes the script, the actors, the ideas of the design-ers—pull it apart and put it back together again. Obviously this "taking apart" is not necessarily physical (although in the plastic arts it might be); it is first and foremost taking apart the philosophical, ideological and aesthetic assumptions of the script. If you are a playwright, the deconstruction process involves questioning your own assumptions, experiences, concepts of the beautiful and/or interesting; taking them apart and putting them together in the process of writing the script. It is a process not of teaching (as Brecht and Friedman are inclined to do) but of discovery. That is precisely what we, as collective playwrights, had been doing with *Tales of the Baal Shem Tov*, in this case the main target of our deconstruction being referentiality.

Another way of looking at the preceding four weeks, I suggested, was as a play that we had been improvising under Newman's direction. After all, if we agreed that performance is key to development, then collective social activity that is developmental is best viewed as play. Our play could have a number of names—*Not Waiting for Answers, The Death of Referentiality, Deconstruction on a Hot Tin Roof, No Beginnings/No Ends*. We had, in a sense, reached the end of the first act. The fourth week had been something of a climax, a breakthrough, an explosion, a leap, and it raised the question of where to go from here. While deconstruction/reconstruction interpenetrate each other and can-not be temporarily (or otherwise) separated, were we now at a point where we could begin reconstructing *Tales of the Baal Shem Tov*? If so what did we need to do to build on what we had created without being conservatized by it?

Newman responded by disagreeing that there was a reconstructive counterpart to deconstruction. Deconstruction, at least in a culture as referential as ours, creates the very aboutness it has taken apart. It is a new aboutness, to be sure, but an aboutness nonetheless—which calls

out for continued deconstruction. While Newman was quite compli-
mentary about the summary I had presented of the first four weeks of
the trimester, he warned that my description of the deconstruction contained, at the same time, a new aboutness. What the class needed to do,
he suggested, was to write new scenes which responded to my presentation. The scenes shouldn't be discussions or commentaries on my summary, but performance pieces that, in Wittgenstein's words, "moved
about around" my summary as a way of continuing the deconstructive
process.

The bulk of the sixth week was taken up by the performance of
scenes. Some of these scenes were written individually and some by
small groups. Some had Dan as a character, Mr. Tov continued to
appear in many of them, some made oblique references to my summary
of the week before, most did not. Overall, it was hard to find a common
thread or theme or focus in the 12 performances presented that week. In
the short time left for discussion after all the performances, Newman
appeared to be tickled pink at the utter pointlessness of the scenes.
"Creativity is not instrumental; it is not a tool for anything else," he
declared. "Developmental theatre's big advance over Brecht is its pointlessness. Part of what makes developmental theatre, including tonight's
performances, so wonderful, is that it goes nowhere." No new assignment was given.

The seventh week consisted of a free-wheeling discussion of the
creative potential of deconstruction, including discussion of the fact
that one of the important things going on in class was the deconstruction of my domination (as playwright) of the theatre activity. We dialogued on why the "creator" of a script staying in control is
fundamentally reactionary. Human creation, after all, is a continuous
collective process; the playwright putting certain words on paper is but
one moment in that ongoing process.

The eighth week consisted of performances of the deconstructive
process, many of them hilarious. One performance that stands out in
my memory, and which embodies for me if not the "lesson" then the
attitude we had learned over the two months together, was that of Sandy
Friedman (no relation), a building contractor and a colleague of

Newman's since his earliest community organizing days. His scene consisted of him performing the tearing down of wall after wall in an unending and constantly changing process of renovation. He ended his performance by facing the audience and declaring, "I've been doing this for 25 years and I'm still not sure what we're building."

ACT III

In the first trimester we had looked at developmental theatre in rela- tion to the institution of theatre, its history and social functions. In the second trimester we had approached developmental theatre from the perspective of how you write it. We participated in a hands-on decon- struction of a script. The third semester, which was only six weeks long, evolved into the most performatory of the three.

It started out with me interviewing Newman about the relationship between his political background and views and his theatre work. While the content of that interview is very interesting and someday may make for an interesting article in its own right, what was signifi- cant about that interview from the perspective of developmental theatre was that it spawned other interviews. The second week consisted of the class collectively interviewing Newman. By then it had became clear to us all that the interview was a form of performatory conversation. During an interview, we noted, both the interviewer and the interviewee perform. Newman suggested that for the third week members of the class interview each other. The interviews needn't, and probably shouldn't, be about developmental theatre. The task was to interview each other as a way of performing together.

In the third week the class began to interview itself. Most of the interviews that week and the next involved small groups, who had pre- pared over the week, interviewing an individual within the group about her or his work. The people being interviewed tended to close the con- versation down with careful, closed, factual, responses. Some of the interviews were more fanciful, with an individual playing a "fictional" character, usually an exaggeration of her or himself. These tended to be more performatory and more fun—and actually more exposing of who the performer was than those in which the interviewees were their "real" selves. For the most part, however, it became obvious that without the support of a script, such as the scenes written in response to *Tales of the Baal Shem Tov* last trimester, people were having a great deal of trouble performing—being who they are and who they are not—in front of the class. This was particularly true for the people being interviewed. About half way through the allotted time of the third class, Newman decided to interview the class about why it was having such a hard time performing. Although there were more interviews among classmates the following week, Newman's interview of the class about performance became the defining activity of the rest of the course.

On one level, what was at issue was the developmental theatre (and postmodern) notion of the character/individual as a constantly unfolding activity, as opposed to a stable, closed entity. Many people spoke of the investment they had in presenting (and being) who they were. Newman challenged them to be who they were not, pointing out that successful interviews, like successful conversations of any kind, including plays, were processes of discovery. If you only presented who you were, there was no place to go, no way to develop. The task of the performer in developmental theatre is to participate in the process of continually creating who s/he is.

In the course of those two weeks of interviews and discussion the class decided that it needed to engage its own resistances to performance as continuous, everyday activity. I summarize the extended discussion we had about barriers to performance within the class, in the hope that it may shed light on the challenges Newman's advocacy of performance as revolutionary activity may face in other contexts as well.

First, there was strong *resistance to contradiction*. Deeply ingrained in Western culture since at least the Greeks, and formally articulated in Aristotelean logic, is the notion that A can only be A; it can't also be B. As Popeye is fond of saying, "I yam what I yam, and that's all what I yam." However, performance is contradictory. It requires that you be who-you-are and who-you-are-not at the same time. The way some people in the class dealt with their resistance to contradiction was to divide themselves in two—the Good Person (who is politically engaged, nice, unreactive, progressive) and the Bad Person (who is not politically engaged, who is reactive and nasty, sexist, racist, classist, etc.). The assumption is that if you are being one, you can't be the other. Of course, as the actuality of any play demonstrates, we are both (and much more) all the time. We talked at length about this refusal to embrace contradiction and concluded that it was, for many, an attempt to impose traditional dualistic moralism on performance. It equated performance with "being good" and not performing with "being bad." It was pointed out that this was hardly developmental. It resulted in continuing to behave as a good girl or boy on our good days, and behaving as a bad girl or boy on our bad days. Performance and development have nothing to do with the moral categories of good and bad, Newman maintained. Being able to perform off-stage involved letting in that you can be anything and everything all at once.

Another common attitude that got in the way of performance was *clinging to the need to know*. This resistance was particularly evident among the people being interviewed, whose answers, as I've pointed out, tended to be so self-conscious (in the negative sense) and constrained. They were very concerned with the image they were projecting. They felt the need to know what they were going to do and say. However, if you know what you're going to do before you do it, then you are almost certain to behave as the status quo has taught/conditioned you to behave. For who/what has taught us what to know? Indeed, who has taught us what "knowing" itself is? Performance is not for cowards. It involves doing what you don't know how to do. It involves risk. It involves embracing mystery. It means living in a perpetual state of uncertainty.[9]

Closely related to letting go of knowing is *letting go of dignity*. Knowing and respectability are closely related in our culture. Someone "in the know" is cool. Yet performance involves doing what you don't know how to do—that's precisely what can make it developmental. A number of people in class talked about how humiliating it felt to perform. Yet each time one performs, one risks losing one's dignity.

I told the class about the first acting and theatre teacher I ever had, Zenobia Alverez, who used to say, "You should fall on your face at least once a day." I never forgot that advice, although I didn't always live up to it, and I certainly didn't appreciate how profound it was. At the time I took it to mean, "Don't take yourself so seriously." Of course it did mean that, but Alverez was also saying a lot about dignity as nondevelopmental. If you're always concerned with dignity, with how you look to others, with how you measure up to society's standards, you will always strive to conform to society's standards and neither you nor society will develop.

The emotion that we learn to feel when we don't conform to society's standards is *humiliation*. We all know this feeling. It's not pleasant. To be a woman, when society holds up masculinity as the ideal, is humiliating. To be Black, in a society that maintains that white is normal, is humiliating. To be a Jew, when society's norms are Christian, is to be humiliated. To be gay, when society considers anything other than heterosexuality to be perverted, is to be humiliated. To be politically progressive in a cynical and conservative age is humiliating. So virtually everyone in our class lived with some form of humiliation daily. It was therefore very understandable that we didn't want to feel any more humiliation. Yet performance is by its very nature humiliating. When you perform, you are doing something other than behaving correctly— and that's humiliating. Whenever we do something new—no matter how beautiful or exciting or developmental that new thing is—we're going to feel humiliated. In fact, the more radical that new thing is the more humiliated we'll feel. However, without humiliation there is no development.

A fourth type of resistance to performance discovered through the work in the third trimester was *clinging to the illusion of self*. This is what was going on when interviewees were more concerned with their answers to questions than with the joint activity of performing an interview. In reflecting back on Zenobia Alverez's advice, I told the class, I now realized that I might not have been so off in understanding it to mean not taking myself so seriously. A more radical (and accurate) way to put it might be—not to take myself at all. "Self" is one of those descriptions which, like all descriptions, captures a process at a particular time and place. For the last several centuries of Western civilization this description of something called "self" has had a certain developmental value. However, to take it as other than a description, to make it into an ontological category, is to confuse the product (self) with the process (human history). Clinging to self might also be described as resisting *process*. The process of human development is fundamentally social, collective, species-wide. Holding on to self means holding on to what you have, clinging to your baggage, so to speak. It means behaving as opposed to performing; it means maintaining your dignity; it means, ironically, allowing the conservative institutions of society to define and shape your so-called self.

Performance, as we experienced time and again in the class, is a social, not an individual, activity. For Newman and those of us who have been working with him for years at the Castillo Theatre and other projects, performance implies being primarily concerned with and connected to the development of the group. In theatre this is called building the ensemble, in politics it is called organizing, in psychology and pedagogy Newman, following Vygotsky, calls it creating the zone of proximal development.

Finally, many people spoke of how much energy it takes to perform all the time, to be "in the show" all the time. We came to call this the *resistance to awareness* because performance is a conscious activity that one must choose to do. You can't perform without being *aware* of performing, and part of that awareness is being conscious of the fact that what one does impacts on others, on the social activity of which we are a part.

In the fifth week, I summed up the resistances we had identified over the previous two classes. In the sixth and final class Newman returned to two points, which he drove home with particular intensity— what he called the "perniciousness of aboutness" and the "riskiness of performance." Aboutness, he emphasized, assumes there is something out there (first principal, God, call it what you will) other than what we human beings have created. Accepting pointlessness means accepting responsibility for our actions. That, after all, is what developmental theatre, and all attempts at development, come down to.

Referencing our weeks of dialogue on the resistances to performance, Newman acknowledged that the fears of performance were quite understandable. It is serious stuff. "Performance as we speak of it would be dangerously psychotic if it weren't anchored in what we're building," Newman explained. "It challenges fundamental assumptions of our culture, assumptions with intense emotions attached to them. It would be irresponsible to advocate performance without there being a growing community to support it, a community involved in an ongoing effort to ignite development and change the world." Assuring that performance liberated from the theatre functions as revolutionary activity instead of a psychotic break depends on the ever-deepening and extensive involvement of the development community in all aspects of contemporary life, or more accurately, it demands the transformation of contemporary life into a vast development community.

Newman ended by reminding his colleagues of the scope of the effort they were undertaking: "Collectively we are engaged in an effort to converse, to perform, to create without commitment to the biases of those who control this culture—that's what it means to be a revolutionary at the turn of the twenty-first century."

EPILOGUE

So ended our 22 weeks of pointless conversation. They were neither the beginning nor the end of the conversation. In reporting them here I have, no doubt, given them a form and continuity that they surely lacked in performance. In my attempt to make these discussions and performances accessible to those not directly involved in them, I fear that I may have over-explained and interpreted, and allowed aboutness to slip in through the back door. Hopefully such impositions have not overdetermined the experience of reading this account of the developmental theatre classes. I invite the reader to consider these pages as simply another scene in an ongoing performatory conversation.

NOTES

1. In addition to myself, other formally trained theatre people who have participated in this ongoing dialogue have included Castillo builders Eva Brenner, Madelyn Chapman, Wilton Duckworth, Roger Grunwald, Gabrielle Kurlander, Maria Moschonisou, David Nackman, Marian Rich, Charlie Spickler, Linnea Tillett, Victoria Wallace and Janet Weigel. Other theatre artists who have engaged in this dialogue with Newman over the years include: Aimé Césaire, Sheila Goloborotko, Bill T. Jones, Amy Pivar, Judith Malina, Heiner Müller, Richard Schechner and Robert Wilson.

2. This analysis is most clearly put forward in Karl Marx and Frederick Engels, *The German Ideology,* Part I, (1973).

3. Most of Newman's plays written between 1986 and 1997 are collected in Dan Friedman (Ed.), *Still On the Corner and Other Postmodern Politcal Plays by Fred Newman* (1998).

4. Whether he is an historic or legendary figure, Thespis, or a person of other name, did have to step out from the chorus in order for drama to develop. Thespis is first mentioned by Horace in "The Art of Poetry." see Barrett H. Clark (Ed.), *European Theories of the Drama* (1974), p. 28.

5. Agit-prop (agitation and propaganda) theatre in the 1920s and '30s attempted to project the mass (the working class) as the collective hero, but wound up individuating the class, that is, imposing an individual personality/psychology on a collective.

6. Newman is not the only playwright in the last 20 years to challenge the traditional approach to character. See the later work of Heiner Müller, the early plays of Sam Shepard, and Carol Churchill's *Cloud Nine.*

7. The Russian actor and director Constantin Stanislavsky, a founder of the world-famous Moscow Art Theatre, is the single most influential theorist and teacher of acting in the twentieth century. Among his major works are: *An Actor Prepares* (1936), translated by Elizabeth Reynolds Hapgood (N.Y.: Theatre Arts Books); *Building a Character* (1949), translated by Elizabeth Reynolds Hapgood (N.Y.: Theatre Arts Books); and *Creating a Role* (1961), translated by Elizabeth Reynolds Hapgood (NY: Theatre Arts Books).

8. For background, the early Hasidic movement and the Baal Shem Tov, see: Martin Buber, *The Origin and Meaning of Hasidism* (1960), translated by Maurice Friedman (NY: Schocken Books) and Martin Buber, *The Legend of The Baal-Shem* (1969), translated by Maurice Friedman (NY: Schocken Books).

9. For a detailed examination of knowing and its potential to hold back further human development see: Fred Newman and Lois Holzman, *The End of Knowing: A New Developmental Way of Learning* (1997).

REFERENCES

Friedman, D. (Ed.) (1998). *Still on the corner and other postmodern political plays by Fred Newman*. New York: Castillo.

Evreinoff, N. (1927). *The theatre in life*, trans. Alexander I. Nazaroff. New York: Brentano's.

Holzman, L. The Developmental Stage. *Special Children*, June/July, 32–35.

Marx, K. (1966). Economic and Philosophical Manuscripts. In E. Fromm, *Marx's Concept of Man*. New York: Frederick Ungar Publishing Co.

Marx, K. and Engels, F. (1973). *The German Ideology*, Part I. New York: International Publishers

Newman, F. (1989). Seven Theses on Revolutionary Art. *Stono, 1 (1)*, 6.

Newman, F. (1991). Talkin' Transference. In F. Newman, *The Myth of Psychology* (pp. 16–44). New York: Castillo International.

Newman, F. (1998). Stories, Plays and Performances: A Preface. In D. Friedman (Ed.), *Still on the Corner and other postmodern politcal plays by Fred Newman* (pp. xii–xxii). New York: Castillo

Newman, F and Holzman, L. (1997). *The End of Knowing: A New Developmental Way of Learning*. London: Routledge.

Thomson, G. *Aeschylus and Athens*. London: Haskell House Publishers Ltd.

Vygotsky, L.S. (1978). *Mind in Society*. Cambridge, MA: Harvard University Press.

What Is to Be Dead?
(Philosophical Scenes)

FRED NEWMAN

Ever since Newman left academia some 30 years ago, philosophy, psychology, politics and theatre have been inseparable activities for him. In this, his mostly explicitly philosophical play, a series of autonomous philosophical dialogues gracefully unfold into a play with political and psychological impact. Yet, the activity of the conversation is what dominates, rather than the ideas separated (abstracted, alienated) from that activity. The failure of Soviet communism, the sorrow and pain of late-twentieth-century American racism, the limitations of cultural identity on human growth, and our contradictory "location" as human beings in both history and society are some of the political and psychological themes of the play (as they are of all of Newman's work).

The play is a contradiction; it contains characters who are and aren't, settings that are where they are and also are somewhere else, lively conversations and warm relationships soaked in a deep despair. It is also a prolonged asking of the question, "What is to be dead?" which attempts no answer.

Newman here explores and critiques the conceptions of self and identity through what Friedman (this volume) calls an approach to "character as other-than-a-specific-one." There is no explanation of (or fight about) how Sprintze could also be Mrs. Golub or how Pearlie could be Hinda. They just are. Rivin (a Jew) and Sam (an African American), whose stories and attitudes—separated by more than a hundred years—parallel each other so closely, may very well be not two *different people with the same history, but the same person with two different histories. This fluid, emergent, transforming vision of the (un)self is taken for granted as simply a part (albeit, not an insignificant part) of the play's larger philosophical investigations which ultimately question the identities of "dead" and "alive."—L. H.*

Characters

(in order of appearance)

SAM
RIVIN
PEARLIE
SPRINTZE
HINDA
MRS. GOLUB

Scene 1: Existentialism: Past and Present

The entire set is a dingy "underground"/shelter setting; the right half of the stage is a Russian turn-of-the-century scene, the left a contemporary inner-city scene. Each side has a small table. Seated at the Russian table is RIVIN (who calls himself Raskolnikov), the underground man; at the other table is SAM, a street person. Each has a stack of papers before him; presumably their own writings. They hold the papers (perhaps) as they "read" (speak) their own words.

RIVIN: I am a sick man . . . I am a wicked man. An unattractive man. I think my liver hurts. However, I don't know a fig about my sickness, and am not sure what it is that hurts me. I am not being treated and never have been, though I respect medicine and doctors. What's more, I am also superstitious in the extreme; well, at least enough to respect medicine. (I'm sufficiently educated not to be superstitious, but I am.) No, sir, I refuse to be treated out of wickedness. Now, you will certainly not be so good as to understand this. Well, sir, but I understand it. I will not, of course, be able to explain to you precisely who is going to suffer in this case from my wickedness; I know perfectly well that I will in no way "muck things up" for the doctors by not taking their treatment; I know better than anyone that by all this I am harming only myself and no one else. But still, if I don't get treated, it is out of wickedness. My liver hurts; well, then let it hurt even worse!

I've been living like this for a long time—about 20 years. I'm 40 now. I used to be in the civil service; I no longer am. I was a wicked official. I was rude, and took pleasure in it. After all, I didn't accept bribes, so I had to reward myself at least with that. (A bad witticism, but I won't cross it out. I wrote it thinking it would come out very witty; but now, seeing for myself that I simply had a vile wish to swagger—I purposely won't cross it out!) When petitioners would come for information to the desk where I sat—I'd gnash my teeth at them, and felt an inexhaustible delight when I managed to upset someone. I almost always managed. They were timid people for the most part: petitioners, you know. But among the fops there was one officer I especially could not stand. He simply refused to submit and kept rattling his sabre disgustingly. I was at war with him over that sabre for a year and a half. In the end, I prevailed. He stopped rattling. However, that was still in my youth. But do you know, gentlemen, what was the main point about my wickedness? The whole thing precisely was, the greatest nastiness precisely lay in my being shamefully conscious every moment, even in moments of the greatest bile, that I was not only not a wicked man but was not even an embittered man, that I was simply frightening sparrows in vain, and pleasing myself with it. I'm foaming at the mouth, but bring me some little doll, give me some tea with a bit of sugar, and maybe I'll calm down. I'll even wax tenderhearted, though afterward I'll certainly gnash my teeth at myself and suffer from insomnia for a few months out of shame. Such is my custom.

And I lied about myself just now when I said I was a wicked official. I lied out of wickedness. I was simply playing around both with the petitioners and with the officer, but as a matter of fact I was never able to become wicked. I was conscious every moment of so very many elements in myself most opposite to that. I felt them simply swarming in me, those opposite elements. I knew they had been swarming in me all my life, asking to be let go out of me, but I would not let them. I would not, I purposely would not let them out. They tormented me to the point of shame; they drove me to convulsions, and—finally I got sick of them, oh, how sick I got! But do you not perhaps think, gentlemen, that I am now repenting of something before you, that I am asking your forgiveness for something? . . . I'm sure you think so. . . . However, I assure you that it is all the same to me even if you do. . . . Not just wicked, no, I never even managed to become anything: neither wicked nor good, neither a scoundrel nor an honest man, neither a hero nor an insect. And now I am living out my life in my corner, taunting myself with the spiteful and utterly futile consolation that it is even impossible for an intelligent man seriously to become anything, and only fools become something. Yes, sir, an intelligent man of the 19th century must be and is morally obliged to be primarily a characterless being; and a man of character, an active figure—primarily a limited being. This is my 40-year-old conviction. I am now 40 years old, and, after all, 40 years—is a whole lifetime; after all, it's the most extreme old age. To live beyond 40 is indecent, banal, immoral! Who lives beyond 40—answer me sincerely, honestly? I'll tell you who does: fools and scoundrels do. I'll say it in the faces of all the elders, all these venerable elders, all these silver-haired and sweet-smelling elders! I'll say it in the whole world's face! I have the right to speak this way, because I myself will live to be 60. I'll live to be 70! I'll live to be 80! . . . Wait! Let me catch my breath.

You no doubt think, gentlemen, that I want to make you laugh? Here, too, you're mistaken. I am not at all such a jolly man as you think, or as you possibly think; if, however, irritated by all this chatter (and I already feel you are irritated), you decide to ask me: what precisely am I?—then I will answer you: I am one collegiate assessor. I served so as to have something to eat (but solely for that), and when last year one of my distant relations left me 6,000 rubles in his will, I resigned at once and settled into my corner. I lived in this corner before as well, but now I've settled into it. My room is wretched, bad, on the edge of the city. My servant is a village woman, old, wicked from stupidity, and always bad-smelling besides. I'm told that the Petersburg climate is beginning to do me harm, and that with my negligible means life in Petersburg is very expensive. I know all that, I know it better than all these experienced and most wise counsellors and waggers of heads. But I am staying in Petersburg; I will not leave Petersburg! I will not leave because . . .

Eh! But it's all completely the Same whether I leave or not.

But anyhow: what can a decent man speak about with the most pleasure?

Answer: about himself.

So then I , too, will speak about myself.

(Lights fade on Russian setting; come up on inner-city setting.)

SAM: I am a sick man . . . I am a wicked man. An unattractive man. I am sure I have AIDS. However, I'm not even sure what it is that hurts me. Y'know. I refuse to be treated—yeah, I refuse to be treated out of my wickedness. Yeah, I am a wicked man—a *homosexual*, a dope fiend, a nigger. Now I assume you liberals will not understand all of this; I assume you think I am "conveying the wrong message to others." But I am no message—I have no message—I send no message. My life, my sickness, my homosexuality, my Black ass, my AIDS is no damn message. Yeah. I know I am unattractive in this way. Ugly. Yes. I am ugly as sin. I like being ugly in your pretty and petty world.

I would like to tell you liberals, whether you do or do not wish to hear it, why I never managed to become even an insect. I have mostly wanted to be a roach—a cockroach. I have mostly wanted to die by being stepped on—from above. Squish. Then dead. Why? You ask why? You think it is because I wish to die quickly? To avoid pain? To avoid my wretchedness? Well, as usual, you are wrong. No. I wish to die like a cockroach so my death, my life, will have no meaning at all; will send no message. Ya see, even you animal-loving liberals—you whale lovers—show no concern for the roach. No pickets. You see no significance in the regular stomping out of roaches in the kitchens of our squalid homes. I want to die as a roach; squished out of existence in a moment, to deprive you of my havin' any significance, of my bein' a message. Yeah. I am a wicked man—a faggot, a nigger, a crack head, and I mean nothing—nothing at all. You will not "make something" of my life.

I have diabetes. I can barely walk. So I go to a clinic in Harlem near where I live. I call for an ambulette. I am told one is not available for 10 days. I say, "I need my shots." They say, "Ten days." Why, I ask? Why so long? They tell me, "The ambulettes go first to the AIDS patients." I will not tell them, "I have AIDS." Diabetes means less. I prefer it. I do not want to be your message, your meaning.

Now, you liberals, you readers of Dostoevsky, will call me a liar— what is your funny word?—disingenuous. *(Laughs.)* You'll say—*(in funny, white-sounding, high-pitched voice)* "He wants to be more significant than everyone else. He wants to be *especially* meaningful. That's what his denial, his desire to be a cockroach is really about." How clever you all are. How hip. How existential. Of course, you are right. I am really an egomaniac. I really think I am more significant than all of you and more significant than others with AIDS, other faggots, other dope fiends, other niggers. Yeah. You liberals got this one right. But so what? That's still not what you want me to mean. You don't want me to be too significant—just a little significant and, most importantly, to be *your* significance—to be significant for you or to you. So I aggravate you even if you are "on to me." For you cannot stand that I know that you are on to me. I have AIDS and it means nothing. Nothing at all. It don't mean shit. And you can't stand that I don't care 'cause you need me to care. Ya see the right-wingers don't care that I don't care. They don't care either. But you liberals got the carin' sickness. Shit. The carin' sickness is worse than AIDS. Kills more people. Got no cure either. But it don't make you ugly and it don't make YOU dead. But the carin' sickness killed more people than the plague. AIDS; AIDS ain't nothin' next to the carin' sickness. Say what, liberal? Oh yeah. I hear ya. Now you sayin' *(in liberal's voice)*,"Well you seem to have the caring sickness, too. You seem to care for us far too much." Yeah. I hear ya. This time you is partly right. I do cares for ya, liberal. But I don't pretend to care *about* ya. Dat's why y'all hate Farrakhan. And why ya hated Malcolm and Fanon. 'Cause they all said, "We don't care what you liberals think. We don't hate you . . . we even care *for* you . . . we just don't care about you. You don't mean nuthin' to us." And Farrakhan, hmm', he don't like me either. Why? 'Cause I don't care about nuthin'. He don't mean nuthin' to me either. And the Minister wants to kick my Black ass 'cause I don't care. But with all due respect, Mr. Farrakhan, I *don't* care. Funny thing, Mr. Farrakhan, you and the liberals, the white liberals you don't care about, *both* got the carin' sickness. Shit. I only got AIDS. I feel sorry for y'all but I don't care about you. I don't care about you and I don't care about me. But I don't care that I don't care. The right-wingers don't care outta hate; the liberals care for me out of guilt. Ya wonder why I'm not so high on white folks! That's one hell of a choice. Farrakhan cares *for* me outta "bow-tie" pride. But me, I just don't care. I don't even feel sorry for myself. I just don't care at all. Jesus, man, if I weren't a poor nigger and a faggot I'd be a goddamned existential hero! Who the fuck woulda believed there would be discrimination even in the "existential hero" business. *(Laughs into cough.)* The damned carin' disease adjusts everything. Even me. *(Pointing to RIVIN.)* He was never adjusted. Back then the world was too ugly, too despairing, too fearful to adjust to. So those poor folks, those poor Russians eventually made a goddamned revolution "to change the world." But only a fool tries to become something; only a fool—or an opportunist—tries to change the world. Nowadays we adjust to everything. No more fear, no more trembling, no more—what's the word—*angst*, no more revolution . . . just bein' adjusted. *(Laughs into coughing.)* I don't *wanna* be adjusted but I am. The damned carin' disease adjusts everything. *(Points to RIVIN.)* Back then the world was uncarin'. You could be an existential hero, a genuine madman. Back then AIDS woulda been a bona fide apocalypse; it could have been what ignited the goddamned Russian Revolution which, we all know, failed anyhow. But AIDS coulda been a first rate tragedy that moved fools to try to do something. Not now. No way. Nowadays— we adjust. But I don't wanna adjust; I don't want to be cared for; I don't want to be someone's message. What can a sick and wretched man do in such a well-adjusted world? He can merely get on with it, I guess. He has no meaning. What can a decent man talk about? Nothing. Not even himself. He can simply move from moment to moment. Life is meaningless. Why? Because we have all adjusted.

And, I'm sick of it. But I am adjusted, too. You liberals won the day.
Now the political reactionaries are taking over 'cause you liberals
won and anything goes. We will adjust to that, too, I guess. Meanin'
don't mean a damned thing no more.

SCENE 2: IDENTITY

*A modest working-class contemporary inner-city apartment, SAM'S sister
PEARLIE'S home; decorated with nationalist icons; pictures, etc. PEARLIE
is sitting on a couch reading. There is a knock at the door. She opens the
door and SAM stands in the doorway totally disheveled.*

SAM: Hey, Pearlie. How ya doing, Babe? *(Pause.)* Oh, hey, I'm sorry,
kid. It ain't Pearlie no more, right? What's it now, sis? Teluma? Is
that it? Teluma. I like that new name. You say it's African, huh.
Teluma. Shit. I got me a damned sister named Teluma. How ya
doin', T-E-L-U-M-A? *(Reaches to kiss her; she pulls away.)*
PEARLIE: You smell like shit. When'd you last take a shower?
SAM: Hey, I don't want no shower, T-E-L-U-M-A.
PEARLIE: It's TAKUMA . . . and you know it . . . and you STINK. Go
take a goddamned shower, brother.
SAM: TAKUMA! Oh yeah. Yeah, I forgot . . . really I did, Pearlie. Those
African names is hard, y'know. Dey sound funny. TAKUMA. I like
it, baby sister. It's cool, TAKUMA. Sounds goddamned authentic,
y'know.
PEARLIE: It was our great grandmother's name, big brother . . . now get
your Black ass cleaned up or get the fuck outta my house. *(Walks
stage left and gets a big black towel that she throws at SAM.)*
SAM: You gonna throw out your big brother if'n he don't take no shower? That's the kinda sister you gonna be? Dat how you treat a sick
African brother? *(Mocking.)* Is you anti-gay, Pearlie . . . oh, I'm
sorry, TAKUMA.
PEARLIE: No, I ain't anti-gay, I'm anti-dirt. *(Pause. Looks at him more
tenderly. Sighs.)* How are ya feelin' anyway? You been in the hospi-
tal again? How's ya T-count? You heard a' this new drug? I read
about it in the *City Sun.* How the hell are ya, man? You look like shit

warmed over. Go take a goddamned shower and I'll fix ya some breakfast. *(Walks over to closet and gets a pair of her sweats; throws them at him.)* Here's a pair of my sweats. Go shower and put 'em on. God, you stink bad.

(SAM walks slowly to offstage bathroom; PEARLIE goes to onstage kitchen to get pan, etc. She turns on the radio, tuned to a Black station. Shower water sound begins; blackout. After 25 seconds, lights up with wet-haired SAM at kitchen table in sweats and PEARLIE serving him eggs and toast.)

SAM: What you been up to, Pearlie? What you tryin' to be nowadays?

PEARLIE: Listen, Sam, I'm just trying to be who I really am . . . an African woman.

SAM: Now, how come you work so hard at tryin' to be who you really is? And why are you so damned proud to be who you simply is? I'd think it would make more sense to be proud of who in the hell you aren't. Y'know. What you made of yourself. Yeah, Pearlie, what d'you thinka that?

PEARLIE: I think that's a lot of your bullshit white philosophy. But no amount of that shit can cover up your Black ass, my brother. You still sleepin' on those damned streets 'cause you a Black man in racist America.

SAM: Now wait a minute, Pearlie . . .

PEARLIE: TAKUMA!

(Sam stares at her.)

SAM: . . . I thought I was on those streets because I'm a lazy good for nothing. Ain't that what you been tellin' me for 10 years now, Pearlie?

PEARLIE: Yeah, my brother, but lazy good for nothin' *white* folks ain't where you are.

SAM: Oh, but they are, Pearlie. They are on the streets. We is knockin' on death's door, my sister. And there ain't no goddamned difference between dead Black and dead white. Pearlie, we all smell the same when we're dead. And as me and those ugly *white* faggots get closer we smell more and more alike. We all stink like shit. Ya see, Pearlie, it don't mean shit when you about to become shit. No. I ain't got no identity, baby. I don't want no identity. This is a kinda freedom I got now, Pearlie. Y'all gotta adjust to me.

PEARLIE: Maybe so, Sam. But for those of us still livin' ya gotta decide who y'are. And I'm an African . . . TAKUMA, an African woman. Y'know Sam, in a certain way I almost agree with you. I mean if ya look forward sometimes there ain't nothin' to see but death. So I choose to look backward to where I come from—and I come from Africa, Sam. I come from Africa. We all eventually go back to the earth, Sam. So it's where we come from that counts.

SAM: Hey, I hear ya, Pearlie—TAKUMA *(said for the first time almost seriously)*—I hear ya, sister. But nuthin' counts. And that's the good news. We're a funny kind of animal, Pearlie. Even before we got AIDS; even before we got the liberal carin' sickness; from almost the very beginnin' us crazy humans done had the countin' disease. That's why I want to be a roach, sister. Ya see, in a way, I wanna go back to my roots, too. I wanna go back to not countin', Pearlie. Does that make any sense to ya?

(PEARLIE is crying; she reaches out for SAM'S hand.)

PEARLIE: *(Sadly and passionately)* Ya counts to me, Sam; ya counts to me.

SAM: I know, my little sister. I know, Pearlie. And it makes me feel bad and sad 'cause I'm gonna be dead in a little bit. (*Stands and kills a roach on the floor by stomping on it. They both freeze, staring at each other.)*

PEARLIE: *(Breaks the sad silence)* I gotta go to a meetin', Sam. We're havin' a big welcome back from Africa celebration for Minister Farrakhan, next month. You gonna hang around here for a while?

(SAM nods yes.)

SAM: My social worker might be comin' over to give me a check.

PEARLIE: Mrs. Golub?

SAM: Yeah, I told her I'd be here. Y'mind, Pearlie? *(PEARLIE shakes her head.)* I could meet her downstairs in the streets.

PEARLIE: I don't mind, Sam. Stay as long as ya like. When you leave, just close the door—it'll lock by itself. *(Starts toward the door; comes back and kisses SAM.)* Now, you take care, Sam. Take care.

SAM: I'm good, Takuma. I'm good. *(Sinks into the couch as PEARLIE exits.)*

SCENE 3: MEANINGLESSNESS

1903 in St. Petersburg, the modest apartment of RIVIN'S sister SPRINTZE, filled with books and Bolshevik icons. There is a knock on the door. It's RIVIN (who calls himself Raskolnikov). Sprintze waits for the correct—coded—knock. None comes. RIVIN keeps knocking. She goes to the door and whispers angrily.

SPRINTZE: Who's there? Who is it?

RIVIN: It's Raskolnikov. Open up. It's your brother Rivin. It's not the police. Open up, Sprintze. Goddamn it . . . open up.

(SPRINTZE opens the door and lets RIVIN in.)

SPRINTZE: *(Whispers)* What are you doing here?

RIVIN: I don't know. I am here.

SPRINTZE: It's dangerous for me. Don't you care?

RIVIN: What are you doing now? Why is it dangerous?

SPRINTZE: These are revolutionary times. You know that. But you don't care about me. You don't care about anything or anyone except yourself.

RIVIN: I do not care about myself. I care about nothing. Everything is meaningless. Nothing can be done, Sprintze, nothing can be done. Why do you risk your life? The Czar is no good. But you people, you socialists, you revolutionaries are no better. You are no better; I am no better. Chernyshevsky was a fool; spending 25 years in Siberia for writing an awful novel. A fool. Tales about new people. What new people? He was a fool. Then your hero Lenin writes an even more awful book with the same stupid title. *What is to be Done?* Nothing. Nothing is to be done. Only a fool thinks he can do something. Only a fool thinks he can be something or someone.

SPRINTZE: Why are you here? What do you want? For 10 years now I have listened to your dead talk; your Dostoevskian despair, your nihilistic nonsense. You have wasted your brilliant mind, your genius, on self-serving empty phrases. *You* can do nothing. Lenin and the Russian masses, the proletariat and the peasantry can do much. And they will. And Lenin will lead them. And you . . . you will still be underground pretending to see the future when, in fact, you are too dead to even see the present. *You* are a fool, Rivin or Raskolnikov—as you stupidly call yourself—pretending to be a philosopher and wasting your life.

RIVIN: No, Sprintze. We are *all* wasting our lives—our wretched lives. We are pretenders—the pretending species. We cannot stop pretending. We are doomed, all of us, to eternal pretense. No insect ever declares its own authenticity. Only us phonies, us fools, us pretenders, do that. Your Lenin might well succeed one day. After all, Russia is a cesspool; the Czar and his ministers are madmen. The Queen and her mystical lover, Rasputin, are more stupid than can be imagined even in a world more imbecilic than can be believed. No. Your Vladimir Ilyich Lenin might succeed. Maybe one day Russia, the darkest of all countries, will become the enlightened, socialist state that you dream of, my dearest sister Sprintze. But it will grow dark again. Everything grows dark again. Socialism will fare no better than Moses or Jesus or Mohammed. It will be corrupted because we are a corruption—pretending eternally that we can be other than a corruption. Socialism, Sprintze, is already—here in its earliest moments—as much a "commodified product" as anything your Mr. Marx writes of in his pompous puffery about Kapital. Progress! Historical progress! *(Laughs.)* There is no progress. Not for us. Not for pretenders like us.

SPRINTZE: Well, then are these words you tell me also pretense?

RIVIN: Of course they are. It is you who insists I am a genius. I am just another man making noises, Sprintze. Another fool. More a fool than others, thinking, perhaps, that my passion in seeing what a fool I am makes me less a fool. But, of course, it doesn't. Maybe they will make statues of Lenin one day. And then, someday, they too will crumble and everyone will rejoice like the fools that we are. *(Laughs.)* Heh, heh. Don't let them frighten you, Sprintze. Everything bad that could happen has already happened. We have nothing to lose . . . only because we have nothing to gain.

SPRINTZE: *(Very angry and confrontational)* I think you are crazy . . . Rivin. A genius, no doubt. And, as well, a fool. Indeed, a philosophical fool. For even if everything you say is true we must still figure out what is to be done. We must still figure out—so long as we have chosen to stay alive and *obviously* both you AND me have made that choice—we must figure out what to do given this dreadful picture you so beautifully paint. If there is nothing to choose between your ceaseless philosophizing and my ceaseless politicizing then so be it. LET'S NOT CHOOSE BETWEEN DIFFERENT VIEWS OF THE WORLD. Perhaps there are no real choices, no better views. They are all, let us agree, phony. Then we must *still* consider the difference between your phony choices, your view and my phony choices, my phony view. *(Pause.)* How easy it is to be negative—critical and philosophically correct. How easy to call Lenin just another phony ideologue. Oh yes. You are right, Rivin. Ideology oversimplifies life and your brilliant negativism exposes the limits of ideology. But no one—no one—is guided by your stupid philosophical truth; your negative insights. Ideology over-simplifies, distorts. Yes, I understand. But we must have ideology to move ahead. And socialism, social democracy, Lenin is our best ideological bet, my brilliant brother, Rivin, my underground man "Raskolnikov."

RIVIN: *(Breathing heavily)* You are a very bright woman, Sprintze . . . very intelligent. For you have identified a real meaning for the stupid question: what is to be done? What does it mean? It means this: given that we foolish humans seemingly cannot go forward without ideology and that ideology so distorts the human situation then how can we go forward without the ideology ultimately destroying us?

(Long pause.)

SPRINTZE: I believe in Lenin.

RIVIN: I envy you. I know him to be a fool.

SPRINTZE: Rivin, enough already. You must rest. You'll stay a few days? You do not look well. How is your liver?

RIVIN: I am sick . . . as always. *(He is breathing heavily.)*

SPRINTZE: We have talked too much.

RIVIN: No. No, dearest Sprintze. You are the only one I can talk to anymore.

SPRINTZE: I must go to a cell meeting. Here is the knock *(raps 1,2,3,— 4)*. Do not let anyone in unless they knock properly.

RIVIN: You let me in.

SPRINTZE: I am your sister. You are my brother.

RIVIN: *(Laughs)* I would have thought that meant nothing to either of us.

SPRINTZE: *(Laughs)* We are silly fools. On this, perhaps, we agree. *(Puts on her coat; RIVIN lies down tiredly on couch. She kisses his fore-head.)* Rest, Rivin, rest. *(Exits.)*

SCENE 4: BEING AND NOTHINGNESS

One hour later. RIVIN is still asleep. There is a "proper" knock on the door; RIVIN does not move. Then a louder knock; two times more. Finally RIVIN awakens, goes to the door and opens it. HINDA (played by the actress playing PEARLIE), an old family friend, once an orthodox Jew, now a Bundist, stands at the door.

HINDA: Rivin? *(With wonder.)* What are you doing here?

RIVIN: Hinda? Is it really you? I haven't seen you in years. Come in. Come in. *(She enters.)* I was just visiting Sprintze. She went off to *(whispers half mockingly)* one of her meetings—you know. I was very tired and she urged me to stay and rest for a while. I fell asleep. *(They stare.)* Do you want something? A glass of wine? *(Looks for wine.)* Where does she keep wine? *(HINDA finds it.)* Where are glasses? *(HINDA finds them; RIVIN pours; they stare.)* What have you been doing? Are you still in school? Look at you, Hinda, you're all grown-up.

HINDA: I finished school over five years ago, Rivin.

RIVIN: You did good? *(Laughs.)* Of course you did. You were always a wonderful student. *(Pause.)* You are married?

HINDA: No.

RIVIN: You are political . . . like, uh, Sprintze.

HINDA: I am political but not like Sprintze. I am a socialist but not a social democrat. I am with the Jewish Bund.

RIVIN: You are still orthodox?

HINDA: No. My family is dead. I am a socialist but still very much a Jew. I could never give that up, Rivin. *(Pause.)* Sprintze tells me you have gone underground; that you have abandoned everything. You do not look well. You have no color. Your old liver ailment is still with you?

RIVIN: I'm afraid so, Hinda. I am sick and . . . yes, I am also wretched. I am underground but unlike Sprintze I have no purpose for being so. I have no purpose at all.

HINDA: You are still a Jew.

RIVIN: I am not a Jew. I am still persecuted like one, but I am not a Jew anymore. I have neither a history nor a future, Hinda. I live for nothing for there is nothing to live for. Sprintze and I spoke of Lenin's new book, *What is to be Done?* A stupid book named after Chernyshevsky's silly novel. For me there is nothing to be done. I merely exist.

HINDA: When we were young together your parents were so wonderful and optimistic. Every one of us children envied you and Sprintze because your mother and father were so alive, so funny, so warm, so caring. And you, Rivin, you were the oldest boy in our crowd; so brilliant, so talented. You played music. You wrote poetry. You read Talmud. I looked up to you. No! I adored you. How could this have happened? What happened to you, Rivin?

RIVIN: *(Walks away a little)* It's good to see you, Hinda. I do not wish to fight with you. But for me—for me, the question is, how come nothing has happened to you? Why are you—and Sprintze—still children—beautiful children dreaming hopefully to change the world, socialists of varying stripes but still infants pretending that you can make a better world; searching to discover what is to be done? *(Smirks.)* Are you also like Sprintze a lover of Lenin?

HINDA: No. I am not. In fact, Mr. Lenin is causing me and the Bund much grief these days. He is insisting that we all must join the RSDLP—you know, *his* social democratic party. He says we can go no further together in coalition. He says there must be a centralized cadre; a single fist and a single mind—and, of course, it is his. And, as well, he is causing grief for me and Sprintze, our friendship. She deeply admires him and respects him—and follows him. I think he is clever and that he has suffered—his brother was murdered by the Czar, you know—but I am wary of him and his politics. He is an atheist. I am a Jew.

RIVIN: Why are you still a Jew? What does it mean that you are a Jew?

HINDA: It's where I come from, Rivin. Without it, I mean nothing. My hopes are for the future. But me, the one who hopes, comes from the past. And it is a Jewish past, a Jewish history. Without it, I am like you; nothing.

RIVIN: *(Ever so slightly critical; almost angry)* And so you *use* being a Jew to keep you from seeing that you are nothing? We are all noth-ing, Hinda. Perhaps we Jews are "the chosen" nothing. You, no doubt, are as committed to being chosen as *(pause)* . . . Mr. Lenin is. He also believes, I assure you, that he has been chosen to lead the starving and struggling masses of the Russian people out of captiv-ity; out of bondage. Your pharaoh is his Czar. Your Moses is his Marx. Your phony Talmud is his phony "scientific socialism." Your god is his godlessness. There is no difference, dearest Hinda. You do not wish to follow him because you already follow another Man—equally tight-fisted and tight of mind. But there is no one to follow. We are quite alone, Hinda. And there is no place to go. So there is no need to have come from anywhere. Your Jewishness is a toy that you will not let go of.

HINDA: And what of *your* past? What have you done with it? This rebel-lion of yours seems to me as authoritarian as Lenin's. He selects which parts of history he is interested in; you deny it all. His follow-ers heed everything he says; yours too. Only he has many followers. You have only one; *you.* But the dogmatism is the same, Rivin, you are an anti-Leninist—but you are much like Lenin; a man too focused on himself.

RIVIN: *(Laughs)* You are right. You're right. But I do not impose me or, for that matter, anybody else, on others. I do not believe in gods precisely because I know how easy it is to be one. A socialist Jew, Hinda, whatever could that mean? How could so brilliant a woman as you be a socialist Jew?

HINDA: Jewishness is my connection to the past; socialism my hope for the future. Together they define me; not unconflictedly, Rivin. But I think I tolerate conflict better than you. Even as a young man you craved consistency. Apparently you have found it—even if you have given up your life to do so.

RIVIN: And where is the woman, Hinda? Where is the woman in you— the socialist part or the Jewish part?

(Pause.)

HINDA: Sprintze and I are lovers. *(Long silence.)* Does that matter to you, Rivin?

RIVIN: I think it might, Hinda. I think it just might.

HINDA: I'm glad. I'm glad something matters to you. How does it matter?

RIVIN: I feel old feelings and old judgments. This news raises for me a kind of moral response that I have not felt in years; a repulsion that is utterly foreign to my current life. I suddenly have pictures in my mind of the two of you naked together and I am at once vaguely excited and nauseated by them. I am surprised. And I am surprised that I am surprised. Nothing has surprised me in a decade.

(The door opens, SPRINTZE enters; she pauses at the doorway; looks at HINDA who nods almost imperceptibly. She goes to HINDA and they embrace.)

RIVIN: I think I am jealous . . . But I will get over it.

SPRINTZE: *(Lovingly)* How are you, Hinda?

HINDA: I am good. Rivin and I have been, uh, "catching up."

SPRINTZE: I met Lenin today—personally—for the first time. Just an hour ago I was talking with him. His eyes looked at me and beyond me at the Same time. He is a strange looking man. One of those people who looks like he is supposed to look. *(Laughs quietly.)* I asked him, Hinda, why he feels so strongly that the Jewish socialists—the Bundists—must abandon their Jewishness. He said we must all give up our pasts if we are to truly create a new human being—a socialist human being. He said it is not negating your past but fully using it to create something qualitatively new. When he said this his eyes looked sad, and I trusted him.

HINDA: I don't think I can give up my Jewishness.

RIVIN: But you have given up your womanliness.

SPRINTZE: *(Defensively)* But it is not the same.

HINDA: No, Sprintze. Rivin is right. It is the same. I must live with this inconsistency. My love for you is greater than my love for socialism. In any event I can have both. But my love for socialism is not as powerful as my Judaism. I don't know why. Perhaps it is spiritual; perhaps cultural. I don't know.

RIVIN: Judaism is your man, Hinda. Don't you see? And socialism is just another man—at that, a Christian man. You will not give up your man. Marx will not replace Moses. But for me, I see no difference between them; or Lenin or Christ. Yes. I am momentarily jealous of you and Sprintze. But I feel nothing for those living and dead phallic icons. Get what you can now, Sprintze, get what you can now out of his sad eyes. Soon enough, I fear, they will turn colder and colder and his successor, I suspect, will have no eyes at all . . . . *(Pause.)* I cannot stay. I must go. Maybe I will see you both again. Maybe not.

(Rivin puts on his coat. The three embrace)

SCENE 5: SEX AND DEATH

PEARLIE'S apartment in Harlem, 1996. SAM is back in his old, dirty clothes. He is folding PEARLIE'S sweats and putting them neatly on a chair. There is a knock on the door. SAM opens the door. Enter MRS. GOLUB (played by the actress playing SPRINTZE), SAM's social worker.

SAM: Mrs. Golub. Good to see ya. I was just gettin' ready to leave.

Come on in.

MRS. GOLUB: Hello, Sam. How are you doing?

SAM: Oh, I'm doin' okay, Mrs. Golub. Can't complain. Nobody really cares anyway . . . y'know.

MRS. GOLUB: Now let's not get into that conversation again, Sam. I never know whether you think people care too much or too little.

SAM: Both, Mrs. Golub, both. *(Laughs.)*

MRS. GOLUB: How's Takuma . . . I mean Pearlie, doing?

SAM: Oh, she's okay. She's off at a Farrakhan meeting. She'll be back in a little while. Maybe you'll catch her.

MRS. GOLUB: Farrakhan's been getting an awful lot of publicity lately, Sam. What do you think of him these days?

SAM: Well . . . I respect him. But I think he's too much like all you white liberals—don't be offended, Mrs. Golub—he's got his own version of the carin' sickness—not to mention the countin' sickness. He cares too much and he thinks things count too much, for my blood—sick as it is. But he's okay. He's doin' his thing. A lot of Black folks like him.

MRS. GOLUB: Well, not many white folks like him, Sam.

SAM: Well, Mrs. G, white folks didn't create him to like him.

MRS. GOLUB: What's that supposed to mean, Sam?

SAM: You know, Mrs. G, the white folks—most particularly the liberals—needed a Black man they could justifiably hate. I mean *(sarcastically)* after all the liberals have done for us in the '60s, they was pissed off when some of us niggers started doin' "our own thing." Thought we was ungrateful, uppity. But it wouldn't do to hate all of us or even most of us—wasn't politically correct for a liberal to be a racist—so they had to create a popular icon who they could justify hatin'. I mean Farrakhan was a small-time preacher before the liberals got ahold of him. And the more the liberals hated him the more Black folks liked him. Now the liberals care too much but they ain't dummies. So they musta known that the more they was hatin' him, the more popular he was becomin'. Yeah. They was makin' him that way; popular and okay to hate. Those liberals are clever. A liberal can get away with hatin' Farrakhan.

MRS. GOLUB: *(Somewhat condescendingly)* Now, Sam, don't you think
that's a little paranoid? A little conspiratorial?

SAM: No. No, Mrs. Golub, I don't. Whenever you liberals don't like
something or don't agree with something, you call it conspiratorial.
That's clever, too. I'm impressed. Actually it's the liberals and Mr.
Farrakhan who do that about the best. I'm tellin' ya. I'm tellin' ya,
white liberals and Farrakhan are very much the same. That's probably part of why they hate each other so much. But no, I ain't paranoid, Mrs. Golub. I'm a sick and dying man. I got AIDS. But I
don't care about the Minister a whole lot more than I care about
liberals . . . *(charmingly)* present company excluded.

MRS. GOLUB: Now, Sam, I know you hate me, too. *(Little laugh.)*

SAM: Not at all, Mrs. Golub. I don't hate you at all. *(Pause.)* You a
socialist. Right, Mrs. Golub?

MRS. GOLUB: Yes, I am, Sam; a democratic socialist.

SAM: Oh, yeah, you mean you're not a communist.

MRS. GOLUB: That's right, Sam. My folks were communists, but they
left the party when Stalin made his deal with Hitler in the late thir-
ties.

SAM: Then you must know somethin' about this demonization business
we was jest talkin' about. That's what the old social dems—really
they was liberals—did with Lenin. The turned him into a demon so
they could hate him while they abandoned socialism. Now you
know that began long before Stalin took over. It's the liberal social
dems that made Lenin and communism into a dirty word long
before the commies went really nasty. Now you must know all this,
Mrs. Golub. You're an old leftist. *(MRS. GOLUB nods.)* Actually, old
Joe Stalin—miserable fuck that he was, pardon my language, Mrs.
Golub—was just the sick child of this Lenin demonization business. You white folks better watch out for Farrakhan's successor.
Someday you all gonna wish old Farrakhan was back. I won't be
around to see it. But it'll be funny as hell. Shit. *(Laughs somewhat
maniacally into a heavy cough.)*

MRS. GOLUB: *(Concerned)* You okay, Sam? We've been talkin' too
much. *(SAM continues to cough. Lies down on couch.)* You want

some water, Sam? Are you okay? *(SAM'S coughing grows more violent. He is becoming sicker. MRS. GOLUB is getting more and more nervous. She is leaning over him on her knees.)* Sam, speak to me, speak to me!

SAM: *(Barely audible and coughing)* I think . . . I think I'm dyin', Mrs. Golub. I think I'm dyin'.

MRS. GOLUB: Let me call a doctor, Sam. *(Moves to get up; he grabs her arm.)*

SAM: No. No doctor. Mrs. Golub. No doctor. No treatment. If I'm dyin', I'm dyin'. *(Pause.)* Maybe I'm not. I don't see my life flashin' before me. So maybe I'm not dyin'! Actually . . . man, this is weird . . . I got a hard-on a mile long—hard as stone. My dick ain't been this big in years. And I ain't been turned on by no woman for decades. This is fuckin' weird, Mrs. Golub.

MRS. GOLUB: *(Looks hard and incredulously at SAM'S crotch)* Sam, this is crazy. This is crazy.

SAM: *(Desperately)* Gimme a blow job, or a hand job, Mrs. G. It's a dyin' man's last request.

MRS. GOLUB: Sam, that's insane. I can't give you no . . . uh, blow job. Are you crazy? You got AIDS. I can't do it, Sam.

(Sam coughs intensely.)

SAM: Please, Mrs. Golub. I ain't never asked you for nothin' like this before and I'll never ask you for nuthin' again. Just touch my dick some way or another. Please, Mrs. Golub. Please.

(She slowly places her hand on his pants, his crotch. SAM'S coughing changes to gradual moaning. She bends over and puts her face [mouth] on SAM'S penis. He groans more and more. Suddenly the door opens and there stands PEARLIE. She sees MRS. GOLUB "down on" SAM.)

PEARLIE: Sprintzy . . . What the hell's going on?

(MRS. GOLUB stands up, humiliated. SAM turns over on the couch.)

MRS. GOLUB: Takuma . . . uh, Pearlie . . . uh, Hindy . . . Hindy . . . uh . . . shit . . . I thought he was dyin' . . . oh God . . . he got . . . uh . . . very

aroused . . . uh . . . very hard . . . and, uh . . . he asked me to touch
him . . . um . . . I thought he was dyin' . . . oh, shit . . . I'm sorry,
Pearlie . . . uh, Hindy. *(Moves to embrace PEARLIE.)*
PEARLIE: That's okay, Sprintzy. That's okay. Don't be so upset. Don't be
so upset. It's no big deal. *(MRS. GOLUB cries hysterically; PEARLIE
comforts her saying "Sprintzy" again and again. Then she looks
up.)* How are you, Sam? You okay?
SAM: I'm okay, Pearlie. I don't think I'm dyin' just yet. I'm okay.
(Pause.) Who's Sprintzy, who's Hindy? How come you call Golub
Sprintzy? And how come she's callin' you Hindy?
PEARLIE: She and I been lovers for years.
SAM: *(Incredulous, disbelieving)* SHIT. And you never told me!
Goddamn. My sister and my social worker been sleepin' together
for years and no one ever told me. Goddamn it.
PEARLIE: Well, it's nice to see there's somethin' you care about, Sam.
SAM: *(To MRS. GOLUB)* Ain't this some violation of social work ethics,
Mrs. Golub?
PEARLIE: Sam . . . the woman was just givin' you a blow job. And you
think us bein' lovers is unethical. Shit. Men.
MRS. GOLUB: Besides, Sam, my personal life ain't none of your damned
business.
SAM: *(Standing)* Well, she's my sister.
PEARLIE: Would you two cut it out.
SAM: *(Shakes his head, sort of agreeing with PEARLIE)* How long you
been together?
MRS. GOLUB: Let's see . . . almost 100 years now. Ain't that right,
Takuma . . . Hindy?
PEARLIE: Yeah, Sprintzy, I think we got an anniversary comin' up. Yeah.
I think we slept together for the first time in the late summer, 1896.
In St. Petersburg.
SAM: What in the hell you two talkin' about? Are you crazy or some-
thin'? Eighteen ninety-six? Neither of you were alive in 1896.
What's wrong with you two?
PEARLIE: What in the hell you know about bein' alive, Sam? You ain't
been alive for years.

MRS. GOLUB: And what do you know about being dead, Sam? Nothin'. Not a damn thing.

PEARLIE: And what do you know about the difference between dead and alive? Zip. Sam, you don't know shit about this stuff.

(Pause.)

SAM: *(Incredulous)* So are you all dead or alive? What are you sayin'? Am I dead or am I alive? Or am I dreamin'?

PEARLIE: Y'know, Sam, there ain't so big a difference between dead and alive as most people make out. Dyin' simply gets ya back to where you was before you was born. Y'ain't here no more. But then again even when you're alive y'ain't a lot a places. You're only where you are. Y'know what I mean, Sam?

SAM: But people don't live forever, Pearlie.

PEARLIE: But people do *live and die forever*. Now don't they?

SAM: What you mean, Pearlie?

MRS. GOLUB: Sam, how come you've suddenly become so unphilo-sophical?

PEARLIE: *(Laughs)* Yeah, Sam, how come? The question we is askin' . . . the topic we is talkin' about is what is to be dead? Wittgenstein, that white philosopher you like so much, said, "The best thing about dyin' is that we don't live through it." Smart for a white guy, I think.

SAM: So, you two sayin' you been together since 1896? Dat's what you're tellin' me?

MRS. GOLUB: Yeah. That's what we're tellin' ya. I mean Takuma and I have our differences. But who doesn't?

SAM: You two are crazy, ain't ya?

PEARLIE: No crazier than you, Sam. No crazier than you. You the only one around here allowed to be crazy, Sam?

SAM: TAKUMA. Hmm. My sister TAKUMA.

SCENE 6: POSTMODERNISM

The setting uses the elements from the Scene 1 set, modified to create a gay club. SAM and RIVIN are standing at the bar. They have obviously "just met." SAM and RIVIN are slightly better dressed.

SAM: You come here often? I don't think I've ever seen ya before.

RIVIN: No. I don't think I've ever been here before.

SAM: You sick?

RIVIN: Yeah. My T-count's pretty damn low. You?

SAM: Fer sure. Been four years now. Where you from?

RIVIN: Originally from Russia. Now I live with my sister in Brighton Beach. How about you?

SAM: Well, I'm on the streets a lot. Shelter sometimes. Every now and again I stay with my sister in Harlem. Y'wanna dance?

RIVIN: Sure.

(They move to the dance floor and begin dancing.)

SAM: What's Russia like?

RIVIN: Corrupt and crazy. Everything has fallen apart. Nationalists, communists, liberals. They all stink. Brighton Beach is better.

SAM: Lotsa queers?

RIVIN: Yeah. In Russia and in Brighton Beach. Is Harlem as scary as they say? I've never been there.

SAM: About the same as a lot of places. A little rough sometimes, especially for a faggot. *(Pause.)* Can I ask you somethin' personal. I mean I don't usually ask this kinda stuff when I'm pickin' someone up, but . . . uh . . . .

RIVIN: Go ahead. No problem.

SAM: Well . . . how old are you?

RIVIN: Let's see . . . I'll be 121 in June.

(SAM stops dancing. They stare at each other.)

SAM: One hundred and twenty-one?

RIVIN: Yes. In June. June 12th.

SAM: How come you ain't dead?

RIVIN: I guess I will be soon . . . unless they got a cure ready for production.

SAM: No, motherfucker. I ain't talkin' about AIDS. I'm talkin' about 121. You don't look a day over 40. No one lives to 121. What's your fuckin' sister's name, brother?

RIVIN: What are you so crazy about?

SAM: What's her name?

RIVIN: Her name is Sprintze.

SAM: She a lesbo?

RIVIN: Yes. How did you know?

SAM: She got a lover named Pearlie . . . or Hindy?

RIVIN: Sure. Takuma's her new name. You know them?

SAM: Pearlie's my sister. Takuma's my sister.

RIVIN: No shit.

SAM: Your sister's a social worker?

RIVIN: Yeah.

SAM: She's my social worker.

RIVIN: Hmm. That's incredible. She used to be straight. She was married for years to a guy named Charlie . . .

SAM: Golub.

RIVIN: Yeah. That's right.

SAM: What is to be dead?

RIVIN: Oh, I guess it's kinda like before you was born. You just aren't *here* anymore.

SAM: Are you dead?

RIVIN: I think so.

SAM: But you are *here*.

RIVIN: I used to be there. That's where *here* used to be.

SAM: Did I know you back then?

RIVIN: Were you there?

SAM: No.

RIVIN: Then I guess not.

SAM: When did you die?

RIVIN: I don't remember.

SAM: You died of AIDS?

RIVIN: No. I died when my liver stopped working. There was no AIDS then. This time I think I'll die of AIDS.

SAM: You mean we die more than once?

RIVIN: Unless we're Christ, we do.

SAM: But we remember who we were?

RIVIN: Some people do.

SAM: I can't remember being anyone else.

RIVIN: Maybe you weren't. Maybe you just can't remember. We all forget things sometimes.

SAM: This is the craziest stuff I ever heard in my life.

RIVIN: I heard crazier . . . *(pause.)* Sam is your name?

SAM: Yeah. And yours . . . how d'ya say it again?

RIVIN: Rivin.

SAM: Rivin.

RIVIN: You got it.

SAM: Rivin, now that you . . . uh, . . . believe all this stuff about dyin' . . . does it change your . . . uh . . . attitude toward life?

RIVIN: Oh, yeah. I used to think that nothing meant anything. Now I don't think about those kinds of things. I used to be an underground man and think that nothing could be done. Now I don't think about those kinds of things. I used to be sick and wretched. Now I am just sick . . . Do you want to dance more?

(SAM looks hard at RIVIN.)

SAM: Yes.

(They dance slowly and sexually as lights fade.)

Contributors

Dan Friedman is one of the founders of the Castillo Theatre in New York City and has been Castillo's dramaturg since 1989. A theatre historian, playwright and journalist, Friedman has been involved for nearly 30 years with political and community-based theatres, including the New York Street Theatre Caravan, the Theatre Collective, and Workers' Stage. He is co-editor with Bruce McConachie of *Theatre for Working Class Audiences in the United States: 1830-1980* and editor of the 1998 *Still on the Corner and Other Postmodern Political Plays* by Fred Newman.

Kenneth Gergen is professor of psychology at Swathmore College in Swathmore, PA. His recent books include *Realities and Relationships: Soundings in Social Constructionism, The Saturated Self* and *Relational Responsibility: Resources for Sustainable Dialogue* (with Sheila McNamee), and as co-editor, *Therapy as Social Construction* and *Historical Dimensions of Psychological Discourse.* Gergen is also editor (with John Shotter) of the Sage series *Inquiries in Social Construction.*

Lois Holzman is director of educational programs, East Side Institute for Short Term Psychotherapy and director, Center for Developmental Learning, New York City. She taught human development and educational studies at Empire State College, State University of New York and has been researcher and program consultant for the Community Literacy Research Project, Inc. She is the author of

Schools for Growth: Radical Alternatives to Current Educational Models; and co-author with Fred Newman of *Lev Vygotsky: Revolutionary Scientist*; *Unscientific Psychology: A Cultural-Performatory Approach to Understanding Human Life* and *The End of Knowing: A New Developmental Way of Learning.*

Fred Newman is director of training, East Side Institute for Short Term Psychotherapy and artistic director, Castillo Theatre, New York City. He is author of *The Myth of Psychology*; *Let's Develop: A Guide to Continuous Personal Growth*; *Performance of a Lifetime: A Practical-Philosophical Guide to the Joyous Life*; and co-author with Lois Holzman of *Lev Vygotsky: Revolutionary Scientist*; *Unscientific Psychology: A Cultural-Performatory Approach to Understanding Human Life* and *The End of Knowing: A New Developmental Way of Learning.* Newman is also the author of 23 plays, including three "psychology plays" written for production at annual conventions of the American Psychological Association.

Index